2nd Edition

BTEC Sport
FIRST

John
Honeybourne

Nelson Thornes
a Wolters Kluwer business

Published in 2006 by:
Nelson Thornes Ltd
Delta Place
27 Bath Road
CHELTENHAM
GL53 7TH
United Kingdom

06 07 08 09 10 / 10 9 8 7 6 5 4 3 2 1

A catalogue record for this book is available from the British Library

ISBN 0 7487 8391 1
Cover photograph: Digital Vision PB RF (NT)
Page make-up by Pantek Arts Ltd, Maidstone, Kent
Printed and bound in Croatia by Zrinski

Contents

Acknowledgements

The publishers are indebted to the following for permission to reproduce copyright material:

UK Sport; Youth Sport Trust; Central Council of Physical Recreation (CCPR); Health and Safety Executive; Health Development Agency.

Crown copyright material is reproduced with the permission of the Controller of HMSO and the Queen's Printer for Scotland. Licence number: C2006009492.

Photograph credits:
Photodisc 10 (NT), p.5; Corel 205 (NT), p.6; Corel 578 (NT), p.8; Photodisc 14 (NT), p.9 (left); Corel 364 (NT), p.9 (right); Corel 745 (NT), p.12 (top); Corel 205 (NT), p.12 (bottom); Corel 364 (NT), p.13 (left); © Photofusion Picture Library/Alamy, p.13 (right); Photodisc 10 (NT), p.33; Stockpix 3 (NT), p.35; Photodisc 40 (NT), p.39; Photodisc 67 (NT), p.40; Photodisc 10 (NT), p.53; Photodisc 51 (NT), p.54; Digital Vision XA (NT), p.55; © POPPERFOTO/Alamy, p.57; Digital Stock SC (NT), p.60; Corel 685 (NT), p.70; © The Photolibrary Wales/Alamy, p.72; Corel 423 (NT), p.76; Corel 772 (NT), p.77 (top); Action Plus Sports Images, p.77 (bottom); © POPPERFOTO/Alamy, p.83; Corel 337 (NT), p.84; Corel 745 (NT), p.85; Photodisc 14 (NT), p.86; Photodisc 14 (NT), p.87; © Index Stock/Alamy, p.89; Photodisc 14 (NT), p.100; Corel 364 (NT), p.106; © POPPERFOTO/Alamy, p109; Photodisc 40 (NT), p.111; Photodisc 51 (NT), p.123; Corel 578 (NT), p.124 (top left); Corel 778 (NT), p.124 (top right); ©Hugh Threlfall/Alamy, p.124 (bottom); © POPPERFOTO/Alamy, p.125; Photodisc 45 (NT), p.129; Digital Vision 12 (NT), p.130 (top); Digital Vision XA (NT), p.130 (middle); Digital Vision 11 (NT), p.130 (bottom); Digital Vision XA (NT), p.131; © Robert Harding Picture Library Ltd/Alamy, p.147; Corel 776 (NT), p.150; Photodisc 10 (NT), p.157; Ingram ILG V1 CD3 (NT), p.158; © Janine Wiedel Photolibrary/Alamy, p.159 (top); © Martin Cushen/Alamy, p.159 (bottom); Digital Vision 11 (NT), p.160; © Richard Wareham Fotografie/Alamy, p.169; Corel 665 (NT), p.171; Digital Vision XA, p.177; Corel 221 (NT), p.182; Photodisc 14 (NT), p.183; © Apply Pictures/Alamy, p.194; Photodisc 67 (NT), p.195; Corel 205 (NT), p.200; © Detail Nottingham/Alamy, p.201; Photodisc 51 (NT), p.202; Photodisc 10 (NT), p.203; Corel 174 (NT), p.206; Corel 745 (NT), p.207; © The Photolibrary Wales/Alamy, p.208; Corel 745 (NT), p.210; Photodisc 51 (NT), p.212; Photodisc 14 (NT), p.221; © POPPERFOTO/Alamy, p.227; © Crash PA/Alamy, p.231; Bananastock E (NT), p. 238; Photodisc 75 (NT), p. 241; © Blend Images/Alamy, p. 242; Bananastock E (NT), p. 246; Photodisc 18 (NT), p. 247 (top); Photodisc 51 (NT), p. 247 (bottom); © Channel Island Pictures/Alamy, p. 248; © Dynamic Graphics Group IT Stock Free/Alamy, p. 250; Corel 364 (NT), p. 254 (top left); Photodisc 67 (NT), p. 254 (top right); Ingram ILSP (NT) p. 254 (bottom); Photodisc 71 (NT), p. 255; © Bubbles Photo Library, p. 256 (top); Photodisc 51 (NT), p. 256 (bottom); Corel 772 (NT), p. 258 (top); Photodisc 67 (NT), p. 258 (bottom); Photodisc 45 (NT), p. 262; Photodisc 51 (NT), p. 263.

Dedication

I would like to thank my wife and family for their support whilst writing this book.

Introduction

Sport is such an important aspect in our world today. A significant number of people watch, take part or work in sport. Millions from around the world watch the Olympic Games, world championships and the Commonwealth Games. Thousands for example, watch football, rugby and athletic events in the UK. Many compete in sports at different levels from Sunday morning games in netball and football, to the elite athletes who train many hours each day to achieve high standards in performance. There is a thriving industry that supports sport with a wide range of related jobs, from sports hall supervisors to top performance coaches and events organisers. To be part of the sports industry it is important to be as qualified as you can be and the BTEC First Diploma can be an important step in your sports education.

How do you use this book?

Covering the units of the new 2006 specification, this book has everything you need if you are studying BTEC First Certificate or Diploma in Sport. Simple to use and understand, this book is designed to provide you with the skills and knowledge for you to gain your qualification. We guide you through your qualification through a range of features that are fully explained over the page.

Which units do you need to complete?

For the BTEC First Diploma in Sport you are required to complete 2 core units and 4 specialist units. You have the choice of following one of three pathways: Performance, Exercise & Fitness and Outdoor Education. Your tutor will probably make the relevant selection of units for you, but for more details please look on the Edexcel website www.edexcel.org.uk

Core Units	Specialist Units
Unit 1 **The Body in Sport**	Unit 3 **The Sports Industry**
Unit 2 **Health, Safety and Injury in Sport**	Unit 4 **Preparation for Sport**
	Unit 5 **Planning and Leading Sports Activities**
	Unit 6 **Practical Sport**
	Unit 7 **Practical outdoor and adventurous activities**
	Unit 8 **Technical Skills and Tactical Awareness for Sport**
	Unit 9 **Psychology for Sport Performance**
	Unit 10 **Nutrition for Sports Performance**
	Unit 11 **Fitness for Sports Performance**
	Unit 12 **Lifestyle and Sports Performance**
	Unit 14 **Instructing Exercise and Fitness**
	Unit 15 **Sports and Leisure Facility Operations***
	Unit 16 **Leading Outdoor and Adventurous Activities***
*not covered in this textbook	Unit 17 **Expedition Experience***

Is there anything else you need to do?

1 Read about sport and leisure in your area – check the local newspapers.
2 Get as much as experience as possible in the sports industry, for example at local clubs or leisure centres.
3 Participate in sport yourself and keep yourself fit and healthy.
4 Read national newspapers including the broadsheets to gain a wider knowledge of sport.
5 Talk to people who are involved in the sports industry, ask them how they got their position and what qualifications /experience they needed.

We hope you enjoy your BTEC course – Good Luck!

Turn over now for your guide to the features of this book.

Features of this book

The Body in Sport

Learning Objectives

At the beginning of each Unit there will be a bulleted list letting you know what material is going to be covered. They specifically relate to the learning objectives within the 2006 specification.

This unit covers:

- the skeleton and how it is affected by exercise
- the muscular system of the body and how it is affected by exercise
- the cardiovascular system and how it is affected by exercise
- the respiratory system and how it is affected by exercise
- the fundamentals of the energy systems

Unit 1 covers the main scientific aspects of how the body responds before, during and after exercise. It relates them to sport in a practical and realistic way. The unit discusses skeletal and muscular structures and describes their functions in producing body movements during sports activity. It also investigates muscle contraction, joint action and levers in relation to sports activity. There is a section on the structure and function of the cardiovascular and respiratory systems, and the unit also briefly describes the short-term adaptations that take place during and after exercise.

Grading Criteria

The table of Grading Criteria at the beginning of each unit identifies achievement levels of pass, merit and distinction, as stated in the specification.

To achieve a **pass**, you must be able to match each of the 'P' criteria in turn.

To achieve **merit** or **distinction**, you must increase the level of evidence that you use in your work, using the 'M' and 'D' columns as reference. For example, to achieve a distinction you must fulfil all the criteria in the pass, merit and distinction columns.

grading criteria	To achieve a **pass** grade the evidence must show that the learner is able to:	To achieve a **merit** grade the evidence must show that, in addition to the pass criteria the learner is able to:	To achieve a **distinction** grade the evidence must show that, in addition to the pass and merit criteria, the learner is able to:
	P1 Describe the structure and function of the skeleton, and how bones grow	**M1** Identify the movement occurring at synovial joints during three different types of physical activity	**D1** Analyse four sporting movements, detailing the musculoskeletal actions occuring and the contractions that are necessary
	P2 Identify the effects of exercise on bones and joints	**M2** Explain the effects of exercise on bones and joints	**D2** Analyse the effects of exercise on the musculoskeletal system
	P3 Describe the different types of muscle, the major muscles in the body and how muscles move	**M3** Give examples of different types of muscular contraction relating to four different types of physical activity	**D3** Analyse the effects of exercise on the cardiorespiratory system

case study 1.2 — BMI indicators

Less than 20	underweight
20–24.9	healthy weight
25–29.9	overweight
30–40	moderately obese
40+	severely obese

There are problems associated with this type of measurement. Body composition is not taken into consideration, which means that someone with a high percentage of lean body tissue may well weigh the same as someone else with similar percentage of body fat (Honeybourne, 2003). The measurement of body fat is more accurate and techniques such as skin-fold callipers or underwater weighing can do this effectively.

(Adapted from Honeybourne *et al.*, 2004)

keyword

Origin
This is the end of the muscle attached to a bone that is stable, such as the scapula. The point of origin remains still when

The fixator is a muscle that works with others to stabilise the **origin** of the prime mover. For example, the trapezius contracts to stabilise the origin of the biceps.

Synergists are muscles that actively help the prime mover or agonist to produce the desired movement. They are sometimes called neutralisers because they prevent any undesired movements. Sometimes the fixator and the synergist are the same muscle. The brachialis, for example, acts as a synergist when the elbow is bent and the forearm moves upwards.

Links to Unit 10, page 120

More information - www.culture.gov.uk.

remember

In sport spinal injuries can be caused by incidents such as a collapsed rugby scrum or falling off a horse in equine events.

progress check

1. Name the four main functions of the human skeleton.
2. What is meant by the synovial joint? Choose one such joint and describe how it functions in a sports activity.
3. Describe the structure of cartilage and what its function is in the human body.
4. Give an example from sport of a movement that involves flexion.
5. Name three major muscles and describe their function.
6. Give an example of a pair of muscles that work together. Name the agonist and the antagonist.
7. Name and describe the three main levers.
8. Draw and label the main structures of the human heart.
9. Describe what happens to air as a person performing a sports activity breathes it in.
10. Give three short-term effects of exercise on the body.

Case Studies

provide real life examples that relate to what is being discussed within the text. It provides an opportunity to demonstrate theory in practice.

Keywords

of specific importance are highlighted within the text in blue, and then defined in a 'keyword' box to the side.

Links

direct you to other parts of the book that relate to the subject currently being covered.

Information bars

point you towards resources for further reading and research (e.g. websites).

Remember boxes

contain helpful hints, tips or advice.

Progress Checks

provide a list of quick questions at the end of each Unit, designed to ensure that you have understood the most important aspects of each subject area.

UNIT 1

The Body in Sport

This unit covers:

- the skeleton and how it is affected by exercise
- the muscular system and how it is affected by exercise
- the cardiovascular system and how it is affected by exercise
- the respiratory system and how it is affected by exercise
- the fundamentals of the energy systems

Unit 1 covers the main scientific aspects of how the body responds before, during and after exercise. It relates them to sport in a practical and realistic way. The unit discusses skeletal and muscular structures and describes their functions in producing body movements during sports activity. It also investigates muscle contraction, joint action and levers in relation to sports activity. There is a section on the structure and function of the cardiovascular and respiratory systems, and the unit also briefly describes the short-term adaptations that take place during and after exercise.

grading criteria

To achieve a **Pass** grade the evidence must show that the learner is able to:	To achieve a **Merit** grade the evidence must show that the learner is able to:	To achieve a **Distinction** grade the evidence must show that the learner is able to:
P1 Describe the structure and function of the skeleton, and how bones grow	**M1** Identify the movement occuring at synovial joints during three different types of physical activity	**D1** Analyse four sporting movements, detailing the musculoskeletal actions occuring, and the contractions that are necessary
P2 Identify the effects of exercise on bones and joints	**M2** Explain the effects of exercise on bones and joints	**D2** Analyse the effects of exercise on the musculoskeletal system
P3 Describe the different types of muscle, the major muscles in the body, and how muscles move	**M3** Give examples of different types of muscular contraction relating to four different types of physical activity	**D3** Analyse the effects of exercise on the cardiorespiratory system
P4 Identify the effects of exercise on skeletal muscles		

To achieve a **Pass** grade the evidence must show that the learner is able to:	To achieve a **Merit** grade the evidence must show that the learner is able to:	To achieve a **Distinction** grade the evidence must show that the learner is able to:
P5 Describe the structure and function of the cardiovascular system and how it is affected by exercise	**M4** Explain the effects of exercise on the cardiovascular system	
P6 Describe the structure and function of the respiratory system and how it is affected by exercise	**M5** Explain the effects of exercise on the respiratory system	
P7 Identify two types of physical activity that use the aerobic energy system and two that use the anaerobic energy systems	**M6** Explain the energy requirements of four different types of physical activity	

The Skeleton and How it is Affected by Exercise

The skeleton has **four** major functions:

- To give shape, support and posture to the body.

- To allow movement of the body by providing areas or sites for muscle attachment. This also provides for a system of levers (addressed later in this unit).

- To give protection to internal organs such as the heart, lungs, spinal cord and the brain.

- To produce red and white blood cells.

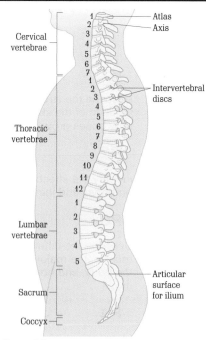

Figure 1.1
Lateral view of the spinal column

The axial skeleton is the main source of support and is the central part of the skeleton. It includes the cranium, the vertebral column and the rib cage including twelve pairs of ribs and the sternum.

The appendicular skeleton consists of the remaining bones and includes the girdles that join these bones onto the axial skeleton.

Figure 1.2
Human skeleton showing major bones

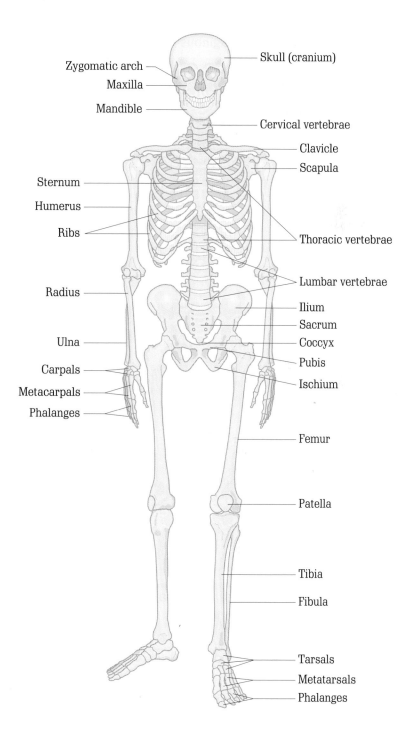

Zygomatic arch
Maxilla
Mandible
Sternum
Humerus
Ribs
Radius
Ulna
Carpals
Metacarpals
Phalanges

Skull (cranium)
Cervical vertebrae
Clavicle
Scapula
Thoracic vertebrae
Lumbar vertebrae
Ilium
Sacrum
Coccyx
Pubis
Ischium
Femur
Patella
Tibia
Fibula
Tarsals
Metatarsals
Phalanges

Joints

There are many different types of joints in the human body, including some that do not allow movement or that allow very little. Joints are very important in movements related to sport. There are three main types of joint:

- **Fibrous or fixed**. This does not allow any movement. Tough, fibrous tissue lies between the ends of the bones. The sutures of the cranium are an example.

- **Cartilaginous or slightly moveable**. This allows some movement. The ends of the bones have tough, fibrous cartilage, which allows for shock absorption but also gives stability. The intervertebral discs in the spine are an example.

- **Synovial or freely moveable**. This is the most common type of joint. It allows for a wide range of movement and so it is very important to sports participants. It consists of a joint capsule and a synovial membrane. The synovial membrane provides lubrication for the joint in the form of synovial fluid, which is secreted into the joint. The knee joint is an example.

Figure 1.3

Diagram of a knee joint

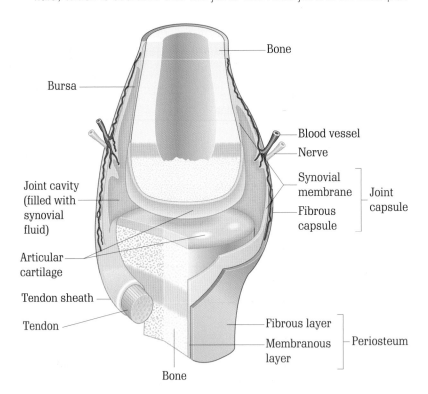

Types of synovial joint

- **Hinge joint**. This allows movement in one plane only (uniaxial). Again, the knee joint is an example.

- **Pivot joint**. This allows rotation only and is therefore also uniaxial. Examples are the axis and atlas of the cervical vertebrae.

- **Ellipsoid joint**. This is biaxial, allowing movement in two planes. The radiocarpal joint of the wrist is an example of an ellipsoid joint.

Figure 1.4

Bones of the knee joint

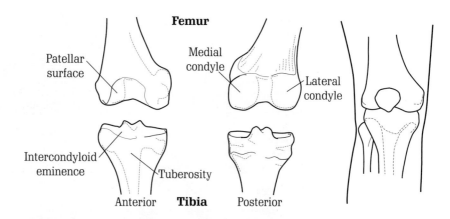

Femur

Patellar surface

Medial condyle

Lateral condyle

Intercondyloid eminence

Tuberosity

Anterior   **Tibia**   Posterior

Figure 1.5

The knee joint is used extensively in many team sports

- **Gliding joint**. This occurs where two flat surfaces glide over one another and can permit movement in most directions, although mainly biaxial. The carpal bones in the wrist are an example.

- **Saddle joint**. This is when a concave surface meets a convex surface. It is biaxial. For example, the carpal-metacarpal joint of the thumb.

- **Ball and socket joint**. This allows a wide range of movement and occurs when a round head of bone fits into a cupped shaped depression, as in the shoulder joint.

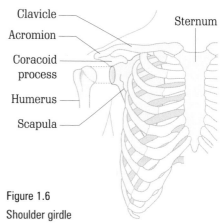

Clavicle

Sternum

Acromion

Coracoid process

Humerus

Scapula

Figure 1.6

Shoulder girdle

Figure 1.7

The thrower of a javelin depends heavily on the shoulder joint

Cartilage

This is soft connective tissue. Newborn babies have a skeleton consisting of cartilage and as they grow older this cartilage is mostly replaced by bone – a process known as ossification. Cartilage has no blood supply but receives nutrition though diffusion from the surrounding capillary network. There are three basic types of cartilage:

- **Yellow elastic cartilage** – flexible tissue. For example, part of the ear lobe.

- **Hyaline or blue articular cartilage** is found on the articulating surfaces of bones. It protects and allows movement between bones with limited friction. Hyaline cartilage thickens as a result of exercise.

- **White fibro-cartilage**. This consists of tough tissue that acts as a shock absorber. It is found in parts of the body where there is a great amount of stress, for example the semi-lunar cartilage in the knee joint.

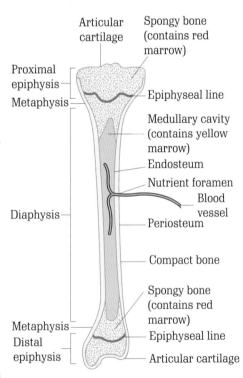

Figure 1.8

Structure of a long bone showing position of articular cartridge

Types of movement

Figure 1.9
Movement

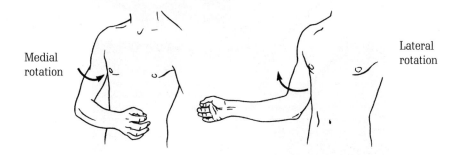

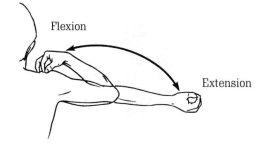

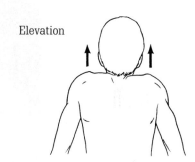

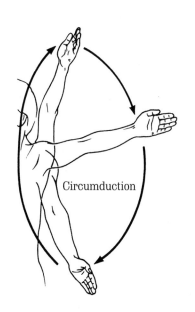

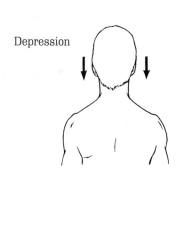

- **Flexion** is a decrease in the angle around a joint, such as when you bend your arm at the elbow and touch your shoulder with your hand.

- **Extension** occurs when the angle of the bones that are moving (articulating bones) is increased, for example when you move from a stooped or squat position to a standing position. The angle between your femur and tibia (upper and lower leg) has increased, thus extension has taken place.

Figure 1.10

When a tennis player hits a forehand the arm shows flexion at
the elbow

- **Abduction** is the movement of the body away from the middle or the midline
  of the body – for example lying on your left side and lifting your right leg
  straight up away from the midline.

- **Adduction** is the opposite of abduction and is movement towards the
  midline. For example, lowering your lifted leg that you have abducted
  towards the middle of your body. In practice, while swimming, the recovery of
  the legs from the breaststroke leg kick involves adduction.

- **Circumduction** is when the lower end of a bone moves in the shape of a
  circle. This is really a combination of flexion, extension, abduction and
  adduction. The only true circumduction occurs at the shoulder and hips where
  there are ball and socket joints.

- **Rotation**. This is when the bone turns about its longitudinal axis within the
  joint. Rotation towards the body is called internal or medial rotation; rotation
  away from the body is called external or lateral rotation.

- **Pronation** occurs at the elbow joint if the palm of your hand is facing
  downwards.

- **Supination** is the opposite of pronation and therefore involves placing the
  palm of your hand upwards.

- **Plantarflexion** occurs at the ankle joint when you point your toes with the
  foot bending downwards away from the tibia.

- **Dorsiflexion**. This is also at the ankle and occurs when you bend the foot up
  towards your tibia.

Figure 1.11

A gymnast in a floor routine may show a balance with pointed toes, or toes that are plantar flexed

Figure 1.12

A table tennis player about to hit the ball with top-spin shows rotation of the lower arm bones

The Muscular System and How it is Affected by Exercise

There are three types of muscle:

- **Involuntary muscle**, or smooth muscle, which is found in the body's internal organs. This is called 'involuntary' muscle because it is not under our conscious control.
- **Cardiac muscle**. This is only found in the heart and it is also involuntary.
- **Skeletal or voluntary muscle**. This is under our conscious control and is used primarily for movement.

The functions of specific muscles

The following muscles are named in the unit specification.

- **Triceps** – this is the elbow extensor (*triceps brachii*) and is attached to the elbow. Its function is to straighten the elbow and to swing the arm backwards, for example in a backhand stroke in table tennis.
- **Biceps** – this is the elbow flexor (*biceps brachii*). Its function is to swing the upper arm forward and to turn the forearm so that the palm of the hand points upwards (supination), for example, a biceps curl in weight training.
- **Deltoid** – this is used in all movements of the arms. Its most important function is to lift the arm straight outwards and upwards (abduction), for instance to make a block in volleyball with arms straight above the head.

Figure 1.13

The muscles of the human body, anterior view

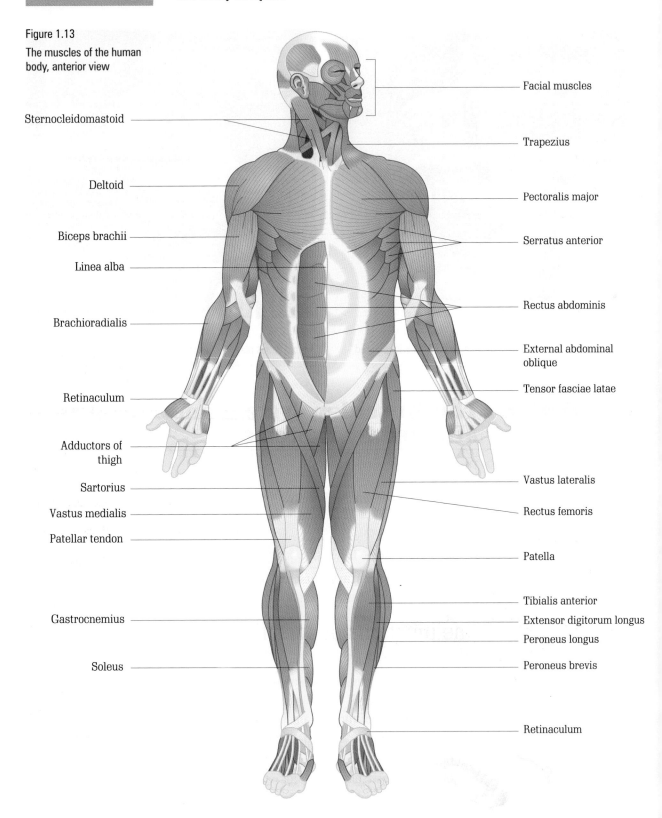

Sternocleidomastoid

Deltoid

Biceps brachii

Linea alba

Brachioradialis

Retinaculum

Adductors of thigh

Sartorius

Vastus medialis

Patellar tendon

Gastrocnemius

Soleus

Facial muscles

Trapezius

Pectoralis major

Serratus anterior

Rectus abdominis

External abdominal oblique

Tensor fasciae latae

Vastus lateralis

Rectus femoris

Patella

Tibialis anterior

Extensor digitorum longus

Peroneus longus

Peroneus brevis

Retinaculum

Figure 1.14

The muscles of the human body, posterior view

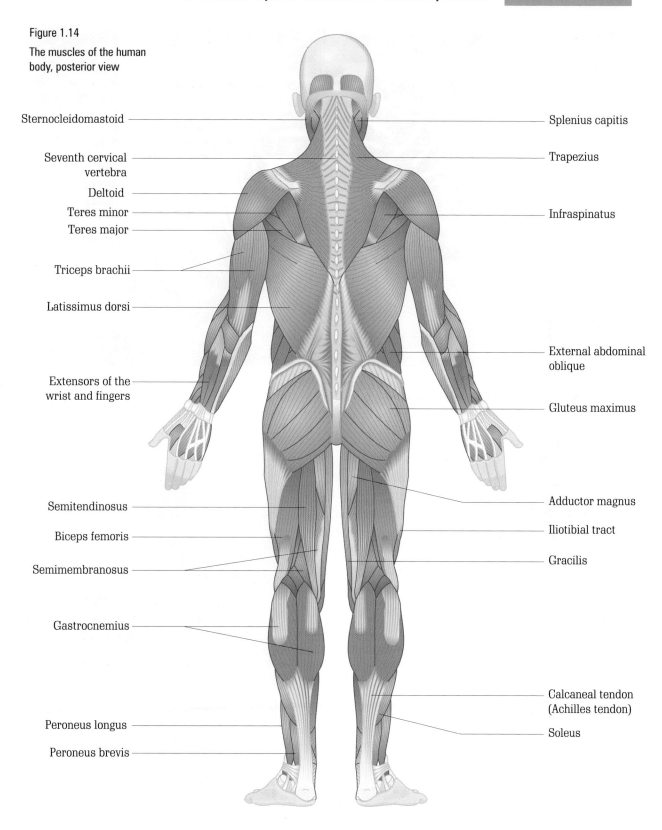

Sternocleidomastoid

Seventh cervical vertebra

Deltoid

Teres minor

Teres major

Triceps brachii

Latissimus dorsi

Extensors of the wrist and fingers

Semitendinosus

Biceps femoris

Semimembranosus

Gastrocnemius

Peroneus longus

Peroneus brevis

Splenius capitis

Trapezius

Infraspinatus

External abdominal oblique

Gluteus maximus

Adductor magnus

Iliotibial tract

Gracilis

Calcaneal tendon (Achilles tendon)

Soleus

Figure 1.15

A rugby player making a tackle would hold on to the opponent using pectoral muscles

- **Pectorals** – there are two sets of chest muscle: *pectoralis major* (greater chest muscle) and *pectoralis minor* (lesser chest muscle). These help to adduct the arm and rotate it inwards, as well as lowering the shoulder blades.

- **Trapezius** – this adducts and rotates the shoulder blade outwards. It also helps to turn the head and bends the neck backwards. A rugby forward in a scrum will use the trapezius to bind into the opponents.

- **Gluteals** – these are the muscles in your buttocks. They straighten and adduct the hip, rotate the thigh outwards and help to straighten the knee.

- **Quadriceps** – this provides stability to the knee joint and extends or straightens the knee joint.

- **Hamstrings** – these muscles will straighten the hip. They will also bend the knee and rotate it outwards

Figure 1.16

A sprinter will use the gluteals in the leg action of sprinting down the track

Figure 1.17

A long jumper when diving off the board will straighten the knee joint at take off using the quadriceps

Figure 1.18

A netball player when running across the court will use her hamstrings in the running action to bend the knees

- **Gastrocnemius** – or the calf muscle. This is used to bend the knee and to straighten or plantarflex the ankle. For instance, swimmers doing the front crawl will point their toes in the leg action using the gastrocnemius.

- **Latissimus dorsi** – the broad back muscle. It will swing the arm backwards and rotate it inwards. Tennis players who, when serving, swing an arm back to hit the ball are using the *latissimus dorsi*.

- **Abdominals** – these bend the trunk forwards and help to turn the upper body. Performing a sit-up exercise will use the abdominals.

Pairs of muscles

The human body can make a vast range of movements. To produce these movements, muscles shorten, lengthen or remain the same length when they contract. Muscles work in pairs. As one muscle contracts the other relaxes. Muscles that work together like this are called antagonistic pairs. This type of action enables the body to move with stability and control.

Examples of antagonistic pairs are:

- **Biceps and triceps** – at the arm joint. As the biceps bends the arms by contacting, the triceps relax. As the arm straightens the opposite occurs.

- **Hamstrings and quadriceps** – at the knee joint. The hamstrings contract, the quadriceps relax and the knee bends. As the knee straightens the quadriceps contract and the hamstrings relax.

keyword

Origin
This is the end of the muscle attached to a bone that is stable, such as the scapula. The point of origin remains still when contraction occurs. Some muscles have two or more origins, for example the biceps muscle has two heads that pull on one **insertion** to lift the lower arm.

keyword

Insertion
This is the end of the muscle attached to the bone that actively moves, for example the biceps insertion is on the radius.

The agonist is the muscle that produces the desired joint movement. It is also known as the prime mover. For example, the *biceps brachii* is the muscle that produces the flexion movement at the elbow.

For movement to be coordinated, muscles work in pairs so that control is maintained. The movement caused by the agonist is countered by the action of the opposing muscle called the antagonist. For example, the action at the elbow caused by the biceps shortening is opposed by the lengthening of the triceps, which acts as the antagonist.

The fixator is a muscle that works with others to stabilise the **origin** of the prime mover. For example, the trapezius contracts to stabilise the origin of the biceps.

Synergists are muscles that actively help the prime mover or agonist to produce the desired movement. They are sometimes called neutralisers because they prevent any undesired movements. Sometimes the fixator and the synergist are the same muscle. The brachialis, for example, acts as a synergist when the elbow is bent and the forearm moves upwards.

Muscular contractions

The following are the types of muscular contraction (adapted from Honeybourne, 2003):

- **Isotonic or concentric contraction**. This occurs when a muscle shortens and creates movement around a joint.
- **Eccentric contraction**. This contraction is when the muscles lengthen as contraction takes place. It acts to control movement.
- **Isometric contraction**. This is when a muscle contracts but neither lengthens or shortens. During this contraction there is no movement around the joint. This is important when the muscle is acting as a fixator.
- **Isokinetic contraction**. This is a type of contraction where the muscle shortens and increases in tension whilst working at a constant speed against a variable resistance.

Levers

Levers are important in movement because they allow efficiency and force to be applied to the body's movements. Levels are made up of a level arm, a fulcrum that is the pivot point, a load force and an effort force.

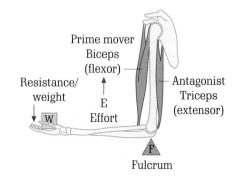

Figure 1.19
The lever system in the forearm

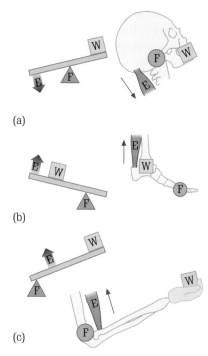

(a)

(b)

(c)

Figure 1.20

Diagrams showing the three types of levers

There are three types of levers:

- **First-class levers**. The fulcrum is located between the effort force and the load force on the lever arm. An example of this type of lever is the neck joint (Figure 1.20a).

- **Second-class levers**. Here the resistance is between the fulcrum and the effort. If you raise up on your toes or plantar flex your ankles then this lever is in operation (Figure 1.20b).

- **Third-class levers**. Here the effort is between the fulcrum and the resistance. This is the most common form of lever in the human body (Figure 1.20c).

Energy needs for muscular contractions

Muscle cells burn carbohydrates and fatty acids when oxygen is present and this causes the production of adenosine triphosphate (ATP), which is essential for the muscles to contract. This process is called aerobic metabolism because oxygen is present.

If the process takes place without oxygen and only carbohydrate is used then it is called anaerobic metabolism.

The greater the intensity of exercise, the more fuel is consumed in the form of carbohydrates. If the intensity is approximately 50% of VO_2 max, then the fuel that is mainly used is fat. As soon as that intensity is raised to 75% of VO_2 max, then carbohydrate is the major fuel source.

See Unit 10 Nutrition for Sports Performance, pages 185–86

The Cardiovascular System and How it is Affected by Exercise

The cardiovascular system involves transporting oxygen around the body and is therefore a very important system for the athlete and coach to understand so that performance can be improved. The cardiovascular system includes the heart, the network of blood vessels and the blood that transports essential material around the body.

The heart

The heart consists of four chambers and is mostly made up of cardiac muscle. The heart has two separate pumps whose main function is to pump blood around the body. The right-side pump sends deoxygenated blood to the lungs and the left-side pump sends oxygenated blood to the muscles of the body.

A muscular wall called a septum separates these two pump systems. The main muscular wall of the heart is called the myocardium and is found between the inner endocardium and the outer membrane called the pericardium.

The two chambers at the superior (top) part of the heart are called atria. The two inferior (lower) chambers are called ventricles.

Figure 1.21

Heart

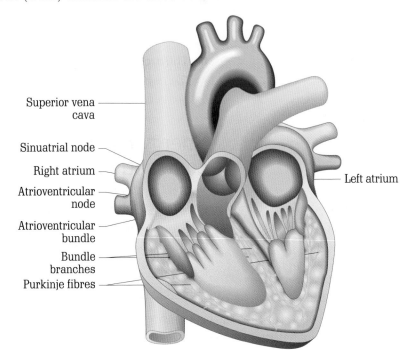

Superior vena cava

Sinuatrial node

Right atrium

Atrioventricular node

Atrioventricular bundle

Bundle branches

Purkinje fibres

Left atrium

There are many blood vessels associated with the heart. The inferior and superior venae cavae bring deoxygenated blood from the body to the right atrium. The pulmonary veins bring oxygenated blood from the lungs to the left atrium. The pulmonary artery takes deoxygenated blood from the right ventricle to the lungs. The aorta takes oxygenated blood from the left ventricle to the rest of the body.

Like other muscles, the heart requires a blood supply and this is transported to the heart via the coronary artery giving oxygenated blood to the heart via capillaries. Deoxygenated blood is taken away from the heart and into the right atrium through the coronary sinus.

The heart also contains valves, which ensure that the blood can only flow in one direction. There are four valves within the heart. Two separate the atria from the ventricles and two are in the arteries carrying blood from the ventricles. As the valves only work one way, this stops the backflow of blood. The blood that flows from the atria to the ventricles pushes the valves open; the valves are then closed by connective tissue called chordae tendineae. The following terms are used to describe the heart's valves:

- **Atrioventricular valves** – a collective term for all the valves between the atria and ventricles.

Figure 1.22

Internal structure of the heart

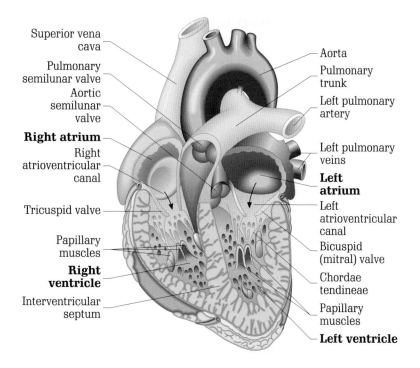

Superior vena cava

Pulmonary semilunar valve

Aortic semilunar valve

Right atrium

Right atrioventricular canal

Tricuspid valve

Papillary muscles

Right ventricle

Interventricular septum

Aorta

Pulmonary trunk

Left pulmonary artery

Left pulmonary veins

Left atrium

Left atrioventricular canal

Bicuspid (mitral) valve

Chordae tendineae

Papillary muscles

Left ventricle

- **Tricuspid valve** – the valve between the right atrium and the right ventricle.
- **Bicuspid valve** – the valve between the left atrium and the left ventricle.
- **Aortic valve** – the valve between the left ventricle and the aorta.
- **Pulmonary valve** – the valve between the right ventricle and the pulmonary artery.
- **Semilunar valves** – a collective term for aortic and pulmonary valves.

The cardiac cycle

The cardiac cycle is a term that refers to the process in which the heart contracts and blood is transported through the heart. The cardiac cycle is a sequence of events during one complete heartbeat, including the filling of the heart with blood and the emptying of the heart. Each cycle takes approx. 0.8 second and is repeated about 72 times per minute.

- **Stage 1 – atrial diastole**. The atria of the heart fill with blood.
- **Stage 2 – ventricular diastole**. The ventricles now fill via the atrioventricular valves.
- **Stage 3 – atrial systole**. The atria contract and all blood is ejected into ventricles. The atrioventricular valves now close.
- **Stage 4 – ventricular systole**. The semilunar valves open, ventricles contract and blood is forced from the right ventricle into the pulmonary artery and blood from the left ventricle into the aorta. Finally the semilunar valves shut and the cycle is completed.

Heart rate (HR)

The heart contracts and relaxes in a rhythm, which produces a heartbeat. This is started by an electrical impulse from the sino-atrial (SA) node, which is the 'pacemaker' of the heart.

Heart rate (HR) is measured in beats per minute (bpm). The average resting HR is 75 bpm.

A decrease in resting heart rate is a good indicator of increasing fitness. A trained athlete's resting heart rate falls below 60 bpm.

Stroke volume (SV)

This is the volume of blood that is pumped out of the heart by each ventricle during one contraction. It is measured in millilitres per beat. Stroke volume varies depending on:

- amount of blood returning to the heart (venous return)
- the elasticity of the ventricles
- the contractility of the ventricles
- the blood pressure in the arteries leading from the heart.

Cardiac output (Q)

This refers to the volume of blood ejected from the left ventricle in 1 minute. It is measured in litres per minute. The cardiac output is equal to the stroke volume × the heart rate:

$$Q = SV \times HR$$

Arteries and arterioles

These are blood vessels that carry blood at high pressure from the heart to the body tissues. The largest artery is called the aorta, which leaves the heart and subdivides into smaller vessels. The smaller of these are called arterioles and have a very small diameter. The walls of arteries contain muscle tissue, which enables the vessels to increase or reduce their diameter.

Vasoconstriction

This occurs when the artery walls decrease their diameter. The vessels can therefore help to change the pressure of the blood, which is especially important during exercise.

Veins and venules

These carry blood at low pressure and return the blood to the heart. Their walls are less muscular but gradually increase in thickness as they approach the heart. The vena cava is the largest vein, which enters the heart through the right atrium. The smallest veins are called venules. They transport the blood from the capillaries. Veins contain pocket valves that prevent the backflow of blood.

Vasodilation

This occurs when the artery walls increase their diameter.

keyword

Haemoglobin
This is iron-rich protein and transports oxygen in the blood. The more concentrated the haemoglobin, the more oxygen can be carried. This concentration can be increased through endurance training.

Capillaries

These only have a single layer of cells in their walls. This makes them thin enough for red blood cells to pass through them. Capillaries occur in large quantities around the muscles and this enables the effective exchange of gases.

Blood and blood vessels

Blood vessels are an integral part of the cardiovascular system and are essential for the transportation of material around the body. During exercise, most of the blood goes to the working muscles so that oxygen can be delivered and carbon dioxide taken away efficiently and effectively. Blood consists of cells and is surrounded by a liquid called plasma. The average total male blood volume is 5 or 6 litres and the average female blood volume is 4 to 5 litres. Blood also consists of erythrocytes, which are red corpuscles containing **haemoglobin**.

The Respiratory System and How it is Affected by Exercise

This system works closely together with the cardiovascular system to ensure a supply of oxygen to the working muscles, which is so important in sports activities. The external respiratory system involves the exchange of gases between the lungs and the blood. The internal respiratory system involves the exchange of gases between the blood and the cells. Cellular respiration is the process that involves the production of ATP (adenosine triphosphate).

Nasal passages

The air enters the body by being drawn in through the nose. The nasal cavity is divided by a cartilaginous septum that forms the nasal passages. Here the mucous membranes warm and moisten the air and the hair filters, and trap dust.

The pharynx and the larynx

The throat contains both the respiratory and alimentary tract so both food and air pass through. Air passes over the vocal chords of the larynx and into the trachea. Swallowing draws the larynx upwards against the epiglottis and prevents the entry of food. Any food is sent down the oesophagus.

The trachea

This is sometimes called the windpipe. It has 18 rings of cartilage, which are lined with a mucous membrane and ciliated cells, which trap dust. The trachea goes from the larynx to the primary bronchi.

The bronchi and bronchioles

The trachea divides into two bronchi. The right bronchus goes into the right lung and the left bronchus goes into the left lung. The bronchi then divide up into smaller bronchioles. The bronchioles enable the air to pass into the alveoli where diffusion takes place.

Figure 1.23

The respiratory system

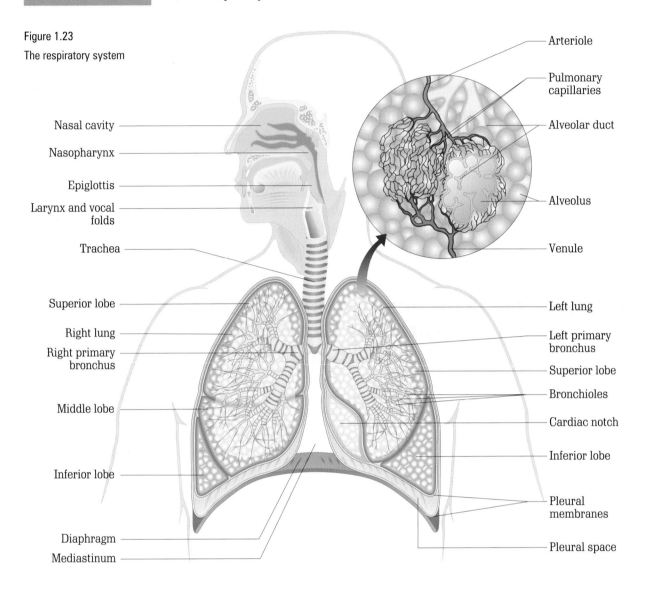

Arteriole

Pulmonary capillaries

Nasal cavity

Nasopharynx

Alveolar duct

Epiglottis

Larynx and vocal folds

Trachea

Alveolus

Venule

Superior lobe

Left lung

Right lung

Left primary bronchus

Right primary bronchus

Superior lobe

Bronchioles

Middle lobe

Cardiac notch

Inferior lobe

Inferior lobe

Pleural membranes

Diaphragm

Mediastinum

Pleural space

Figure 1.24

The exchange of oxygen

Capillary wall

Alveolar wall

Alveolus

Red blood cell

Red blood cell in capillary

Respiratory membrane

Diffusion of O_2

Diffusion of CO_2

Alveoli

These are responsible for gaseous exchange between the lungs and the blood. They are tiny air-filled sacs and there are many million of these in the lungs, which provides an enormous surface area (some have estimated it to be the size of a tennis court!). The walls of the alveoli are extremely thin and are lined by a thin film of water, which allows the dissolving of oxygen from the inspired air.

The lungs

These lie in the thoracic cavity, which is a protected area surrounded by the ribs and the diaphragm, and separated into two by the mediastinum, which contains the heart. The pleural membrane, which lines the pleural cavity, surrounds each of the two lungs. The pleural cavity contains pleural fluid, which reduces friction by lubricating. The diaphragm borders the bottom of the lungs and is a sheet of skeletal muscle.

Breathing

Inspiration

Inspiration, or breathing in, occurs when the respiratory muscles contract. These muscles include the external intercostal muscles and the diaphragm. The external intercostal muscles are attached to the ribs and when they contract the ribs move upwards and outwards. The diaphragm contracts downward and thus the area of the thoracic cavity is increased. The lungs are pulled outwards through surface tension along with the chest walls, which causes the space within the lungs to increase. The pressure within the lungs decreases and becomes less than the pressure outside the body. Gases move from areas of high pressure into areas of low pressure and so air is inspired into the lungs.

Figure 1.25

Inspiration and expiration

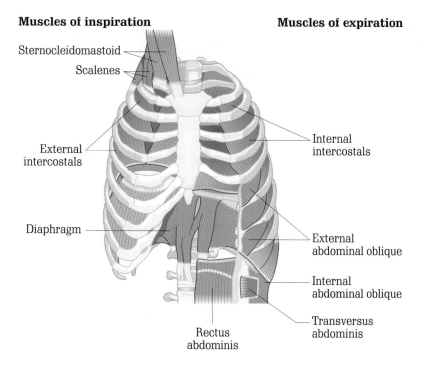

Muscles of inspiration

Muscles of expiration

Sternocleidomastoid

Scalenes

External intercostals

Diaphragm

Internal intercostals

External abdominal oblique

Internal abdominal oblique

Transversus abdominis

Rectus abdominis

During exercise the sternocleidomastoid lifts the sternum; the scalenes and the pectoralis minor both elevate the ribs. These actions help to increase the size of the thoracic cavity.

Expiration

This is more of a passive process than inspiration and is caused by the relaxation of the respiratory muscles. When the external intercostal muscles relax, the ribs are lowered and the diaphragm relaxes. The area of the lungs decreases and the pressure within the lungs becomes greater than the pressure outside the body. Air is now forced out to equalise this pressure and expiration takes place.

Gaseous exchange

At the lungs

There is a movement of gases across the respiratory membrane because of the imbalance between gases in the alveoli and the blood. Oxygen moves from the alveoli into the blood and carbon dioxide diffuses from the blood into the alveoli. Athletes who are involved with more endurance events have a greater ability to diffuse oxygen because of an increase in cardiac output and an increase in the surface area of alveoli.

At the muscles

This is a similar process. The high pressure of oxygen in the blood enables oxygen to pass through the capillary wall and into the muscle cytoplasm. Carbon dioxide moves in the opposite direction. When oxygen is in the muscle it attaches itself to myoglobin, which takes the oxygen to the mitochondria, and glycolysis takes place. Glycolysis is the term used to describe the breakdown of glucose.

The Fundamentals of the Energy Systems

Short-term responses of the cardiovascular system

The following are short-term responses of the cardiovascular system to exercise.

There is a rise in heart rate prior to exercise called an anticipatory rise, which is designed to prepare the body for activity. This is due to hormonal action. Then there is a sharp rise in the levels of these hormones due to stimulation from the sense organs and hormones. The heart rate remains high due to the need for physical exertion and there is a period when it remains steady before it declines due to the withdrawal of stimuli and the drop in hormone levels. The heart eventually returns to its resting rate.

Figure 1.26

The heart rate

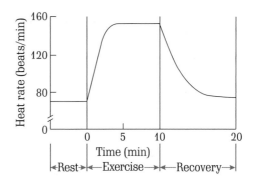

Short-term responses of the respiratory system

The breathing rate rises during exercise due to demands for more oxygen.

■ **Tidal volume (TV)** is the volume of air either inspired or expired per breath. This increases during exercise.

■ **Inspiratory reserve volume (IRV)** is the maximal volume inspired in addition to the tidal volume. This decreases during exercise.

■ **Expiratory reserve volume (ERV)** is the maximal volume expired in addition to the tidal volume. This decreases slightly during exercise.

■ **Residual volume (RV)** is the amount of air left in the lungs after maximal expiration. This increases slightly during exercise.

■ **Total lung capacity (TLC)** is the vital capacity plus the residual volume and is the volume at the end of maximal inspiration. This decreases slightly during exercise.

■ **Vital capacity (VC)** is the maximum amount of air that can be exhaled forcibly after maximal inspiration. This decreases slightly during exercise.

Long-term adaptations

The following are long-term adaptations that may occur due to exercise (Honeybourne, 2003):

■ increase in bone density

■ increase in capillary density and efficiency.

■ lower resting heart rate

■ increased vital capacity

■ increase in stroke volume at rest and during exercise

■ cardiac output increases

■ decrease in resting blood pressure

■ increase in haemoglobin, which helps carry oxygen along with an increase in red blood cells.

Effects of exercise on the muscular system

The following are the long-term adaptations of the muscular system after a period of exercise:

- There are aerobic adaptations in the muscles. Activities like swimming or running can enlarge slow twitch fibres, which gives greater potential for energy production.

- The size and number of mitochondria increase.

- There is an increase in myoglobin content within the muscle cell.

- The onset of fatigue is delayed because of higher maximum oxygen uptake (VO_2 max).

- Anaerobic adaptations in muscle occur: activities like sprinting or weight lifting can cause hypertrophy of fast twitch muscle fibres.

- The size of the heart increases – this is called cardiac hypertrophy.

case study 1.1

A decrease in resting heart rate for a trained person

A trained person's resting heart rate is usually lower than average at 50 – 60 bpm. The heart of a trained person will beat fewer times to produce the same cardiac output (amount of blood pumped out per minute). The trained person will also have an increase in stroke volume (amount of blood pumped out of the heart by each ventrice during one contraction.

Cardiac output = stroke volume × heart rate.

Tests exist to establish whether adaptations have taken place. For example:

- **Heart rate**. This can be monitored by taking the pulse rate before exercise using a heart rate monitor. These monitors can also be used to assess the intensity of the training, to set goals and to record heart rate patterns during exercise.

- **Breathing**. Use of a spirometer will measure lung volume. (See Unit 11 on fitness testing.)

- **Anaerobic capacity**. This can be tested by using a bicycle ergometer, which is a static bike with controllable intensity of exercise. Subjects perform a 30 second bout of exercise, sprinting as hard as they can (called maximal exercise) on the bike. The computer linked to the bike records the peak power reached. The peak power is an indication of the ability of the body to work at a high rate for as long as possible. Those who have a high level of power are more anaerobically fit.

- **Blood pressure**. This is usually measured at the brachial artery in the arm using a sphygmomanometer. This records the systolic pressure over the diastolic pressure. A typical reading for a male at rest is 120 mmHg/80 mmHg.

- **Weight**. Energy balance is realised when input (food eaten) equals output (energy expended). When input exceeds output, then the excess energy is stored as fat unless extra activity burns it up. The simple answer to weight gain is to eat less and exercise more (Honeybourne, 2003). In sport we have already recognised the importance of a ready availability of energy and so the right energy input must be maintained.

A common way of measuring whether you are the right weight is to calculate your body mass index (BMI). Before a training regime you may simple weigh yourself and then reweigh after exercise but remember that your weight alone does not indicate fitness. Muscle weighs more than fat, so training that increases muscle size is bound to result in weight gain.

Body mass index (BMI)

Your BMI is a measurement of your weight in kg divided by your height in square metres:

$$\text{BMI} = \frac{Weight\ (Kg)}{Height\ (M^2)}$$

A BMI greater than 25 indicates that you are overweight. If it exceeds 40 then there is a severe health risk. A BMI over 30 for adults indicates obesity.

---

case study

1.2

BMI indicators

Less than 20 – underweight
20–24.9 – healthy weight
25–29.9 – overweight
30–40 – moderately obese
40+ – severely obese

There are problems associated with this type of measurement. Body composition is not taken into consideration, which means that someone with a high percentage of lean body tissue may well weigh the same as someone else with similar percentage of body fat (Honeybourne, 2003). The measurement of body fat is more accurate and techniques such as skin-fold callipers or underwater weighing can do this effectively.

(Adapted from Honeybourne *et al.*, 2004)

*progress
check*

1   Name the four main functions of the human skeleton.

2   What is meant by the synovial joint? Choose one such joint and describe how it functions in a sports activity.

3   Describe the structure of cartilage and what its function is in the human body.

4   Give an example from sport of a movement that involves flexion.

5   Name three major muscles and describe their function.

6   Give an example of a pair of muscles that work together. Name the agonist and the antagonist.

7   Name and describe the three main levers.

8   Draw and label the main structures of the human heart.

9   Describe what happens to air as a person performing a sports activity breathes it in.

10   Give three short-term effects of exercise on the body.

UNIT 2

Health, Safety and Injury in Sport

This unit covers:

- the different types of injuries and illnesses associated with sports participation
- dealing with injuries and illnesses associated with sports participation
- the risks and hazards associated with sports participation
- undertaking a risk assessment relevant to sport

This core unit, which has close links with many other units in this qualification, covers theoretical elements related to health, safety and injury. It investigates major risk factors that can affect sportsmen and women in different sports settings. Causes of injury in sport are covered, along with measures to prevent them. The importance of recognising situations that require immediate expert advice is also emphasised. The unit highlights the main relevant laws and regulations that deal with health and safety, and includes useful material to support your own risk assessment of a given sports activity.

grading criteria

To achieve a **Pass** grade the evidence must show that the learner is able to:	To achieve a **Merit** grade the evidence must show that the learner is able to:	To achieve a **Distinction** grade the evidence must show that the learner is able to:
P1 Describe the six risks and hazards associated with sports participation	**M1** Explain risks and hazards associated with sports participation	**D1** Give a detailed account of why participants are at risk of injury whilst taking part in sport
P2 Describe prominent rules, regulations and legislation relating to sports participation	**M2** Explain prominent, rules, regulations and legislation relating to sports participation	**D2** Analyse the use of specialist equipment to minimise the risk of injury
P3 Describe four different types of injuries associated with sports participation	**M3** Explain why certain injuries and illnesses are associated with sports participation	

grading criteria

To achieve a **Pass** grade the evidence must show that the learner is able to:	To achieve a **Merit** grade the evidence must show that the learner is able to:	To achieve a **Distinction** grade the evidence must show that the learner is able to:
P4 Describe types and signs of illnesses related to sports participation	**M4** Deal with casualties suffering from three different injuries and/or illnesses	
P5 Deal with casualties suffering from three different injuries and/or illnesses, with teacher support	**M5** Describe contingency plans that can be used in a risk assessment	
P6 Complete a risk assessment relevant to sport		

The Different Types of Injuries and Illnesses Associated with Sports Participation

Types of common sports injuries

Head injuries

In sport it is common for participants to be knocked unconscious and to suffer from concussion. Concussion is possible in many contact sports but it is most common in boxing, skiing, rugby and football. It is caused by a hard blow to the head or by the head striking an object. When there is a violent blow to the head the brain bounces against the rigid bone of the skull. The brain's stabilising connective tissue and blood vessels may tear and this stops the normal passage of messages in the brain. The result is a feeling of headache, nausea and dizziness, together with an increase in pupil size, sickness and confusion. A player who has suffered light concussion can return to play after about 15 minutes of rest following a medical check. If a player is unconscious then check that the airway is clear and call a trained first aider. A hospital visit is advisable. A full recovery might take a week after severe concussion. Post-concussion syndrome can occur after weeks or months if proper treatment is not given after the injury.

case study 2.1

Concussion

Professional rugby players are not allowed to play for three weeks after experiencing concussion.

Wales's rugby player Alix Popham nursed a sore head after being knocked unconscious during his team's match against South Africa [in 2004]. The No.8 had to be stretchered off the pitch and spent the night in hospital. Luckily Popham escaped serious injury thanks to the quick thinking of teammate Ceri Sweeney who stopped him swallowing his tongue. Head injuries can occur in all sports and must be treated seriously.

(Source: www.bbc.co.uk/sportacademy)

remember

In sport spinal injuries can be caused by incidents such as a collapsed rugby scrum or falling off a horse in equine events.

Spinal injury

Any injury to the spine should be treated extremely seriously. There could be lasting damage to someone's health, which could prevent that person from playing sport or even living normally. Damage to the spinal cord may cause very painful conditions. A break high up in the spinal cord usually causes death. If there is a suspected injury to the spine then it is important to get expert help immediately without moving the injured person. Moving a person who has a spinal injury could make matters much worse.

Fractures

Bone fractures can be serious injuries. As well as damaging the bone they often injure the tissues around the bone such as tendons, ligaments, muscles and the skin.

Anyone involved in contact sports is in danger of sustaining a fractured bone. For example Martin Keown broke his leg before the football World Cup in 2002.

A fracture occurs when there is a physical impact to the arm, leg or bone or an indirect blow.

There are different types of fracture:

- **transverse** – straight across the bone
- **oblique** – diagonal break across the bone
- **spiral** – around the bone
- **comminuted** – the bone is shattered.

A compound fracture is also called an open fracture. This is a more serious fracture because the bone breaks through the surface of the skin. This fracture causes much more damage to the surrounding tissue and there can be serious bleeding. The exposed broken bone is also open to infection if it is not treated immediately.

case study 2.2

Lower back stress fracture for a cricket bowler

A cricket bowler can be put out of action for as long as a year if they suffer from a stress fracture in the lower back.

The nature of bowling can place terrible strains on the spine, literally cracking a bone. Most commonly, bowlers with a faulty technique or those who have bowled too much may suffer from this injury. The stress fracture means an extended period of rehabilitation, which requires hard work from both the physiotherapist and the injured bowler.

It is comparatively rare to see bowlers with highly developed stomach muscles (or six-packs) as for some time this has been known to develop muscles that only strengthen the stomach and do not support the lower back. Working with the physiotherapist, the bowler needs to develop the deeper stomach muscles, which effectively hold the vertebrae in place. Gradually this strengthens the support given to the lower back.

After injury the bowler must be cautious and take reasonable steps not to aggravate the injury. They will take a day off after training and avoid indoor bowling practice, as the hard floor increases the impact on the joints. Warming up, and loosening the spine before exercise, remains essential.

(Adapted from www.bbc.co.uk/sport, 2004)

When there is a fracture there is swelling and progressive bruising and a lot of pain during movement. You may also be able to see that the limb with the suspected fracture looks awkward and that the bone is not in the right place.

To treat the fracture, cover and elevate the injured limb and keep it completely still. Go to hospital. The medical staff will probably put the limb in a cast to keep it completely still while the bone heals. This can be made of plaster, which can be quite heavy, but doctors are increasingly using lightweight plastic casts. The injured player can be back in training after 5 to 12 weeks.

Metatarsals are the five long bones in the forefoot. These bones can be fractured through impact (such as someone stamping on your foot) and through overuse (stress fractures).

The symptoms include pain in the bone during exercise and swelling and tenderness in the foot.

Treatment involves rest. An injured person may be asked to wear walking boots or stiff-soled shoes to protect it while it heals. Recovery from a metatarsal fracture can take between 4 and 6 weeks.

case study

2.3

Fractures to the metatarsals

Striker Wayne Rooney was forced to limp off after 27 minutes in the Euro 2004 quarter-final against Portugal. He had to watch England be knocked out of the competition after his collision with the Portuguese player, Jorge Andrade.

Rooney had suffered the same fate as both David Beckham and Gary Neville; they had been stricken with metatarsal injuries just before the World Cup finals in 2002.

All three England players suffered a direct blow to the foot, or were affected by a stress fracture in the same area. Unfortunately metatarsal injuries are common in both football and other athletic sports.

(Adapted from www.bbc.co.uk/sport, 2004)

Dislocations

These involve movement of a joint from its normal location and are caused by a blow or a fall. When a joint has a lot of pressure put upon it in a certain direction, bones in the joint disconnect. The joint capsule often tears, along with ligaments, because of this movement of bones. A dislocated joint looks misshapen and out of place. The sufferer will have limited movement and will experience severe pain.

Soft tissue injuries

These are injuries that affect muscles, tendons, ligaments and skin.

Sprains

This is a tear to a ligament and is often caused by overstretching. Ankles, knees and wrists are very susceptible to sprains.

The ankle sprain

This is common for anyone involved in sport or outdoor activities. Going over on your ankle causes it. Sometimes a 'snap' or 'tear' is felt or heard.

There are three grades of severity:

- **Grade 1** – pain is experienced when turning the foot in or out.
- **Grade 2** – swelling.
- **Grade 3** – huge swelling and problems walking.

An ankle sprain may be treated using rest, ice, compression and elevation (RICE). Do not remove the shoe until ice has reduced the ankle swelling.

Recovery takes between 1 week and 3 months, depending on the grade of injury. The usual recovery time is 2 weeks.

Strains

These are twists or tears to a muscle or a tendon. Overusing the joint, force or overstretching causes it. There are three degrees of strain:

- **First degree** – this is when only a few muscle fibres are torn and there is mild swelling. There is only a little pain.

- **Second degree** – this is when there is a little more tearing of the muscle fibres. There is much more pain and there is swelling and stiffness.

- **Third degree** – this is when there is a total rupture or tear in the muscle. There is a considerable amount of pain and there is severe swelling.

Other injuries

Blisters

Blisters can be a real nuisance to sports performers, especially in team games. A blister is the body's way of trying to put protection between the skin and whatever is causing friction, for example, in a footballer's case, the boot.

The skin consists of various layers. Friction and force causes these layers to tear. Fluid called serum flows in between the damaged skin layers, producing a bubble of liquid. The pain occurs when this swelling rubs against another surface.

---

case study **2.4**   ## Blisters in Portugal (Euro 2004)

Blisters forced David Beckham, Sol Campbell and Steven Gerrard to miss training ahead of England's Euro 2004 game against Switzerland.

This could have been due to the very hot weather – heat causes the foot to swell. It can be made worse if the players have been wearing sandals or walking around bare-foot. If this is the case then their boots may not fit comfortably. Footballers put their feet through an enormous amount of stress.

For example, when they go up for a header, the body's entire weight is coming down on such a small area. That's a huge amount of pressure.

To treat blisters, the first thing you have to do is cleanse the skin with a sterilising solution. Then, with a sterilised needle, puncture the blister. Having done that, make sure you do not damage the skin otherwise it could create further problems. The next step is to put a protective covering over the blister to prevent infections. Chiropodists use something called hydro gel to cover the blister. It is like a second skin and protects the foot from further damage.

The amount of time it takes to heal depends upon how big the blister is, but on average a couple of days is enough.

You can get blood blisters, which are a mix of blood and serum. Some can get as big as 3 or 4 inches in width and length. The most important thing to remember is to put a protective barrier around them until they heal.

You can prevent blisters by wearing your football boots in properly to soften up the leather. Wear them around the house as this will help to mould the boot around your foot's shape.

Tennis elbow

This is a very painful injury that occurs to the outside of the elbow where the tendons that cock the wrist become inflamed. These tendons attach to the bony part of the outer elbow bone called the 'lateral epicondyle'. The scientific name for the injury is 'lateral epicondylitis', meaning inflammation to the outside elbow bone. We refer to it as tennis elbow as it is tennis players who mainly suffer from it.

It is caused by the repetitive action of hitting thousands and thousands of tennis balls. Tiny tears develop in the forearm tendon attachment at the elbow. The pain starts slowly but increases to a point where hitting the ball, especially a backhand shot, becomes just about impossible. If you rest your arm when the discomfort first appears then these micro-tears will heal. However, if you keep on playing, the micro-tears will become bigger, eventually causing pain and swelling that completely prevents you from hitting a ball.

Pain can stretch down the forearm to the hand, and simple things like holding a cup of tea or carrying a case become painful, forcing the sufferer to use the other hand.

Figure 2.1

The scientific name for tennis elbow is 'lateral epicondylitis', meaning inflammation to the outside elbow bone. We refer to it as tennis elbow as tennis players mainly suffer from it

To treat this condition, the first thing to do is rest from tennis to allow the micro-tears to heal. The main cause for the injury is playing too much, so the sufferer will have to cut out hitting balls altogether.

Other reasons may be equipment-related, such as too large a handle or a racket that is strung too tightly.

The best treatment for tennis elbow is a combination of:

- ice to reduce swelling
- anti-inflammatory tablets from a doctor
- soft tissue massage to the tight forearm muscles and the injured tendons once the pain has gone down
- stretching the forearm muscles to help blood to flow and tissues to heal
- ultrasound therapy
- strengthening exercises for the forearm muscles and tendons.

Sometimes top tennis stars require cortisone injections or an operation if the injury does not respond to rest and physiotherapy.

Strengthening the forearm muscles that grip the racket and stiffening the wrist during backhand shots should help to prevent the injury from happening again. The player should stretch the forearm muscles and tendons when warming up and might want to try an elbow brace to take the pressure off the injured tendon.

Technique adjustments may also help. For example, one could try playing the backhand shot more from the shoulders and less from the wrist. One could try to reduce the amount of straight-arm shots by bending the arm at the elbow. This will bring the shoulder and arm muscles more into play and take the pressure off the wrist and forearm muscles and tendons.

Dealing with Injuries and Illnesses Associated with Sports Participation

The following help to prevent the injuries or health problems identified above:

- Make sure that you are fit for sport. If you are to play an activity requiring stamina, make sure that you have good cardio-respiratory fitness (more on this later in the book). If you are required to stretch suddenly in basketball, for example, make sure that you have worked on your flexibility to prevent injury. Be aware of the main principles of fitness training that will be covered later. Any training programme must take the individual into account. The person's age, the time available, equipment available and skill level must all be taken into consideration before the principles of training are applied.
- Each player must reach a particular skill level and have good skill technique before performing seriously in sport. Training should include basic skills that,

when practised enough, become almost second nature. Injury is much less likely the higher your personal skill level. Ensure that skills and techniques follow technical models of how the skill ought to be performed to ensure personal health and safety.

■ Whatever the level of the sport, whether it is serious competition or just recreational play, you should be prepared for the activity by carrying out an effective warm-up. This often includes some light activity to raise the body's temperature and to ensure better flexibility in muscles and ligaments. In team games the activity may include light jogging followed by a series of stretching exercises to prepare the muscles for sudden and prolonged movement. A cool-down is equally important and should take place immediately after exercise. The cool-down normally involves similar exercises to the warm-up – steady jogging and stretching. This enables lactic acid to be dispersed and prevents muscle soreness during the days following the activity.

■ Always ensure that your training is safe. After warming up sufficiently your exercise regime should suit your age, ability and physical fitness. You should also ensure that you do not push yourself too hard and that you 'listen' to your body and stop if any exercise hurts or you are becoming unduly fatigued.

case study 2.5 — Warming up for golf

Nick Dougherty, Golf professional

Upcoming golf star, Dougherty, recommends stretching your arms by raising them above your head, keeping your palms together. He then stretches the fingertips on the left hand higher than the right and then those on the right higher than the left. To loosen up he hits around fifty practice shots before beginning a round.

(Adapted from www.bbc.co.uk/sport, 2004)

Figure 2.2

You should be prepared for any activity by carrying out an effective warm-up

Training safely

The following are essential components of any training programme (source: Honeybourne *et al.*, 2000):

- identify the individual's training goal
- identify the macro, meso and micro cycles
- identify the fitness components to be improved
- establish the energy systems to be used
- identify the muscle groups that will be used
- evaluate the fitness components involved
- use a training diary
- vary the programme to maintain motivation
- include rest in the programme for recovery
- evaluate and reassess goals.

See Unit 4 Preparation for Sport, page 84

Eating and drinking correctly

Participants in sport, like everyone else, should have a balanced diet that ensures they have all the nutrients and enough water. Unit 10 will deal with diet in more detail. A healthy diet should contain enough fruit and vegetables. This helps to reduce the likelihood of coronary heart disease and some cancers. Government guidelines suggest that you should eat at least five portions of fruit and vegetables each day. Most healthy eating guidelines warn against eating too much salt. If your diet contains too much salt then this may lead to high blood pressure, which can cause heart and kidney disease (Honeybourne, 2003). The athlete may lose up to 1 litre of water per hour during endurance exercise so rehydration is essential, especially if there are also hot environmental conditions. The athlete needs to drink plenty during and after exercise even if little thirst is experienced.

A sports person, whether a serious competitor or a casual participant, must not drink too much alcohol because this interferes with health and fitness levels. Fitness-enhancing drugs are, of course, banned and they should never be taken because of the many health risks and because anyone caught using them is likely to be banned from competition and be labelled as a cheat!

Safe equipment, clothing and environment

Make sure that all equipment is 'fit for purpose' – in other words that it is in good working order and is safe to use. Clothing for sport should also be suitable for the activity to provide enough warmth and also to not be hazardous to the owner and others around them. Any playing surfaces should also be safe. For example football pitches should be checked for broken glass or large stones and the basketball court should be dry and not slippery.

Correct lifting and carrying procedures

If you have to lift or carry sports equipment ensure that you follow the guidelines for lifting and carrying such equipment. For example a heavy piece of equipment should be lifted with other people or a machine/device which helps you to lift. Instructions/guidelines must be strictly followed, otherwise injury can occur.

---

case study

2.6

Injury statistics

The injuries in the report cover the five-year period from 1994/95 to 1998/99.

There were three fatal injuries occurring in the sports and recreation industry: one death involved being struck by a vehicle; another resulted from an explosion; and one resulted from coming into contact with moving machinery.

Fatal injuries to members of the public include:

'A child was crushed by an unsecured mobile goal post while playing on a football field. Children moved the posts from their usual secured storage place so that they could use them. The goal posts were very heavy and unstable, and needed secure fixing before use.'

'A man died when his jet ski collided with a similar water craft piloted by a friend. The jet skis had been inspected and serviced by the proprietor of the jet ski centre. Observers said the two men were not observing sufficient caution while piloting the craft. The coroner reported a verdict of accidental death. No blame was attached to the proprietors. An engineer found the craft to be in perfect working order.'

'A member of the public was killed when he crashed at a motor racing circuit. The man had been taking part in a motorcycle "experience" activity. The rider died as a result of head injuries sustained in the accident. The investigation revealed that there was no obvious cause of the accident.'

Non-fatal injuries

In the five-year period to 1998/99 there were 3675 non-fatal injuries to members of the public in the sports and recreation industry.

Of these 3675 non-fatal injuries:

- 1430 (39%) injuries resulted from a slip or trip (762 involved slipping whilst playing sports);

- 228 involved slipping on a slippery surface (148 involved lost footing and 122 involved falling over an obstruction);

- 1347 (37%) injuries resulted from a fall from a height (640 involved falling from an animal, 297 involved falling whilst playing sport and 126 involved a fall from a motor vehicle);

- 319 (9%) injuries resulted from striking a fixed object (216 involved walking into a fixed object, e.g. a wall, 43 involved walking into or striking another person and 21 stepped on a nail or other similar object).

Major injuries
Of the 999 major injuries:

- 349 (35%) injuries resulted from a slip or trip (106 involved slipping on a slippery surface);

- 75 (4%) involved lost footing (62 involved falling over an obstruction and 60 involved slipping whilst playing sports);

- 227 (23%) injuries resulted from fall from a height (97 involved a fall from an animal, 30 involved a fall down stairs and 25 resulted from a fall from another object);

- 95 (10%) injuries resulted from being struck by a moving or falling object (17 involved being struck by an object falling from a shelf, table or stack, 15 were struck by a door or ramp, 11 involved being struck by a falling piece of structure and 11 involved being struck by flying chips or nails);

- 79 (8%) injuries resulted from handling, lifting or carrying a load (of which 39 involved an awkward or sharp object and 24 involved a heavy object);

- 68 (7%) injuries resulted from being injured by an animal.

(Source: Health and Safety Executive)

Alternative treatments
The medical profession is increasingly aware and more accepting of alternative treatments for injured sportspeople. There is no reason why they should not be tried as long as the practitioner is appropriately qualified. Personal recommendation is best. If you hear of someone who has benefited from such treatment find out details about the therapist.

Acupuncture
Acupuncture is a traditional form of Chinese medicine that has been in existence for over 3000 years. It involves inserting needles into the skin in strategic places called acupuncture points, situated along energy channels called meridians. The Chinese believe that energy flows around the body in these channels. If it flows freely, the body is in a healthy state but if there is a problem energy stagnates and pain and other symptoms may develop. The stimulation of these acupuncture points frees this stagnation and allows the body to continue to return to a healthy state.

Figure 2.3

If it flows freely, the body is in a healthy state but if there is a problem, energy stagnates and pain and other symptoms may develop

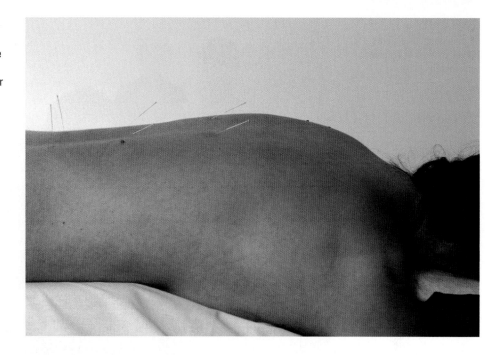

Yoga

Yoga, was developed in India and is a system of personal development involving body, mind, and spirit that dates back more than 5000 years. The aim of this integrated approach of mind and body control is ultimate physical health and happiness, together with mental peace and tranquillity.

Today, yoga is practised for general health, and for its preventive and curative effects.

There are various types of yoga, all of them leading ultimately to the same goal – unification with the Divine. The yoga paths can be broadly classified into:

- **bhakti yoga** – the path of devotion
- **karma yoga** – the path of selfless action
- **jnana yoga** – the path of transcendental knowledge
- **asthanga yoga** – the path of Patanjali (eight-step path).

In the Western world yoga is recognised mainly as hatha yoga, which is a combination of *asanas* (physical exercises and postures), *pranayama* (breathing techniques) and meditation. Hatha yoga is said to provide a balanced and wholesome approach to achieving perfect physical and mental health, happiness and tranquillity.

Eastern yogis believe that *asanas* are simply a stepping-stone to higher paths and that working only on the body is a waste of time as the body is mortal whereas the soul is immortal. Hatha yoga is in fact a single step in the eight-step path of asthanga yoga.

Figure 2.4
Yoga is good for general fitness as well as helping with injuries in sport

Many people learn yoga by attending classes; however, videos and books teaching yoga are also popular. As with all exercises, technique is very important and for this reason it is advisable for beginners to seek out a reputable teacher.

Yoga can be practised by anyone, at any age, it develops flexibility and muscular endurance and, like many of the martial arts, incorporates techniques to relieve stress and bring the mind and body into harmony. Yoga is a Sanskrit word for 'union' and means an experience of oneness or union with your inner being (self).

Homeopathy

Homeopathy is the treatment of 'like with like'. Minute doses of substances that can cause signs of illness in a healthy person are used to treat the same symptoms in a sick person. Tiny doses of plant, animal or mineral materials are soaked in alcohol and then diluted and shaken vigorously. The more a substance is diluted, the stronger its therapeutic or helpful effect. Testing the substance on healthy volunteers and noting the symptoms produced has determined the effect of each remedy.

Chiropractic

The most common forms of **manipulation** practised in complementary medicine are osteopathy and chiropractic. Physiotherapists also use manipulation techniques. Manipulation is the use of various manual techniques to rebalance the spine and joints of the body, to increase the range of movement of the joints and to stretch and relax the muscles. Chiropractic focuses on the links between the spine and the nervous system. Corrections of spinal imbalance are believed

keyword

Manipulation
The term 'manipulation' comes from Latin. Manipulate means 'to handle'. It covers a range of techniques, using the hands to realign the structural system of the body, relax the muscles and improve circulation.

to help restore the nervous system and improve internal organ function. Chiropractors generally use direct manipulation or quite vigorous massage techniques whereas osteopaths also use direct techniques but often favour gentle manipulations, soft-tissue massage and subtle cranial (head massage) techniques as well. Manipulation has been shown to be beneficial for joint and back problems, especially low back pain, neck stiffness and pain, and knee problems. It can also help relieve headaches and ear, nose and throat problems that are caused by restriction of the spine and muscle tension.

The Risks and Hazards Associated with Sports Participation

The main risks for participants in sport are:

- **Poor physical fitness/inappropriate physique for the activity**. Sports activities require at least some level of fitness of the participant. For example to be involved in gymnastics you need to have some flexibility and the ability to support your own weight. A netball player needs to have some stamina and the ability to run up and down a netball court. Most sports are quite physically demanding and any person who has an injury or has health problems should seek advice from a qualified medical practitioner before participating. If you wish to play rugby football as a forward you will need to be physically strong to be able to withstand the physical demands of scrimmaging to prevent the risks of injury.

- **Poor level of skill or technique**. There are many cases of injury caused through inexperience. Some players new to sport will not know how to participate safely. There are, for example, more injuries sustained in hockey at lower ability levels related to inappropriate use of the hockey stick – a novice player does not have the stick control of a more experienced player. Club squash players suffer more eye injuries than international players because the ball is more likely to be struck in an inappropriate or unpredictable manner. Sports performers also sustain injuries because of poor technique. A golfer who has an inefficient golf swing can sustain back injuries. A tennis player who uses the wrist too much in shots may suffer wrist sprains. A javelin thrower in athletics who does not throw with a correct technique can suffer arm, leg and back strains.

- **Lack of effective preparation for sport – for example warming up and cooling down**. It is crucial that all performers in sport take appropriate steps to prepare for vigorous activity through an effective warm-up and following the activity a cool-down. This applies to all sports activities at all levels. If you are merely a beginner it is just as important to warm up properly. The benefits of an effective warm-up and cool-down are well documented. The warm-up enables the body to prepare for exercise. It decreases the likelihood of injuries and muscle soreness. There is also a release of adrenaline that will start speeding up the delivery of oxygen to the working muscles. There is also an increase in muscle temperature, which will help with the supply of much-needed energy. The muscle also becomes more flexible and this helps to prevent injury. The cool-down is also important for effective training. If light exercise follows training, then the oxygen can more effectively be flushed through the muscle tissue and will oxidise lactic acid, which needs to be dispersed. Cool-downs also prevent blood pooling in the veins, which can cause dizziness.

See Unit 4 Preparation for Sport

■ **Dangerous training practices**. There are many different training methods. Some of the more conventional ones will be dealt with later in this book. There are, however, some methods not recognised by sports professionals, which may prove to be dangerous and cause injury or illness. There are also types of training only suited to the very best performers whose bodies are able to take – and indeed need – the extra stresses and strains for top competition. If a novice performer attempts advanced training methods without working up towards them then injury is much more likely. Training methods will be dealt with in later units but it is important that certain safety issues should be addressed, whatever the method of training. Health and safety are very important whatever level you are at in your sport.

■ **Inadequate or inappropriate diet**. It is very important that a sports performer eats and drinks appropriately. You must maintain the right balance in a diet for good health and fitness. The intake of water before, during and after exercise is very important, otherwise you may become dehydrated. Studies show that individuals who are dehydrated become ill. The body's systems become inefficient if there is dehydration and the body cannot provide adequate bloodflow to the skin. This essential to prevent heat exhaustion. Fluids must be taken in during prolonged exercise. This will make dehydration less likely and will slow the rise in body temperature. Water is the most important constituent in any drink taken before, during and after exercise because it empties from the stomach extremely quickly and reduces dehydration associated with sweating.

See Unit 4 Preparation for Sport, pages 80–81

■ **Dangerous environment, for example broken bottles on a playing field**. The playing field, court or track all have potential hazards associated with them. Many recreational pitches may have litter that is dangerous to sports participants. Large stones, broken glass and even discarded hypodermic syringe needles can cause serious injury.

case study 2.7 — Dangerous training practices

Serious injuries and even deaths have occurred in javelin training. In long-distance running there have been athletes who have not prepared properly and who have suffered from severe heat exhaustion. Even very simple activities such as shooting at a goal in hockey can be dangerous if safety is not emphasised by players waiting for appropriate moments to shoot. In gymnastics horrendous spinal injuries have been caused by pushing young gymnasts too far and getting them to attempt moves that they are not ready for.

keyword

Hypothermia
Hypothermia results from a reduction in the body's core temperature. If the core temperature drops to 35°C or below then you are deemed to be suffering from hypothermia. If the core temperature continues to drop then there is a real risk of death.

- **Weather conditions**. The weather can cause problems for the athlete. For example, if there is a thunderstorm there is a risk of being struck by lightning especially in water based activities. Severe hot weather can cause dehydration and heat exhaustion and severe cold weather can cause **hypothermia**.

- **Inappropriate or dangerous clothing**. When you participate in sport you must wear the correct clothing for the activity. This is true whether the activity is a 'kick around' in the park or preparation for an Olympic final and whatever the level of your ability. Certain items of clothing can be dangerous – for example training shoes must be correctly laced to avoid them coming off. Jewellery should not be worn if you are participating in activities where it might hurt you or others. For example a necklace could become caught in the clothing of an opponent giving you a serious cut to the neck, or other people could hurt themselves on your rings. Clothing should also be appropriate to the weather conditions. If the weather is very hot then obviously you would wear lighter clothes and if it is very cold then it is important to wear enough clothes to keep warm.

case study 2.8 — Anabolic steroids

Anabolic steroids are man-made drugs that increase muscle growth if taken with vigorous training. This enables the athlete to recover quicker and therefore to be able to train even harder. The main problems with taking such drugs are: the liver and kidneys can develop tumours; the liver ceases to act properly causing major health problems; high blood pressure, severe acne or spots; shrinking of the testicles, reduced sperm count and the development of breasts in males; the growth of facial hair, baldness and deepening of the voice in females. There is also an increase in aggression and other psychological problems.

- **Lifting and carrying equipment**. There are many instances of back strains and even broken limbs caused by the incorrect methods of lifting and carrying sports equipment. For example, heavy gymnastic equipment, if carried incorrectly, is a hazard to the health and safety of the carrier and also to others who may be around at the time. Correct techniques should be used for lifting equipment – those working in sports centres are taught to bend their legs rather than their back to lift, protecting the back from injury. Trampolines, for instance, should only be put up by those who have been trained to do so because of the danger of the trampoline's legs springing up and causing injury.

- **Inappropriate or damaged equipment**. The equipment used in sport should be correct for the activity and the age/ability of the people involved. For example, in gymnastics the vaulting box should be at an appropriate height. For very young novice tennis players the rackets may be lighter and smaller than full size. If the equipment is inappropriate then injury may occur – for example if a vault is too high then there is a greater chance of the gymnast colliding with the vaulting box. A tennis player who has too heavy a racket may well experience muscle strains in the arm. Damaged equipment can also cause injury. For example a basketball backboard, if damaged, may well become loose and fall upon a competitor, causing serious injury.

- **Behaviour of other participants**. In sport it is particularly important to behave correctly in order to prevent injury. If a child throws a discus out of turn then this may well hit another child, causing a nasty injury. If a team player becomes overly aggressive and hits out at an opponent then again injury will occur. In outdoor activities if a participant in canoeing decides to tip someone else out of their canoe then there is a risk of serious injury or even drowning. It is important to establish codes of behaviour so that all participants know what is expected of them when playing a particular sport.

Rules and Regulations in Sport

Rules and regulations have been designed to protect individuals in the workplace and also those who participate in sport. If the laws, regulations and guidelines are checked thoroughly and followed properly then it is much less likely that an accident will happen or that lives will be put at risk.

Health and Safety at Work Act (HSWA) 1974

This Act has led to big improvements in the quality of sports buildings and equipment. It has also led to better staff working conditions.

The Act includes measures for:

> . . . Securing the health, safety and welfare of persons at work and for protecting others against risks to health or safety . . . controlling the keeping and use of dangerous substances . . . controlling emissions into the atmosphere . . .

Health and Safety at Work Act

The HSWA has been called an 'enabling Act'. In other words it allows for further regulations without full legislation via parliament. For example after the tragedy in Lyme Bay in 1993, when four canoeists died following an outing from an outdoor activity centre, a further Act came into force – Activity Centre (Young Persons' Safety) Act 1995.

European Directives 1992

The European Community passed the following directives relating to health and safety:

- Management of Health and Safety at Work regulations (MHSW) – this concerns how employers and employees manage their facilities so that there are adequate health and safety procedures.

- Personal Protective Equipment at Work regulations (PPE) – this concerns the wearing of appropriate safety equipment such as goggles and ear defenders.

- Manual Handling Operations (MHO) – this concerns the finding of ways to make manual handling of equipment less hazardous.

- Health and Safety (Display Screen Equipment) regulations (DSE). It is now commonplace for workers to be in front of a computer display screen for many hours each day. These regulations are designed to protect such workers by ensuring adequate training, work breaks and a suitable environment.

Control of Substances Hazardous to Health regulations (COSSH) 1994

A hazardous substance is one that is toxic, harmful and corrosive or an irritant. In the leisure and recreation industry there is widespread use of chemicals, used for cleaning, hygiene and disinfecting. Swimming pools, in particular, use chlorine and ozone to keep pool water clean. These regulations concern their storage and use.

Employers must:

- have a code of practice for the control of hazardous substances
- have a trained risk assessor
- inform all staff of regulations and published guidance
- make sure that only absolutely necessary hazardous substances are used
- train staff adequately in the use of personal protection and emergency procedures
- have a system of maintaining control of these substances e.g. how long they are to be stored
- monitor the handling of hazardous substances.

Health and Safety (First Aid) regulations 1981

A procedure for treating injuries must be in place to conform to these regulations. The leisure and recreation industry involves supervising and participating in activities that have risks associated with them. At times there are those who do not follow rules, they may themselves suffer from a known or unknown existing medical condition and there are many chance circumstances that may result in injury.

One of the most important elements of these regulations is that they require efficient record keeping of incidents, including the circumstances and possible causes of accidents. These records are important if risk assessments are to be reviewed and accidents can be prevented from happening again. In the present climate of increased litigation, it is also very important to keep records in case there are legal proceedings following an accident.

There are accidents or outbreaks of disease that have to be reported to the appropriate authority such as the local authority's environmental health department. The reporting of serious incidents is necessary if regulations are to be followed. The regulations in this case are the 'Reporting of Injuries, Diseases and Dangerous Occurrences regulations' 1995, also known as RIDDOR.

Children Act 1989

This had a huge impact on the sport industry, especially play work. The Act contributed significantly to a greater emphasis on care provision and child protection. The Children Act was aimed at children under the age of eight but its interpretation has had an impact on the provision for all school-aged children. There has been a growing demand for trained and qualified play workers, for instance, because of the fit person to child numbers ratios, such as a staff ratio of 8:1 for children under eight. Records must be kept of accidents, attendance and names of all employees and volunteers.

There is an increase in awareness of child abuse and there are many positions of trust with children associated with the sport and leisure industry. This Act protects not only the children but also employees who can be accused falsely or accidentally of abuse.

Examples of guidance include:

- do not get into isolated situations with children
- physical contact must be minimal and involve only non-sensitive areas of the body, such as hands
- use physical restraint only in emergencies
- show appropriate role model behaviour – not swearing, smoking or drinking alcohol.

Safety at Sports Grounds Act 1975

This Act is concerned with large sports stadia that have at least 10 000 spectators. The owners and managers of such stadia are criminally liable if the Act is not implemented and so it is a strong and important legislative Act. It requires that:

- a stadium can only be used after a safety certificate has been issued
- this certificate is only for the activities applied for in the stadium
- there is a stated number of spectators allowed in the stadium
- there is a record of attendance
- there are records of maintenance to the stadium.

In crowds people's behaviour can be erratic and if there is panic there may well be crush injuries resulting in death. There has been a growth of very large sports stadia in the UK since the beginning of the twentieth century and there was little control over the numbers that were let into each stadium or how spectators were controlled. Consequently there have been some dreadful disasters:

- 1924 Football Cup Final – injuries and loss of crowd control
- disasters at Bolton Wanderers (1946) and Ibrox stadium (1971) prompted a public inquiry
- 1986 Bradford – fire disaster with 56 deaths
- 1989 Hillsborough – disaster involving 96 deaths.

These disasters prompted more legislation to be enacted.

Undertaking a Risk Assessment Relevant to Sport

Situation assessment

When you are faced with a situation where there is someone injured in a sports activity, then it is important to prioritise your actions. In other words what is it important to do first and what next?

Anyone who has some knowledge of first aid can be very helpful if the injured person is to recover quickly. It is best to try to obtain a recognised first aid qualification.

When an accident occurs it is important to establish what is wrong with the injured person:

1 Make an assessment of the situation. What risks are there to you, the injured person and to others around?

2 Ensure that the area is safe. Make sure play has stopped or other activities close by have moved away or have stopped. If someone has been electrocuted then turn off the electric switch.

3 Give first aid – if you know what you are doing! Identify whether the victim is conscious and then check the 'ABC':

A – Airway should be open.

B – Breathing should be OK.

C – Circulation – check their pulse.

(This will be covered in more detail on a recognised first aid qualification course.)

4 Get help.

5 Call an ambulance if necessary:

- dial 999
- ask for the ambulance service
- make sure you give an accurate location
- give clear, simple details about what has happened
- give some simple details about the injured person, such as gender and age.

Risk assessment

To be able to prepare a **risk assessment** it is important to identify:

- **The health and safety hazards in a given situation** – this includes identifying equipment faults, use of chemicals, other substances hazardous to health and the possibility of spillages.

- **The purpose of the assessment. Identify the level of risk**. The assessment is designed mostly to minimise injury to participants and workers. It is also designed to ensure that the activity involved can be successful with no injury or accident but hopefully keeping the excitement and thrill of a sports activity. A safe environment is crucial if the activity is to be successful.

- **The risks involved**. Participants, coaches, supervisors and others involved must be aware of their responsibilities in limiting the risks in any sports activity. The risks should be calculated, specialist equipment used and record sheets and other documents kept up to date.

- **Procedures for monitoring or checking that risks are kept to a minimum**. If there are any changes to the planning of an activity, these should be reviewed to identify their levels of success. There may be other equipment to buy to make the environment safe or new procedures to be used. All this must be planned within an identified timescale.

Identifying hazards

The area in which the activity takes place must be examined carefully to identify hazards that may be present. The facilities and equipment that are used in sports activities often carry warnings of possible injuries and these must be taken into account.

There may be obvious risks associated with the activity, the equipment or the facilities provided – for example, in a swimming pool or in an athletics session related to throwing.

There are many risks associated with sports activities and without those risks sport would lose its excitement and popularity but the risks can still be minimised with sufficient care and attention to detail. The main causes of accidents are:

- **objects falling** – for example, a container falling off a shelf in a leisure centre
- **trips and falls** – for example, a path leading up to a sports facility may be uneven
- **electric shock** – perhaps from a hi-fi music machine used for an aerobics session
- **crowds** – supporters at a football match
- **poisoning** – toxic chemicals used in a swimming pool
- **being hit by something**, such as a javelin
- **fire** – in the changing rooms of a sports centre
- **explosion** – in the store area of a leisure centre
- **asphyxiation** – chemicals used for cleaning.

Identify who might be harmed

Care must be taken to identify and protect those who may not be fully aware of obvious risks, for instance children or those with learning difficulties, or those new to a job in a leisure centre, or a beginner in a sports activity. Once those who are at particular risk are identified, there needs to be an assessment of how they might be harmed and safety procedures should be put into place to make sure that those involved are protected from harm.

Evaluate whether existing safety measures are adequate

There must be an assessment of how dangerous a particular **hazard** is and then whether the **risks** associated with that hazard is high, moderate or low. If the hazard is particularly dangerous and the risks are high, then clearly the more serious the situation and the more care has to be taken.

In many cases it may be possible to remove the hazard altogether. For instance the path that is uneven can be put out of bounds or a broken indoor football goal can be removed from the sports hall.

In some cases the hazard would have to be made safer in some way to lower the risks. For example glass in a door that is frequently can be replaced by non-breakable plastic, or additional safety mats can be provided for a trampoline.

The risks arising from some hazards can be limited by using protective equipment, for example the wearing of protective gloves when handling cleaning equipment or a rugby player wearing a gum-shield. Another example of a piece of protective equipment in sport is a squash player wearing protective goggles to minimise the risk of impact with the ball.

The hazard is often supervised so that the risks are minimised, for example a lifeguard at a swimming pool, or spotters around a trampoline or a coach supporting a gymnast on the beam.

keyword

Hazard
Something that has the potential to cause harm.

keyword

Risk
The chance that someone will be harmed by the hazard.

Make a record of your judgements

It is a legal requirement for an organisation that has five or more employees to record the risk assessment.

Monitor, evaluate and revise the risk assessment regularly

Assessments are often soon out of date, so it is important that assessments are reviewed regularly. Procedures should also be reviewed after any incident that may have caused or nearly caused injury. If there was any aspect of risk assessment that was not accurate or realistic then there should be a reassessment and procedures reviewed and changed if necessary.

---

case study 2.10

Risk assessment pro-forma

OPERATOR ....

ADDRESS ....

TEL ....

DATE OF ASSESSMENT ....

ASSESSMENT REVIEW DATE ....

SIGNED..

DATE ....

Activity – Flat water kayaking
Introductory session
(May–August)
Location site: 'Safe practice lake'

(Source: adapted from British Canoe Union Guidelines, 2004)

Figure 2.5

Hazard	Who might be harmed?	Is the risk adequately controlled?	What further action is necessary to control the risk?
Drowning (generic risk)	Staff Clients	Buoyancy aids to be worn at all times on the water. B's comply with CEA standards. BAs undergo flotation monitoring to standards laid out in BCU guidelines. Kayaks are also monitored to this same BCU standard. Staff are BCU qualified for type of water. Ratio of 1:8.	All clients given a pre-session briefing – action in the event of a capsize is explained here. BAs sized and fitted. Checks are made by staff.
Hypothermia (generic risk)	Staff Clients	All staff/clients to wear warm clothing as appropriate. Wetsuit long-johns can be issued at the discretion of the instructor in charge of the session. All staff/ clients are issued with a waterproof kayak cag. A head covering is always used.	Staff judgement calls to be upheld. Established 'cut offs' for sessions i.e. wind onshore force 3, offshore force, 2 max (Beaufort Scale). Green Bay is a 'Sheltered' site (in BCU terms of reference) with generally good landing points.

progress check

1   Name ten of the main risks associated with sport.

2   Choose one of the above risks and give an example from a sports activity.

3   Give three ways in which you can minimise the chance of an injury in sport.

4   What factors should be taken into account when planning a safe training programme for a sports activity of your choice?

5   Outline the Health and Safety at Work Act 1974.

6   Give two regulations that are included in the Control of Substances Hazardous to Health Regulations (COSSH) 1994.

7   Identify three points for guidance that you would give to anyone working with children in sport.

8   Name a sports injury that you or a friend has had recently. Give details of the injury and how you would treat it immediately after the injury took place.

9   What factors should you take into consideration when planning a risk assessment in sport?

10 Give examples of low, moderate and high risks in sport.

The Sports Industry

This unit covers:

- understanding the nature of the sports industry
- how and why people participate in sport
- how the sports industry is funded
- the impact of different key issues upon the sports industry

The material in this unit is central to the course and will be useful to refer to when studying other units. It covers the nature of sport and what it means to us in our society, as well as who plays sport and who does not and why. The unit also discusses how sport is organised and funded in the UK. There are important influences on sport in our society and this unit explores the role of the media, professionalism and the misuse of drugs in sport.

grading criteria

To achieve a **Pass** grade the evidence must show that the learner is able to:	To achieve a **Merit** grade the evidence must show that the learner is able to:	To achieve a **Distinction** grade the evidence must show that the learner is able to:
P1 Describe the local provision of sport	**M1** Compare local and national provision of sport, identifying areas for improvement	**D1** Evaluate local and national provision of sport, suggesting ways in which local provision could be improved
P2 Describe the national provision of sport	**M2** Explain how a chosen sport is organised and funded, identifying areas for improvement	**D2** Evaluate the organisation and funding of a chosen sport, suggesting ways in which it could be improved
P3 Describe how a chosen sport is organised and funded	**M3** Explain strategies used by a chosen sport to encourage participation	**D3** Evaluate strategies used by a chosen sport to encourage participation
P4 Describe ways in which people participate in sport and reasons for participation	**M4** Explain the impact of four key issues on sport	
P5 Describe factors that affect participation in sport		

Understanding the Nature of the Sports Industry

> **keyword**
>
> **Sport**
> This involves competition between individuals or teams that is organised and includes physical activity.

It is important to recognise what we mean by the term '**sport**'.

Sport involves competitive activity. Competitions can involve individuals, for example in skiing one person competes against another. In the high jump one individual tries to jump higher than another. Competitions can also involve teams, for example a hockey or football team playing against another team. Sport often involves people watching – spectators. The audience or spectators often pay to watch if professional sport is involved. For example those who wish to watch county cricket have to pay to enter the ground.

At times both individual competitions and team competitions can exist at the same time. For example, in rugby one prop forward is competing against another to push harder in the scrummage, but the prop forward is also part of the whole rugby team in competition against the other team.

Figure 3.1

A tennis net may contribute to a 'lucky' shot …

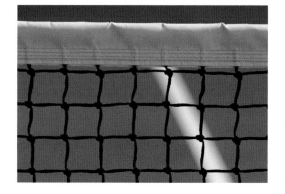

In most sports you have a winner or a loser, or in some sports you can have a draw where there is no clear winner. Sports also involve rules so that the competition that takes place is fair and there is no unfair advantage to a team or an individual. This helps to prevent cheating. In sport there is also usually a defined place to play, for example a netball court or a football pitch. These sports places usually have boundaries, for example the sideline on a hockey pitch. Sport also involves a certain amount of luck or chance, for example the ball in tennis may hit the net cord and travel over to the other side rather than your side, thus winning you a point.

The Sports Industry

We use lots of different terms when describing activities related to sport. For example sport is often divided into the following different types:

- Invasion games. The object of these types of games is to invade the opponent's territory, as if you are war with the opposition – which of course you are not! Rugby, netball and football are examples of invasion games.

- Target games. As the name suggests the aim of the game is to hit certain targets. They involve accuracy of judgement often called 'marksmanship'. Target games include golf and archery.

- Court games. These games include tennis, squash and volleyball. There is usually no contact between the players because they are kept apart by a net, although in squash both players occupy the same space.

- Field sports. These are often associated with rural areas, but not always. Sports such as shooting and fishing are field sports and are linked with killing animals for food, although the point of most field sports is the competition between the human being and the animal he or she wishes to kill. Many people who participate in field sports describe the 'thrill of the chase' as the most enjoyable aspect of this type of sport. Others oppose this activity and view it as cruel and unsporting because the animal has no choice in its participation and it is not a fair competition.

Figure 3.2

Invasion games involve invading the opponents' territory

Amateurs and professionals

Sport can be played as an amateur or a professional. An example of an amateur player would be a netball player who plays for her local club or a rugby player who plays for his local club. Both of these players would not receive any money for playing the sport. An example of a professional would be a county cricket player or a football player who plays in the football league. Both of these players play for a living – it is their job to play the sport and therefore they are called professional players. There are some players who are called semi-professionals who receive money for playing but do not earn enough to make a living from the sport and therefore have other jobs to support them.

keyword

Leisure
'An activity, apart from the obligations of work, family and society, to which the individual turns at will, for either relaxation, diversion, or broadening experiences.'
(Source: adapted from Honeybourne et al., 2004)

Leisure

This is a term that we use for many different activities, which may involve sport, but sport is different to **leisure**. Leisure is a wider term used to describe activities we are involved in that are nothing to do with work or home/family commitments such as cleaning your room. We choose to be involved in leisure, we do not have to do it. Leisure activities then include watching TV, going to the cinema, skateboarding in the park or reading a book. For many of us the time we have for leisure has been increasing over the last 100 years. More recently with the invention of computers and machines that do many of our tasks for us, we have much more time on our hands to be involved in leisure activities.

People participate in leisure activities for a number of reasons, for example to escape the stresses of everyday life and do something enjoyable. Some become involved in leisure activities to meet other people and make friends.

Outdoor and adventurous **recreation** activities involve individual challenge, for example climbing and canoeing.

Many of these activities are in the natural environment.

keyword

Recreation
The active aspect of leisure. Recreation involves a state of mind and involves us viewing the activity as not work but active enjoyment that helps us to relax and escape stress.
(Source: Honeybourne et al., 1998)

There has been an increase in interest in outdoor and adventurous sports with the term 'extreme sports' also used to describe sports that have elements of danger associated with them. Mountain biking, climbing and windsurfing and skateboarding are very popular now.

Lifetime sports

These are sports such as badminton and golf that can be carried on throughout our lives. Just because you get old it doesn't mean you cannot be involved in such sports, thus keeping fit and active and also being socially involved with other people.

Figure 3.3
Adventurous recreation involves personal challenge

The leisure industry

The **leisure industry** has grown rapidly over the last 20 years. As we have discovered, we have more leisure time and are now more willing to spend our money on leisure activities. When money is to be spent, an industry of selling us goods and services grows, hence the growth of the leisure industry. Sport is very commercialised with events and sports competitors themselves being sponsored for large sums of money.

keyword

Leisure industry
This involves the products and services that surround leisure activities.

Products for leisure include, for example, trainers and other sports clothing, DVDs and videos.

Leisure services include cinemas, sports stadia, skateboard parks and leisure centres.

Large multinational companies such as MGM often control the business of leisure.

Leisure centres and health clubs

There has been a tremendous growth in the number of health clubs and leisure centres both in the private sector, owned by a commercial company, or in the public sector, run by local councils and subsidised by the taxpayer. Later in this unit the private and public sectors will be explored in more detail. Private clubs have certainly seen a massive growth since 2001 – for example Livingwell, LA Fitness, Fitness First and the David Lloyd Centres. There is now a demand for private trainers: fitness professionals who work with individuals for an hourly fee. Other services that have benefited from this health and fitness boom nutrition advice and beauty treatment.

case study 3.1 The private and public sectors

The local LA Fitness health club is in the private sector. Members pay a membership fee, usually for the year, and in return they receive open access to the club's health and fitness facilities.

The local leisure centre is in the public sector and is partly funded by the taxpayer. It also charges for the use of its facilities but the fees are not as expensive as private health clubs.

Sports clothing and equipment

Along with this massive rise in interest in the health and fitness industry, the clothing and equipment requirements have also increased. Sports clothing has also become highly fashionable and even those who do not participate in any sport can spend money on sports clothing to be fashionable.

Sports equipment manufacturers have also tried very hard to compete against each other to gain more sales, for example, to sell the latest training shoes or the high spec tennis rackets. There is also a big market for fitness equipment for the home. Boots stores for example now sell punch bags, exercise machines and yoga mats!

How and Why People Participate in Sport

There are many influences on whether people either participate or watch sport. There are, of course, those who show no interest in sports whatsoever but even they may be interested in keeping healthy and may well do some exercise or consider what they eat carefully.

There is still a difference in the participation levels between men and women in sport. Far more men become involved in sport either to participate or to spectate. It is still thought by some people that being good at sport or interested in sport is unfeminine, thus reinforcing male dominance in sport and sport coverage (Honeybourne, 2003).

case study

3.2

Women's tennis

In tennis there is a huge discrepancy in prize money, with women receiving far less. The media show a lot of interest in women tennis players because of their looks.

Figure 3.4

The media focus on the looks of female players rather than their sporting abilities

See Unit 12 Lifestyle and Performance, page 225.

Of course there are many positive aspects of female sport. More women are now involved in physical exercise and there is far more interest in health and fitness matters. The participation rates for women in sports such as football and rugby are now much larger and continue to grow.

People become involved in sport for many reasons including:

■ **Benefits to our health and fitness**. Sport can make us fitter and therefore healthier.

■ **Benefits to our wellbeing**. Many people report that they feel better after participating in sport. It is accepted that certain hormones are released during exercise and that these can help us to feel more optimistic about life and better about ourselves.

■ **Combating stress**. Many people often use sport as an escape from their working life. It has been recognised that by playing sport we can release some of our pent-up frustrations and aggressions – the squash ball can be hit hard to get rid of anger caused by frustrations at work or at college.

■ There are benefits in learning new skills, again giving a sense of accomplishment, and also being able to compete eventually at a higher level and increasing our satisfaction when we overcome challenges and barriers.

■ There is of course the huge benefit of meeting other people and participating with them. New friends can be made through sport. That is important for our sense of wellbeing.

case study 3.3   The London Marathon

This is an event that combines seriously competitive runners, those who are looking for a personal challenge and those who are running to make money for charity.

More than 35 000 runners took part in the 24th London Marathon on a Sunday in April 2004. The event doubled as British Olympic trials, with runners needing to record a time below 2 hours 15 minutes for the men and 2 hours 37 minutes for the women to qualify for Athens.

Sport is hugely enjoyable for all the reasons mentioned and because many of us seek competition that is fair and tests our own capabilities.

Reasons why many do not get involved in sport could include:

- **Time** – work commitments can get in the way of finding enough time for sport.
- **Resources**. There might not be appropriate facilities or sports clubs nearby. This can dictate whether you participate in sport or not. Some local authorities lay on a transport service for those who wish to visit a sports facility. For example the elderly may catch a special bus to a local leisure centre.

case study 3.4   The benefits of sport – some facts

Sport is taking youngsters away from crime and helping to fight drug abuse according to reports commissioned by Sport England.

In Bristol, there has been a 40% reduction of crime levels on the Southmead Estate since the first sport development worker was appointed.

Sports development

The organisation UK Sport, formally called the Sports Council, produced a report called *Better Quality Sport for All*. This highlighted the need to enable people to learn basic sports skills that could be built upon to achieve sporting excellence.

The report highlighted the following strategies:

- to develop the skills and competence to enable sport to be enjoyed
- for all to follow a lifestyle that includes active participation in sport and recreation
- for people to achieve their personal goals at whatever their chosen level of involvement in sport
- for developing excellence and for achieving success in sport at the highest level. (Adapted from www.sportengland.org, 2000.)

The report stated that everyone has the right to play sport. Whether it is for fun, for health, to enjoy the natural environment, or to win, everyone should have the opportunity to enjoy sport. The challenge was to make 'England the sporting nation' (Honeybourne, 2003).

The sport development continuum

This was called the 'pyramid of participation' at first and was developed into a continuum when it was recognised that most adults do not participate in sport. This non-participation has stemmed from a non-active lifestyle and often being deterred from sport by school PE experiences.

A new strategy was developed following the *Better Quality Sport for All* report. This included:

■ working with schools to encourage children to become active sporting adults

■ working with non-participating adults to encourage them to take up sport.

1 **Foundation**. This stage is concerned with the development of basic skills in sport. Good exercise habits with appropriate knowledge and understanding also help to develop positive attitudes to sport. The aims of this section of the continuum were identified as:

- to increase curriculum time for PE in schools
- to increase the numbers of children taking part in extra-curricular sport
- to increase the percentage of children taking part in out-of-school sport
- to generate more positive attitudes to sport, especially by girls
- to increase the percentage of young people taking part in a range of sports on a 'regular' basis.

2 **Participation**. This stage is concerned with involving as many people in sport as possible. The aims of this section of the continuum were:

- to increase the numbers of people taking part in regular sporting activity
- to reduce the number of people who drop out of sport as they get older
- to reduce barriers to participation in sport.

Figure 3.5

Sport development continuum model

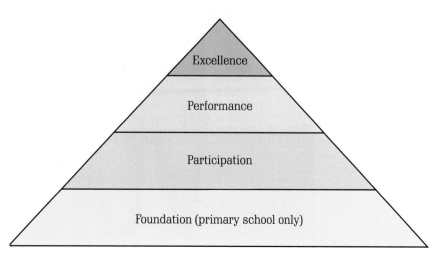

59

3 **Performance**. This refers to the improvement of coaching standards. It relates to competitive sport and encourages people to obtain fulfilment by improving their performance. The aims related to this section of the continuum are:

- to increase the numbers of participants who are trying to improve their sporting skills
- to increase the numbers of sports' club members.

4 **Excellence**. This stage is concerned with reaching the top standards in sport, such as national and international competition. The aims of this section of the continuum are:

- to achieve improved levels of performance in terms of world rankings, win–loss records, national and international records and individual personal bests
- for English teams to achieve success in international competition.

Target groups

Target groups are often identified and particular strategies put in place to ensure that everyone in society has an equal chance to become involved in sport. Sports organisations in the UK have identified particular groups of people whose **participation rates** in sport are below those of other groups. For example, in a school the participation rates for girls in extra-curricular sport could be 30%. This means only three out of every ten girls are regular members of a sports team or club.

There are many examples of inequality, or those not having an equal chance, in sport.

keyword

Participation rates
This refers to the number of people within a group who are involved in sport compared with those who are not.

Figure 3.6

The 'excellence' stage is concerned with individual personal-bests

The following are generally recognised as being groups of people who are not being given a fair chance in sport. They are not the only people who are not getting a fair chance:

- ethnic minority communities
- people with disabilities
- women
- the 50+ age group.

Sports equity concerns fairness and access for all. In sport, as in life, there are many individuals and particular groups who may feel discriminated against.

UK Sport has a written statement regarding equity in sport:

> UK Sport recognises that discrimination is unacceptable and will not tolerate discrimination on the grounds of race, special needs, including learning and physical disabilities, class or social background, religion, sexual orientation, ethnic or national origins, gender, marital status, pregnancy, age, colour or political persuasion.

> UK Sport will take positive action to eliminate individual and institutional discrimination; to comply with its statutory and legislative obligations; to meet the needs of its staff and partners and to make equality and equal treatment a core issue in the development, delivery and refinement of our policies, initiatives and services and in the way we manage our staff.

> UK Sport is committed to achieving equality in sport and is taking a proactive approach in this area. It is central to the Modernisation Programme and progressive, dynamic sports organisations are those that can demonstrate effective equality strategies and programmes.

> To underline our commitment, UK Sport:

> Has developed an Equality Strategy and Race Equality Scheme that will ensure we meet our legal obligations as well as establishing equality principles and policies within UK Sport and our work with partner organisations

> Has appointed an Equity Co-ordinator to support the organisation and its partners in developing and implementing equality strategies and programmes

> Will seek to collate and disseminate good practice from across the UK, including the work of Home Country Sports Councils and equity organisations

> Developed the Equality Standard for sport for governing bodies and sports organisations

> Co-ordinated the development of the UK Strategy Framework for Women and Sport

> Will continue to represent the UK in equality issues and good practice to the international sport and equality movement

> Is working with disability sports organisations to develop appropriate processes for drug-testing

(Source: www.uksport.gov.uk, 2004)

keyword

Sports equity
This is concerned with fairness in sport, equality of access, recognising inequalities and taking steps to address them. It is about changing the culture and structure of sport to ensure that it becomes equally accessible to all members of society.
(Source: www.sport england.org, 2002)

Barriers to participation

There are still examples and practices that are against the sense of sports equity or fairness of opportunity that has been described above.

---

case study 3.5

'Kick Racism out of Football'

This was a slogan adopted by a campaign started in 1993 to cut racial harassment in football by fans and by players. The Commission for Racial Equality and the Professional Footballers Association both backed the campaign.

Barriers also exist because many people cannot afford the equipment, facilities or membership fees to participate in many sports. It may also be very difficult for people to afford the time away from work and family commitments to be involved in sport.

Influences of sports development

The sports development policies of local authorities (the role of local authorities will be explored later in this unit) include a variety of methods to promote and develop sport at all areas of the sports development continuum. Local authorities will support local schools and colleges with help and advice from sports development officers.

Sports development officers

These are experts in a particular sport who also have coaching expertise. They can include general officers who deal with a variety of sports and activities with a particular target group and also specific sport officers who concentrate on increasing participation in one specific sport.

Organisation of sport

Organisations that are associated with sport in the UK can be divided into public, private and voluntary. We all pay our taxes to the government, which in turn funds the public organisations (funding will be dealt with later in this unit). The private sector organisations include commercial businesses trying to make a profit and non-profit-making voluntary organisations such as the Youth Hostel Association or amateur sports clubs.

Those who want to keep fit and wish to find appropriate facilities to train and exercise could use public, private or voluntary facilities:

- Public facilities include the local leisure centre, run by the local authority and funded via the taxpayer.
- Private facilities include the local private health and fitness club.
- The voluntary sector facilities includes the local athletic club where people can train to keep fit. The Youth Hostel Association is another example of a voluntary organisation that can provide information and concessionary rates to stay at youth hostels, so that people can walk or ramble to keep fit.

The public sector includes local authorities and their sports development officers, which we covered earlier in this unit. The local authorities promote sport according to local needs – for example, to promote basketball to improve levels of participation and excellence or to improve basketball court facilities.

The private sector provides sport again according to local needs and often strives to involve as many people as possible, to raise attendance levels and, very importantly because they are money-making organisations, to improve their profits. An example of a private club would be LA Fitness, a health and fitness club that provides the equipment, instruction in fitness activities and also, increasingly, personal training.

The voluntary sector also aims to provide support for local needs. It may promote specific sports – for example the local hockey club could strive to persuade as many people to play hockey as possible and might try to attract men and women from all walks of life to the game of hockey. Such a club would run teams in local leagues and hold training sessions for their members.

Other agencies

SPRITO – the national training organisation

This is the national training organisation for sport and recreation. It includes the training for leisure attractions, health and fitness instructors, outdoor activities, the caravan industry, playwork with children as well as sport and recreation.

Department for Culture, Media and Sport (DCMS)

This is a government department with responsibility for government policy related to sport. The department has a minister associated with it, responsible for sport. In the year 2000/2001, for instance, the budget for the department was approximately £1 billion, 90% of which went directly to service providers in cultural and sporting sectors.

The budget is forecast to be approximately £1.6 billion by 2005/6; this includes £25 million for coaching; £6 million for talent scholarships; £20 million per year for facilities at Community Amateur Sports Clubs and a guarantee on maintaining levels of funding through the World Class Performance Programme (CCPR, 2002).

Department for Culture, Media and Sport:
www.culture.gov.uk

UK Sport

In 1972 the national sports councils were formed by Royal Charter. In 1996 there was a reorganisation of the Sports Councils and UK Sport or the UK Sports Council was formed. UK Sport is accountable to parliament through the Department for Culture, Media and Sport and provides support for elite sports people who have a high level of performance or have the potential to reach the top. The organisation not only distributes government funds, including lottery money but also supports world-class performers and promotes ethical standards of behaviour including the fight against the use of performance-enhancing drugs through its anti-doping programme.

UK Sport works in partnership with each home country sports council and other agencies to lead sport in the UK to world-class success. The home country sports councils are:

- Sport England
- Sportscotland
- Sports Council for Northern Ireland
- Sports Council for Wales.

UK Sport:
www.uksport.gov.uk

Figure 3.7
The UK SPORT emblem

world class success

case study 3.6   UK Sport

UK Sport states that:

Our purpose is to lead the UK to sporting excellence by supporting winning athletes, world-class events, and ethically fair and drug-free sport. Our aim is that the UK will become one of the world's top five sporting nations by 2012, measured by performances at World Championships, Olympic and Paralympic Games.

Accountable to parliament through the Department for Culture, Media and Sport, UK Sport became a lottery distributor in 1999 and is responsible for the allocation of 9.2% of the Lottery Sports Fund through the World Class Performance and World Class Events Programmes.

UK Sport receives Exchequer funding in order to fulfil our role as the UK's national anti-doping agency, as well as funding a number of support programmes including International and Modernisation.

UK Sport also takes the lead among the Home Country Sports Councils in aspects requiring UK-wide strategic planning and administration, co-ordination or representation.

(Source: www.uksport.gov.uk, 2004)

UK Sports Institute (UKSI)

The aim of this organisation is to provide the very best sportspeople with appropriate facilities and support. It provides sports science advice, coaching expertise and top training facilities. The UKSI comprises of a number of centres located around the UK. Each individual home country sports council has responsibility for the development of the UKSI in its own area.

Youth Sport Trust

The Youth Sport Trust is a registered charity established in 1994 to support the education and development of all young people through physical education and sport.

It has developed and expanded a variety of linked schemes called the TOP programmes, which are designed to create a sporting pathway for young people aged 18 months to 18 years. These programmes promote the roles PE and school sport play in improving the lives and futures of all young people. The Youth Sport Trust also plays a central role in the development and support of Specialist Sports Colleges and School Sport Partnerships.

Youth Sport Trust:
www.youthsporttrust.org

Figure 3.8
The Youth Sport Trust emblem

Governing bodies

The majority of sports that we know today were developed and organised in the late nineteenth century. The participants needed to agree rules and regulations for their sports and so they met and formed their own committees called governing bodies (Honeybourne, 2003). Examples include the FA, LTA, ASA and RFU. There are over 265 governing bodies in the UK. The teams and clubs pay a subscription to the governing body, which in turn administers the sport nationally and organises competitions and the national team. There are still many amateur positions within each governing body but, increasingly, salaried members of staff are involved.

The national governing bodies are also members of international governing bodies for example UEFA and FIFA. These international bodies control and organise international competitions.

Central Council of Physical Recreation (CCPR)

The aim of the CCPR is to promote, protect and provide for the interests of the national governing bodies for sport and physical recreation in the UK. This organisation is completely independent from government control and has no responsibility for allocating funds.

Central Council of Physical Recreation:
www.ccpr.org.uk

Figure 3.9
CCPR emblem

One voice for sport and recreation

British Olympic Association (BOA)

The BOA was formed in 1905. Great Britain is one of only five countries that have never failed to be represented at the Olympics since 1896. The BOA supplies the delegates for the National Olympic Committee (NOC). The BOC is responsible, amongst other things, for the planning and execution of the Great Britain Olympic Team's participation in the Olympic and Olympic Winter Games.

British Olympic Association:
www.olympics.org.uk

International Olympic Committee (IOC)

The IOC was created by the Paris Congress in 1894. It owns all the rights to the Olympic symbol and the Games themselves. This is the world body that administers the Olympic movement. Its headquarters is in Lausanne, Switzerland. Members are appointed to the IOC and are responsible for selecting the host cities of the Olympic Games, both summer and winter.

English Federation for Disability Sport (EFDS)

This is a national body that is responsible for developing sport for people with disabilities in England. It works closely with other national disability organisations recognised by Sport England:

- British Amputees and Les Autres Sports association
- British Blind Sport
- British Deaf Sports Council
- British Wheelchair Sports Foundation
- Cerebral Palsy Sport
- Disability Sport England.

How the Sports Industry is Funded

Sports organisations have a number of different sources of funding.

Grants

These are usually made available to public and voluntary sectors (although there is an increase in private sector projects being funded as long as the project benefits the local population) and are made by local and national government and the European Union. Such bodies typically fund buildings and equipment. Many grants involve the sports organisation putting forward a percentage of the cost itself – for example the government might fund 50% of a project with 50% of the costs funded by the sports organisation itself.

Subsidies

If local authorities or councils tried to cover all the costs of sport then few people would be able to participate, for example, in swimming. There is therefore a system of subsidies whereby the members of public pay a certain cost and the local authority pays the rest. Taxpayers fund these subsidies via local government.

Membership fees

All sports organisations that have a membership – usually the voluntary sector – can take a significant proportion of their income from membership fees. For example to join a hockey club an annual membership fee is paid by each player and often there is a 'match fee' paid by the player for each game he or she plays.

The National Lottery

This is regarded as a grant for sport. The relatively newly formed (2002) English Institute of Sport, which supports world-class performers, is also funded through the lottery. UK Sport is lottery funded and this in turn funds high-performance sport in the UK. Sport England, Sports Council for Scotland and Sport Wales are also lottery funds and these fund sport at all levels.

Sponsorship

The influence of sponsorship on the development of sport has been enormous. Sport is now big business, with large amounts of money being spent by commercial companies on sports participants and events. For example a company such as Adidas might sponsor a top-class tennis player to wear a particular style of training shoe. At the other end of the scale, a local hockey club might attract a small amount of money to go towards the first team kit.

There has also been a significant increase in sponsorship due to sports clothing being fashionable. There has been a huge increase in sales for instance in training shoes. Many people wear 'trainers' who would never dream of participating in sport! Nevertheless commercial companies recognise that top sports stars can be fashion role models for the young and therefore use them in advertising campaigns (Honeybourne, 2003).

case study 3.7

British Olympic Association

The British Olympic Association (BOA) has announced Easynet as its Official Broadband Network Partner. Easynet will support the BOA for the next three years, throughout the Olympic Games in Athens 2004 and the Winter Olympics in Turin in 2006. Simon Clegg, Chief Executive of the BOA, said:

'The BOA provides the infrastructure that enables elite British athletes to compete at the highest level. Easynet provides the infrastructure that will enable British business to compete in the global marketplace of the future. Easynet's sponsorship is a great example of British business getting behind British sport, and they will be joining our Olympic family which includes Adidas, Rover and Heineken.'

Easynet is also supporting the BOA's Schools Programme, which as part of the National Curriculum, aims to raise awareness of the Olympics.

(Adapted from www.uksport.gov.uk, 2004)

Sports sponsorship is increasingly difficult to find for the 'middle-ranking sports', according to independent research commissioned by the Sports Sponsorship Advisory Service.

A new report – presented to national governing bodies at a seminar at the offices of the Central Council of Physical Recreation in 2002 – blames the current climate on sports' inability to attract sufficient media coverage.

'Sports sponsorship can be a vital ingredient of the financing of governing bodies' activities', explained Howard Wells, Chairman of the CCPR.

'Many sports however are unable to attract sponsors because they cannot get television coverage. Sport must also begin to understand the value of its intellectual property rights and how best to market them in a rapidly changing market place.'

The main points in the report are:

1 Sponsors continue to seek image enhancement and brand awareness through sponsorship and see this to be largely dependent on broadcast and other media coverage

2 Sponsors are also looking to sell their products, develop promotional opportunities and demonstrate that they are good corporate citizens

3 Sponsors continue to be attracted to the 'top ten' sports and/or to community based activity and 'middle ranking' sports are rarely considered

4   Women's sport has the potential to attract more sponsors but to date most of that potential is unfulfilled

5   Many sports are becoming more commercially aware but some demonstrate naivety over valuing their rights and approaching sponsors.

'The current market place is difficult in particular for middle ranking sports and even greater efforts are needed to develop their true potential,' added Mike Reynolds, Director of the Institute of Sports Sponsorship. 'This is an increasingly competitive market and some sports have to become smarter and more professional.'

(Adapted from www.uksport.gov.org, 2002)

Charging for products and services

Sports organisations charge for playing, coaching and for watching. The amount that is charged is often related to how popular the sport is, especially in the case of watching.

Income from the mass media

The mass media provides an enormous income for professional sport in the UK. Media include satellite and terrestrial television companies and radio stations.

The Impact of Different Key Issues upon the Sports Industry

Some of the key issues in sports participation and development are related to barriers to access, in other words: what stops people being involved in sport. Here are some of the barriers and issues related to them:

■ **Social inclusion** – this is a phrase that relates to the need for all to have an equal chance of being included in sport, whatever their background or social standing.

■ **Racism** – most sports are determined to stamp out any racist activities, for example not allowing black participants to join their clubs. Racism is related to discriminating against someone or acting against his or her best interests because of that person's racial background.

■ **Sexism** – this is about discriminating against people because of their gender, for example not permitting women to have equal playing rights in certain golf clubs.

■ **Ageism** – this is discriminating against people because of their age, for example a health club failing to put on activities or classes suitable for their older clientele.

Access

The growth of sports facilities has increased access but, although there are more low-cost courses available, there is still the problem of being able to afford to participate in sport. For many the most important questions that influence access are:

■ What is available?

■ What is affordable?

■ How do I feel about myself?

This is sometimes identified in the three words: provision; opportunity; esteem.

The following are the main issues related to access:

■ **Opening times**. These might not be convenient for shift workers, for example.

■ **Age**. Sport is often perceived as a 'young person's activity' and the elderly may feel undignified if they participate in sport.

■ **Race**. Racial discrimination may be reason for lack of confidence to get involved in a predominantly white environment such as a golf club.

case study 3.8   Sport and disadvantaged communities

'People on low incomes living in a disadvantaged community in the north of England demonstrate some of the lowest levels of participation in sport ever measured'

(headline from *The Player*, summer 2002).

■ 71% of people from social groups D and E take part in at least one sport but in Liverpool the figure is only 51%

■ in Bradford the proportion of children swimming, cycling or walking is less than half the national average

■ 43% of British children play cricket but in Liverpool only 3% play it

■ however, in these areas the vast majority of children have a very positive view about the value of sport.

Figure 3.10
Only 3% of children in Liverpool play cricket

Drugs in sport

There is much pressure on sports performers to win. At times this can lead to a temptation to win at all costs – including running the risk of personal harm and of an outright ban with public shame. These risks are associated with the use of drugs and banned substances, which help sports performers do even better. Many top or elite sportspeople have been tested positive for banned substances. Some took them by accident and some because they wished to cheat. There are regular checks by governing bodies of sports but the availability and use of performance-enhancing drugs has been on the increase. The main categories of drugs that are used to enhance performance illegally are:

- anabolic steroids – enabling athletes to train harder and longer and increasing strength and aggression
- amphetamines – a brain stimulant, which increases alertness
- narcotic analgesics – enabling athletes to work harder and longer and not feel the pain of training or injury as much
- beta-blockers – these help to control the heart rate and help to keep the athlete calm
- diuretics – taken by athletes to control or lose weight.
- there are also sports performers who have taken illegal 'recreational' drugs such as cocaine.

See Unit 12 Lifestyle and Sports Performance, pages 216–19

Influences of the media

Television companies spend an enormous amount of money to secure the broadcasting rights to sports events. To view certain events such as boxing the subscriber must often make an extra payment (pay-per-view). Sky, for example, holds the rights to many Premiership football games, which can only be viewed if you subscribe to a Sky package. Digital TV has also influenced sport and not always to anyone's benefit. The collapse of ITV Digital in 2002 meant that many football teams were facing financial disaster, having been promised a considerable amount of money that was then not forthcoming.

The terrestrial channels such as BBC and ITV have lost many of the major sports events and the ludicrous situation arises whereby the BBC's news programme is unable to show a clip of a boxing match because the rights to that match are owned by another company. There has never before been so much coverage of sport on TV but, because of satellite TV dominating this coverage, only those who can afford to subscribe have access to many sports events. Football receives the most coverage but coverage for other sports can be quite limited. Male sport also still dominates, although there is a refreshing interest in women's football, for instance.

The needs of the TV companies have led to revised event programming. Football fans, for instance, are finding that their team may play on a Sunday at

6.00 p.m., which has not traditionally been a timeslot for the game. Events at the Olympic Games are often scheduled at unsuitable times because of the demands of TV companies, which are beaming the event around the world across different time zones.

The media have influenced the rules of sport. For instance, in cricket the third umpire in the form of a video replay analysis has come into force, largely due to the influence of TV. There has been a similar development in rugby football. The armchair spectator can now see the event at every angle and the officials' decisions are laid bare for scrutiny, hence the need for new technology to aid the decision makers on the field of play (Honeybourne, 2003).

The extent of media involvement has also influenced the amount of sponsorship and advertising revenue available to participants, clubs and other sports organisations.

Figure 3.11

Advertising revenue is a significant source of income

This has brought much-welcomed money into sport but some may argue that it has only gone to a small number of participants in a small number of sports and may well have led to the decrease in participation in minority sports.

The media can increase participation in sport. You only have to see the increased activity on municipal tennis courts during the Wimbledon fortnight to appreciate that watching sport can stimulate participation.

Our interest in playing a sport increases when the media highlights the success of UK sports performers. There was a surge of interest in curling, for instance, after the success of the women's team in the Winter Olympics in 2002 and more recently with the men's team just missing out on a bronze medal in the 2006 Winter Olympics in Italy.

Types of media involved in sport include:

- television: BBC, ITV, Channel 4, Channel 5, Satellite, Cable, Digital, factual/fiction/advertising
- press: broadsheets, tabloids, local, weekly, magazines, periodicals
- radio: national, local, commercial
- cinema: documentaries, movies.

progress check

1   What are the main differences between sport and recreation? Give examples.

2   Give examples of amateur and professional sports.

3   Why are sports such as badminton and golf called 'lifetime sports'?

4   Give some of the possible reasons for people participating in the London Marathon.

5   Give examples of sports provision in the public, private and voluntary sectors.

6   Describe the activities of one of the following organisations: UEFA, Youth Sport Trust, Central Council for Physical Recreation, SPRITO.

7   Describe the different types of funding available for sport in the UK.

8   What are the benefits and drawbacks of sponsorship in sport?

9   What is meant by racism, sexism and ageism in sport? Give examples.

10 What are the advantages and disadvantages of the influence of the media on sport?

Preparation for Sport

This unit covers:

- the fitness and lifestyle of an individual sports performer
- planning a simple fitness training programme for an individual sports performer
- the nutritional requirements of effective sports performance
- the psychological factors that affect sports training and performance

Unit 4 examines the essential theoretical and practical issues involved in preparing effectively for sports performance. You are expected to be able to investigate the fitness level and lifestyle of an individual and to be able to administer simple fitness tests. The unit provides all the information necessary to complete this task. You will be able to discuss the effects of lifestyle on sports performance and be able to identify the different methods of training. This unit also enables you to plan a physical fitness-training programme and to identify the nutritional requirements of sports performers. It covers fascinating psychological factors, such as personality and motivation, which affect sports performance.

grading criteria

To achieve a **Pass** grade the evidence must show that the learner is able to:	To achieve a **Merit** grade the evidence must show that the learner is able to:	To achieve a **Distinction** grade the evidence must show that the learner is able to:
P1 Describe components of fitness and their effect on sports performance	**M1** Explain the effects of fitness and the lifestyle of sports performers on sports performance	**D1** Evaluate the effects of lifestyle factors on sports performance, providing recommendations for changes
P2 Describe four different lifestyle factors that can affect sports performance	**M2** Independently select and conduct three suitable tests, related to different areas of fitness, in order to assess the fitness of a selected sports performer, accurately recording and interpreting results	**D2** Analyse the fitness test results drawing valid conclusions and making recommendations for future sports performance

To achieve a **Pass** grade the evidence must show that the learner is able to:	To achieve a **Merit** grade the evidence must show that the learner is able to:	To achieve a **Distinction** grade the evidence must show that the learner is able to:
P3 Select and conduct three suitable tests, related to different areas of fitness, in order to assess the fitness of a selected sports performer, with teacher support, recording results accurately	**M3** Independently plan a six-week training programme for a selected sports performer	**D3** Analyse psychological factors that affect sports training and performances
P4 Plan, with teacher support, a six-week training programme for a selected sports performer	**M4** Explain dietary guidelines and meal plans	
P5 Prepare and present dietary guidelines for a selected sports performer providing suitable daily meal plans over a two-week period	**M5** Describe psychological factors that affect sports training and performance and what the effects on sports training and performance could be	
P6 Identify psychological factors that can affect sports training and performance and what the effects on sports training and performance could be		

The Fitness and Lifestyle of an Individual Sports Performer

Components of physical fitness

The term 'fitness' is often used very loosely to refer to aerobic endurance or how far someone can run without becoming too breathless. However, fitness is more complex than that. It involves many different components or parts. Depending on the type of sport you are involved with you might be very fit in one component but not another. For example, strength and power is very important to the discus thrower in athletics but is less important in archery. All sports activities, however, require a good general level of fitness for all components. In some team games, for example, all components of fitness are equally important, although this may vary depending on what position you play. The following are recognised as the main components of physical fitness:

Figure 4.1

Strength is the ability of a muscle to exert force for a short period of time

- **Strength**. This is the ability of a muscle to exert force for a short period of time. The amount of force that someone can exert depends on the size of the muscles and the number of muscles involved, as well as the type of muscle fibres used and the co-ordination of the muscles involved.

- **Muscular endurance**. This is the ability of the muscle or group of muscles to repeatedly contract or keep going without rest.

- **Aerobic endurance**. This is the ability to exercise continuously without tiring. The more the oxygen can be transported around the body and the more the muscles can use this oxygen, the greater will be the level of aerobic endurance you have.

- **Flexibility**. This is the amount or range of movement that you can have around a joint. The structure of the joint restricts movement, as well as the muscles, tendons and ligaments.

- **Power**. This is often referred to as fast strength. Power is a combination of strength and speed.

- **Speed**. This is the ability of the body to move quickly. The movements may involve the whole body or parts of the body – for example arm speed in cricket bowling.

- **Body composition**. This refers to the way in which the body is made up. The percentages of muscle, fat, bone and internal organs are taken into consideration. There are two main components: body fat and lean body mass, which is body mass without the fat.

- **Other components**. These are also important in determining how fit you are for sport and include:

  - **Agility**. How quickly you can change direction under control.

  - **Co-ordination**. Ability to perform tasks in sport, for example running and then passing a ball in rugby.

- **Balance**. The ability to keep your body mass over a base of support. For example, a gymnast performing a handstand on a balance beam.
- **Reaction time**. This is the time it takes someone to make a decision to move, for example how quickly a sprinter reacts to the gun and decides to drive off the blocks.

Figure 4.2

Good reaction time is important for a sprinter to get a good start

Fitness tests

Fitness testing is important if you are going to find out the present fitness level of a performer. It also serves as a basis for progress. In other words, a training programme may be followed after testing, and then after a few weeks another fitness test will reveal how effective the training has been and whether the performer has increased their fitness. As we have discovered, physical fitness involves a number of different components, therefore fitness tests must be designed to test a specific component.

It is important that individuals view the tests as benchmarks for their own improvements instead of comparing them against the results of others.

Figure 4.3

A grip dynamometer

Strength tests

The use of dynamometers such as the handgrip dynamometer, which measures the strength of the handgrip, can give an objective measure of strength.

Make sure that the handgrip is adjusted to fit the subject's hand. The subject should stand, holding the dynamometer parallel to the side of the body, with the dial facing away from the body. The handle should be squeezed as hard as possible without moving the arm. Three trials are recommended with one minute's rest between each trial.

Speed

This can be measured by the 30 m sprint test. This should be on a flat non-slippy surface to prevent accidents. The sprint should be from a flying start back from the beginning of the marked out stretch. The time is taken from the beginning of the 30 m stretch to the end.

Cardiovascular endurance

The level of endurance fitness is indicated by an individual's VO_2 max – that is, the maximum amount of oxygen an individual can take in and use in one minute.

VO_2 max

Top endurance athletes, such as marathon runners, usually have a very high VO_2 max – approximately 70 ml/kg/min. The average performer is about 35 ml/kg/min. A low VO_2 max of 25 or less would probably indicate that you are not going to be an endurance athlete. The more endurance training you do, however, the higher your VO_2 max scores will generally become.

The potential VO_2 max of an individual can be predicted via the multistage fitness test (sometimes called the 'bleep' test). This test involves a shuttle run that becomes progressively more difficult.

The test is in the form of a cassette tape. Subjects run a 20 m shuttle as many times as possible but ensure that they turn at each end of the run in time with the 'bleep' on the tape. The time lapse between each bleep sound on the tape gets progressively smaller and so the shuttle run has to be completed progressively quicker. At the point when subjects cannot keep up with the bleeps, they are deemed to have reached their optimum level. The level reached by the subject is recorded and used as a baseline for future tests or can be compared to national norms.

case study 4.1 — The 'bleep test'

The test usually consists of 23 levels. Only the very top or elite athletes can get into the top three levels. Cyclist Lance Armstrong and footballer David Beckham are two such examples.

The test is often recommended for players of sports that involve a lot of stop–start sprinting, such as tennis, rugby, football or hockey.

Muscular endurance

Testing the endurance of one particular muscle group can assess an individual's muscular endurance. One such test again comes from the National Coaching Foundation and is called the abdominal conditioning test. This tests the endurance of the abdominal muscle group by measuring the number of sit-ups an individual can perform by again keeping to a 'bleep' indicated on the cassette tape. When individuals cannot complete any more sit-ups in time with the bleep then it is deemed that they have reached their optimum level. Again this test can be used as a benchmark for training or used for comparison with national norms.

Flexibility

This can be tested via the sit and reach test. The subject sits on the floor with legs outstretched in a straight position. The subject reaches as far forward as possible but keeping the legs straight and in contact with the floor. The distance between the ends of the fingers and the feet (pointing upwards) is measured. Using a 'sit-and-reach' box ensures more accurate measurements. Once again, this test can provide measurements that can be used in assessing any future training and also that the subject can use to compare performance with national norms.

Figure 4.4
The sit and reach test

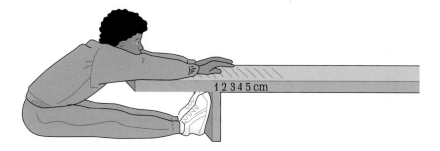

Power

An individual's power can be measured by using the vertical jump test. There are commercial jump-test boards that can be fixed to the wall. The subject jumps vertically, using both feet, and then touches the calibrated scale on the board with one hand. The position of the touch is noted; the test is completed three times and the maximum height attained is recorded.

Body composition

This can be assessed in a number of different ways:

- **Skinfold measurement of body fat**. Completed using a skinfold calliper. Measurements of body fat are taken from the areas around the biceps, triceps, subscapular and supra iliac. The total measurements are added together and recorded to compare with national averages (called norms) or, more importantly, to assess training or weight-management programmes.

- **Hydrostatic weighing**. Completed by measuring the water displacement when the subject is submerged in water.

- **Bioelectrical impedance**. A small electric current is passed through the body from the wrist to the ankle. Fat is known to restrict the flow of the electrical current, therefore the greater the current needed, the greater the percentage of body fat.

The influence of lifestyle on physical fitness

Training for fitness is only one, albeit very important, aspect of becoming and keeping physically fit. Out lifestyles – in other words the way in which we conduct our everyday lives – can affect significantly our overall fitness for sport. There is an increase in people being overweight. When extreme this is called obesity. Many of us now live more sedentary lives; in other words, we are less active. We use the car more for getting from A to B even if B is just up the road to the local shop! There are more instances of type 2 diabetes and coronary heart disease, which is affected by the food we eat. The main 'lifestyle' factors that can affect our physical fitness are given below.

Stress levels

There is now an increase in stress-related ailments. These are often due to our hectic lives, which leave little room for relaxation. Modern life is very competitive and, for many, becoming involved in competitive sport is the last thing they wish to do. Many, however, find that sport is a great release from everyday life and they find participating or watching sport refreshing and relaxing.

Alcohol consumption

Alcohol is a concentrated source of energy but cannot be available during exercise for our working muscles. Therefore many elite performers in sport do not drink alcohol and most drink very little.

The Health Development Agency recommends for adults (not necessarily sporting adults):

- **males**: 3–4 units per day
- **females**: 2–3 units per day.

A unit is half a pint of 'ordinary strength' beer (3.0%–3.5 % alcohol = 90 calories), or one standard glass of wine (11% alcohol = 90 calories), or a single measure of spirits (38% alcohol = 50 calories).

'Binge drinking', which is a growing habit amongst teenagers and young adults, is particularly bad for health. It is better to spread alcohol consumption across the week and to leave some alcohol-free days.

Smoking

Few serious sportspeople smoke. There is overwhelming evidence that health and fitness are affected adversely by smoking, whatever age you are. Cigarettes contain tar, nicotine, carbon monoxide and other irritants that cause coughing for instance. Normally haemoglobin in the blood carries oxygen. Haemoglobin seems to prefer carbon monoxide when it is present in the body and once it has taken up carbon monoxide it is unable to take up oxygen again, therefore less oxygen is available for the body to work effectively. Up to 10% of the oxygen-carrying capacity can be lost in this way.

remember

Smoking and sport
- The time needed to complete exercise trials increases after smoking.
- Endurance and capacity for exercise is reduced in proportion to the cigarettes smoked – the more you smoke the less fit you will be.
- Training has less effect on smokers – so you can train really hard but smoking can undo all the good work.

Smoking is the biggest cause of preventable death in the Western world. It kills more than 120 000 in the UK every year, with most dying from three main diseases: cancer, chronic obstructive lung disease (bronchitis and emphysema) and coronary heart disease. Around 29% of men and 25% of women in the Great Britain smoke. However, these figures are an average for the population as a whole – the figures for those on low incomes and from poor backgrounds are much higher. One in every two regular cigarette smokers will be killed by their habit.

Drugs

The use of drugs whether they be recreational (for example cannabis) or performance-enhancing (for example anabolic steroids) is widespread and can seriously affect the health and wellbeing of a sports performer.

Drug taking involves the use of chemicals that alter the way we feel and see things and is one of the oldest activities of the human race.

Even when there are serious consequences to their use – of tobacco, alcohol, cannabis, heroin or performance-enhancing drugs in sport – those consequences will not always make people wish to stop using their drug of choice. If and when they do decide to give up they may find that this is harder than they thought.

There is often more to an addiction than the physical withdrawal symptoms. Addiction includes anxiety, depression and lowering of self-esteem. The pattern of these symptoms will depend not only on the drug used but also on the psychological makeup of the person and the circumstances in which that individual is attempting to remain drug free.

UK Sport has been designated by government to deliver its policy objectives as the national anti-doping organisation, to represent government in international meetings and to co-ordinate the national anti-doping programme of testing and education and information for sport throughout the UK.

The core aim of anti-doping policy in the UK is the planning and delivery of an effective programme that:

- protects athletes' rights to participate in drug-free sport
- actively encourages the support of medical professionals and administrators
- is publicly accountable for its plans and outcomes.

    A major landmark in the fight for drug-free sport was achieved in January 2002 when UK Sport published its Statement of Anti-Doping Policy. This was the result of widespread consultation both nationally and internationally and took over two years to develop. The policy set out the requirements of governing bodies and sports councils to deliver effective anti-doping systems. It brought the UK in line with all phases of the International Standard for Doping Control.

(Adapted from www.uksport.gov.uk)

case study 4.2   Prohibited substances in sport

Prohibited substances may vary from sport to sport. It is the athlete's responsibility to know their sport's anti-doping regulations. In cases of uncertainty, it is important to check with the appropriate governing body or UK Sport and be sure to read carefully the anti-doping rules adopted by the relevant governing body and international sports federations.

(Adapted from www.uksport.gov.uk)

Athletes are advised to check all medications and substances with their doctor or governing body medical officer. All substances should be checked carefully when travelling abroad as many products can, and do, contain different substances from those found in the UK.

Substances and methods are prohibited in sport for various reasons:

■ **Performance-enhancing effects**, which contravene the ethics of sport and undermine the principles of fair participation.

■ **The health and safety of the athlete**. Some drug misuse may cause serious side effects, which can compromise an athlete's health. Using substances to mask pain/injury could make an injury worse or cause permanent damage. Some drug misuse may be harmful to other athletes participating in the sport.

■ **Illegality**. It is forbidden by law to possess or supply some substances.

Most sporting federations have anti-doping regulations to ensure that all athletes compete by the same principle of being drug free. The regulations aim to achieve drug-free sport through clearly stated policies, testing and sanctions. They are also intended to raise the awareness of drug misuse and to deter athletes from misusing prohibited drugs and methods.

Prohibited classes of substances include:

■ stimulants

■ narcotic analgesics

■ anabolic agents

■ anabolic androgenic steroids

■ other anabolic agents

■ diuretics

■ peptide hormones, mimetics and analogues

■ substances with anti-oestrogenic activity

■ masking agents.

Prohibited methods include:

- enhancement of oxygen transfer
- blood doping
- administration of products that enhance the uptake, transport and delivery of oxygen
- pharmacological, chemical and physical manipulation
- gene doping.

Classes of substances prohibited in certain circumstances:

- alcohol
- cannabinoids
- local anaesthetics
- glucocorticosteroids
- beta blockers.

Other lifestyle factors

There are other lifestyle factors that affect your fitness levels. The amount of sleep you have can affect the way you feel as well as your sports performance. It is important to get enough sleep.

case study 4.3

The sleep habits of a top athlete: Haile Gebrselassie

The athlete keeps a regular routine, waking up at 6 a.m. and ensuring that he is in bed by 9.30 p.m. each day. With young daughters, he finds it difficult to sleep during the day and contents himself with a rest, usually lasting for about 2 hours in the afternoon.

Gebrselassie finds massage helps him, particularly in recovering from training and has a massage every day during his heavy training periods.

(Adapted from www.bbc.co.uk/sport, 2004)

Figure 4.5

The very best athletes ensure a healthy lifestyle – including getting enough sleep

Physical fitness is also affected by the type of job you have. Some people have jobs that involve sitting at a desk all day – this is know as a sedentary type of work. Others who have active jobs may be more physically fit even before training for sport. The type of diet also affects physical fitness and this will be explored later in this unit.

Planning a Simple Fitness Training Programme for an Individual Sports Performer

For an effective training programme, it is important to understand the theory on which that training is based. Useful training is based on what are called 'principles of training'.

Principles of training

Training programmes must take into account the needs and personality of the particular individual. The aims or goals of the training should be agreed – what are you trying to do? Are you wishing to prepare over a short or long time? An individual's goals must be understood. Does the performer want to become generally fit or fit for a particular sport? The individual's current activity level must be assessed by doing an initial fitness test (see tests earlier in this unit). The age, time available, equipment available and skill level must all be taken into consideration before the following principles of training are applied.

The principles of training include specificity, overload, progression, reversibility and variance.

Specificity

This principle indicates that the training should be specific and therefore relevant to the appropriate needs of the activity or the type of sport involved. For

Figure 4.6

Training should be specific and therefore relevant to the appropriate needs of the activity or the type of sport involved

example, a marathon runner would carry out more aerobic or stamina training because the event is mostly aerobic in nature. It is not just energy systems that have to match the training: muscle groups and actions involved in the training also have to be as specific as possible. For example, a high jumper would work on power in the legs. There is, however, a general consensus that a good general fitness is required before any high degree of specificity can be applied.

Overload

This principle states that you need to work the body harder than normal so that there is some stress and discomfort on the body's systems and parts. The body will become fitter and physical progress will follow overload because the body will respond by coping or adapting to the stress experienced. For example, in weight training the lifter will eventually attempt heavier weights or an increase in repetitions, thus overloading the body. The weightlifter will then in the future adapt to this stress and be able to lift heavier weights.

Overload can be achieved by a combination of increasing the frequency (how many times), the intensity (how hard you train) and the duration (how long each session is) of the activity. These aspects are important if the **'FITT'** programme is to be followed.

Progression

The work in training should become progressively more difficult so that progress can be made. If the same level of exercise is attempted week in and week out, then the athlete will only reach a certain level of fitness and then stay there. Once adaptations, or changes to the body's fitness, have occurred then the performer should make even more demands on the body and do more strenuous work. It is important not to make too many demands of the body too early. Training must be sensibly progressive and realistic if it is to be effective, otherwise injury may occur and there would be a fall in fitness levels instead of progression.

keyword

FITT
F = frequency of training (number of training sessions each week)
I = intensity of the exercise undertaken
T = time or duration that the training takes up.
T = type of training to be considered that fulfils specific needs.

Figure 4.7

In weight training the lifter will eventually attempt heavier weights or an increase in repetitions, thus overloading the body

Reversibility

This principle states that fitness can deteriorate and get much worse if training stops or decreases in intensity for any length of time. If training is stopped, then the fitness gained will be largely lost. For instance VO_2 max and muscle strength can decrease. Therefore it is important to 'keep going' with your training. It is better to have days of light training rather than no training at all if you wish to improve your fitness significantly.

Variance

This principle states that there should be variety in training methods. A lot of different types of training or different activities will make training interesting and exciting. If training is too predictable then performers can become demotivated and bored. Overuse injuries such as muscle strains (see Unit 2) are also common when training is too repetitive with one muscle group or part of the body. Variance in training can therefore be motivating and also helps to prevent injury.

Training methods

Warm-ups and cool-downs

The warm-up enables the body to prepare for exercise. It reduces the likelihood of injury and muscle soreness. There is also a release of adrenaline that will start the process of speeding up the delivery of oxygen to the working muscles. An increase in muscle temperature will help to ensure that there is a ready supply of energy and that the muscle becomes more flexible to prevent injury.

The cool-down is also important for effective training. If light exercise follows training, then the oxygen can more effectively be flushed through the muscle tissue and oxidise lactic acid. Cool-downs also prevent blood pooling in the veins which can cause dizziness.

Figure 4.8

The warm-up enables the body to prepare for the onset of exercise

Aerobic and anaerobic fitness training

Aerobic capacity can be improved through continuous, steady-state (submaximal) training. The rhythmic exercise of aerobics is an example. Continuous swimming or jogging are also good for aerobic fitness.

This low-intensity exercise must take place over a long period of time from 20 minutes to 2 hours. The intensity of this exercise should be 60% to 80% of your maximum heart rate.

Anaerobic training involves high-intensity work that may be less frequent, although elite athletes will frequently train both aerobically and anaerobically.

Interval training

This is one of the most popular types of training. It is adaptable depending on individual needs and sports. Interval training can improve both aerobic and anaerobic fitness. It is called 'interval training' because there are intervals of work and intervals of rest. There should be slower intervals for training the aerobic system. This is suitable for sports like athletics and swimming and for team games like hockey or football. For training the anaerobic system, there should be shorter, more intense intervals of training.

The following factors have to be taken into account before the design of a training session:

- **Duration** of the work interval. The work interval should be between 3 seconds and 10 seconds at high intensity for anaerobic training and 7 minutes and 8 minutes for aerobic training.

- **Speed** (intensity) of the work interval. This should be between 90% and 100% intensity for anaerobic and moderate if aerobic.

- Number of **repetitions**. This depends on the length of the work period, but if repetitions are short, then up to 50 repetitions three appropriate for anaerobic. For aerobic, three to four are more appropriate

- Number of **sets** of repetitions. Repetitions can be divided into sets. If there are to be 50 repetitions then these could be divided into sets of five.

- Duration of the **rest interval** or the length of time that the heart rate falls to about 150 bpm. Aerobic training will require a shorter rest interval for effective training.

- **Type of activity** during the rest interval. If the energy system is anaerobic, then only light stretching – if it is aerobic then some light jogging may help to disperse lactic acid.

Fartlek training

This is also known as 'speedplay' training. This training is good for aerobic fitness because it is an endurance activity. It is good for anaerobic fitness because of the speed activities over a short period of time. Throughout the exercise, the speed and intensity of the training are varied. In an hour session, for instance, there may be walking activity, which is low in intensity, or very fast sprinting, which is high intensity. Cross-country running with sprint activities every now and again is a simplistic but reasonable way of describing fartlek.

Muscular strength, muscular endurance and power training

For strength and power training, the performer needs to work against resistance. The training is effective only if it is specific enough. In other words the training needs to be targeted depending on the type of strength that needs to be developed, for instance, explosive strength for a thrower in athletics, or strength endurance for a gymnast.

Circuit training

This involves a series of exercises that are arranged in a particular way called a circuit because the training involves repetition of each activity. The resistance that is used in circuits relates mainly to body weight, and each exercise in the circuit is designed to work on a particular muscle group. For effective training, different muscle groups should be worked on, with no two muscle groups being worked on one after the other. For instance, an activity that uses the main

Figure 4.9

Training needs to be targeted depending on the type of strength that needs to be developed, such as explosive strength for a thrower in athletics

muscle groups in the arms should then be followed, for example, by an exercise involving the muscle groups in the legs.

The types of exercises that are involved in circuit training are press-ups, star jumps, dips and squat thrusts.

Circuit training can also incorporate training in the skills that are used in particular sports. For example hockey players may include dribbling activities, flicking the ball, shuttle runs and shooting activities.

The duration and intensity depends on the type of activities that have been used. An example would be a circuit with one minute's activity, followed by one minute's rest. The whole circuit could then be repeated three times. The score at the end of the circuit may be related to time or repetitions. It can be used to provide motivation in training. It is also easy to see progression in fitness as the weeks go by when more repetitions can be attempted or times are improved.

Weight and resistance training methods

For strength to be developed more resistance can be used in the form of weight training or the use of pulleys. Weight training involves a number of repetitions and sets, depending on the type of strength that needs to be developed. For throwing events in athletics, for example, training methods must involve very high resistance and low repetition. For the strength endurance that you may need in swimming or cycling then more repetitions need to be involved with less resistance or lighter weights.

Plyometrics

This type of training is designed to improve dynamic strength. Plyometrics involves bounding, hopping and jumping. It improves the speed with which muscles shorten. If muscles have previously been stretched then they tend to generate more force when contracted. Any sport that involves sprinting, throwing and jumping will benefit from this type of training, as will players of many team sports like netball or rugby.

One type of jumping used in this training method is called in-depth jumping, which is when the athlete jumps on and off raised platforms or boxes. This type of training is very strenuous on the muscles and joints and a reasonable amount of fitness must be present before this training is attempted. As usual it is important that there is sufficient stretching of the muscle before attempting this type of training. It is also important to have the right sort of footwear so that impact injuries do not occur.

Flexibility training

This is sometimes called mobility training. It involves stretching exercises of the muscles and this can help with performance and to avoid injury. There are two types of flexibility exercises: active stretching and passive stretching.

Active stretching is when there are voluntary muscular contractions that are held by the performer for 30 seconds to one minute. When the muscle is relaxed at the limit of the stretching range, muscle elongation may occur if this practice is repeated regularly. The stretching must be under control and muscles should be suitably warmed up before stretching begins.

One method of active stretching is called the ballistic method. In ballistic stretching the subject actively uses the momentum or movement of the limb to propel the body. This is achieved through a bouncing-type movement and should only be attempted by those who are extremely flexible such as gymnasts or certain athletes because muscle tissue damage is easily experienced with such active stretching.

Passive stretching incorporates an external 'helper', who pushes or pulls the limb to stretch the appropriate muscles. This is obviously potentially dangerous so the subject must be thoroughly warmed up and should go through some active stretching to begin with. Gymnasts often favour this particular type of stretching.

One type of passive stretching is called proprioceptive neuromuscular facilitation (PNF). This method tries to decrease the reflex shortening of the muscle being stretched when the muscle is fully stretched:

- the limb is moved to its limit by the subject
- the limb is then taken to its passive limit by the partner
- just before the point of real discomfort, the muscle is contracted isometrically for a few seconds, then relaxed
- it will be possible to stretch the muscle a little more during the next stretch.

Figure 4.10

Stretching can help with performance

The Nutritional Requirements of Effective Sports Performance

Components of a healthy diet

People should follow a diet that is balanced and contains the right amount of nutrients necessary to live a fit and healthy life, whether or not they are involved in sport. The main nutrients are carbohydrates, fats, protein, water, vitamins and minerals. Loading up on fuel before any event is vital for success.

Carbohydrates

These are made up of the chemical elements carbon, hydrogen and oxygen. They are primarily involved in energy production and exist in two forms:

- **simple sugars** – these provide a quick energy source and include glucose and fructose
- **complex starches** – these have many sugar units and are much slower in releasing energy.

Carbohydrates are very important to the athlete, especially in very intense exercise. They also determine fat metabolism and are essential to the nervous system.

Carbohydrates are stored in the muscles and the liver as glycogen but in limited amounts that need to be replenished.

Carbohydrates are the body's most important source of fuel. Endurance runners need lots of them. Two to three days before a race they will eat pasta, rice, potatoes, noodles, bread and cereals to build up their reserves.

Sprinters need some carbohydrates but they should not overload because they will not feel the benefit running over a short distance.

Examples of sources of carbohydrates:

- **Complex** – cereal, pasta, potatoes, bread, fruit.
- **Simple** – sugar, jam, confectionery, fruit juices.

When exercise takes place, glycogen is broken down to glucose, which supplies muscles with energy. When glycogen stores are depleted, there is less energy available and the athlete will become fatigued. It is recommended that about 60% of a sportsperson's diet should consist of carbohydrates.

Fats

Fats are also very important and are a major source of energy, especially for athletes performing low-intensity endurance exercise. Fats or lipids are made up of carbon, hydrogen and oxygen but in different proportions to carbohydrates. There are two types:

- **Triglycerides**, which are stored in the form of body fat

- **Fatty acids**, which are used mainly as fuel for energy production. These are either **saturated** or **unsaturated fats**.

> **keyword**
>
> **Saturated fat**
> A saturated fat is in the form of a solid, such as lard, and is primarily from animal sources.

> **keyword**
>
> **Unsaturated fat**
> An unsaturated fat is in the form of liquid, such as vegetable oil, and is from plant sources.

Both sprinters and endurance athletes will need to stay lean and not take in too many fat calories. On the last day before the race, both will eat lighter, compact, low-fat snacks for energy. (Carbohydrate snacks like dried fruit, bananas, pancakes, malt loaf, fig rolls are perfect. Jellied sweets and sports drinks are ideal for final race build-up.)

When muscle cells are readily supplied with oxygen then fat is the usual fuel for energy production. This is because the body is trying to save the limited stores of glycogen for high intensity exercise and therefore delays the onset of fatigue. The body cannot solely use fat for energy and so the muscle is fuelled by a combination of fat and glycogen.

One explanation of marathon runners 'hitting the wall' is that there is a complete depletion of the athlete's glycogen stores and the body attempts to metabolise fat which is a slower way of producing energy and therefore extreme fatigue is experienced and muscles struggle to contract.

Fat consumption should be carefully monitored and can cause obesity, which will be examined later in this unit. Fat is very important to protect vital organs and is crucial for cell production and the control of heat loss. It is generally accepted that a maximum of 30% of total calories consumed should be from fatty foods.

> **remember**
>
> An endurance athlete and a sprinter are two incredibly different sporting animals and have different nutritional requirements.

Examples of sources of fats:

- **saturated fats** – meat products, dairy products, cakes, confectionery
- **unsaturated fats** – oily fish, nuts, margarine, olive oil.

Protein

Proteins are composed of carbon, hydrogen, oxygen and nitrogen and some contain minerals such as zinc. They are chemical compounds that consist of **amino acids**. Proteins are known as the building blocks for body tissue and are essential for repair. They are also necessary for the production of haemoglobin enzymes and hormones. Proteins are also potential sources of energy but are not used if fats and carbohydrates are in plentiful supply. All athletes need them to help maintain and develop muscles – more so than individuals who do not participate so much in sport.

> **keyword**
>
> **Amino acids**
> These are present in protein. There are eight amino acids that the body is unable to make for itself and these are called essential amino acids, for example leucine and threonine. The essential amino acids should be part of our dietary intake. The other 12 amino acids are called non-essential, for example glycine and glutamine.

Proteins break down more readily during and immediately after exercise. The amount of protein broken down depends upon the duration and intensity of exercise. Increased protein intake may be important during the early stages of training to support increases in muscle mass and myoglobin.

Many people think sprinters need more protein because they have larger muscle mass but it is the endurance athletes who suffer most muscle damage and protein helps this.

case study 4.4

Proteins

Protein should account for approximately 15% of total calorie intake. If protein is taken excessively then there are some health risks, for example kidney damage due to excreting so many unused amino acids. Meat, fish and poultry are the three primary complete proteins. Vegetables and grains are called incomplete proteins because they do not supply all the essential amino acids.

Both types of athletes need protein. It can be found in eggs, fish, meat, poultry, nuts, peas and lentils. However athletes should avoid fat-heavy proteins like burgers, sausages and bacon because they need to stay lean and trim.

Fluids

It is important to preload on liquid with as much as 500 ml to 1 litre up to an hour before running. Dehydration causes performances to dip. Water is lost through sweat and this comes from the blood and will cause stress on the heart. Sprinters need to make sure they do not drink too much water to avoid weighing more before a big race but they will need to rehydrate between heats.

Athletes should replace their weight loss – caused by sweating – after a race with the equivalent weight in fluid. When they sweat they lose salt as well as water. This can lead to cramp, so water and a salty snack or sports drink will help.

Athletes would normally lose between 0.5 litre and 1 litre depending on their size and the intensity of work. Fluid loss in the Olympic Games in cases Athens was reported to be as much as 1 to 2 litres.

Vitamins

Vitamins are non-caloric chemical compounds that are needed by the body in small quantities. They are an essential component of our diet because they are vital in the production of energy, prevention of disease and our metabolism. With the exception of vitamin D the body cannot produce vitamins. Vitamins A, D, E and K are fat soluble. Vitamins B and C are water soluble.

A well-balanced diet will ensure sufficient vitamin intake. Vitamins can be found in fresh fruit and vegetables.

Minerals

These are also non-caloric and are inorganic elements essential for our health. There are two types:

- **macro-minerals** – needed in large amounts e.g. calcium, potassium and sodium.
- **trace elements** – needed in very small amounts e.g. iron, zinc and manganese.

Many minerals are dissolved in the body as ions and these are called electrolytes. These are essential for healthy cells, the nervous system and for muscle contraction. Minerals can be lost through sweating and so there are implications for those who exercise. Minerals should be replaced quickly to ensure good health.

Examples of important minerals include:

- **Iron**. This is an essential component of haemoglobin, which carries oxygen in the blood. Iron-deficiency anaemia can impair performance in endurance events. Research has shown that 36% to 82% of female runners are anaemic and therefore should seek iron-rich foods in their diets. It should be noted that only a qualified medical doctor should prescribe iron supplements because too much iron can be dangerous. Iron can be found in meat, fish, dairy produce and vegetables. Main sources are from red meat and offal.

- **Calcium**. This mineral is essential for healthy bones and teeth. If there is a deficiency in calcium then there is an increased likelihood of osteoporosis and bone fractures. For calcium to be absorbed there needs to be sufficient vitamin D, which is found in sunlight. Calcium is found in milk and dairy products, green vegetables and nuts. Calcium deficiency can be found in females who are underweight, smokers, alcoholics, vegetarians and those who overdo training in sport.

Water

This is crucial for good health and in particular for those who participate in sport. It carries nutrients in the body and helps with the removal of waste products. It is also very important in the regulation of body temperature. The body loses water readily as urine and sweat. This water loss accelerates depending on the environment and the duration and intensity of any exercise that is being undertaken. On average, daily consumption of an individual should be about 2 litres. Those involved in exercise should take more to ensure a good state of hydration.

Studies show that individuals who are dehydrated become intolerant to exercise and heat stress. The cardiovascular system becomes inefficient if there is dehydration and there is an inability to provide adequate blood flow to the skin, which may lead to heat exhaustion.

Fluids must be taken in during prolonged exercise. This will minimise dehydration and slow the rise in body temperature.

There are a number of sports drinks available commercially, which contain electrolytes and carbohydrates. Some of the claims that are made about these drinks have been misinterpreted. A single meal, for instance, can replace the minerals lost during exercise. Water is the primary need in any drink taken before, during and after exercise because it empties from the stomach extremely quickly and reduces hydration associated with sweating. Thirst is not a reliable indicator for fluid intake; therefore it is best to drink small amounts regularly even if you are not thirsty. Under cooler conditions a carbohydrate drink may give the extra energy needed in events lasting over an hour.

Dehydration in sport

Dehydration is the loss of water and important blood salts like potassium. If you are suffering from dehydration, vital organs such as the kidneys, brain and heart cannot function because they require a certain minimum of water and salt.

The body tries to stay around a temperature of 37 °C by sweating. This results in the loss of body fluid. If fluid levels are reduced it can lead to dehydration and heat stroke. You are probably dehydrated if you are thirsty, have dry lips and a dry mouth.

A more serious form of dehydration occurs if you have blue lips, a weak pulse, quick breathing and confusion.

---

remember

- You should start drinking early on a match day.
- With 2 hours to go until the match starts, drink up to 600 ml of fluid.
- Then, with 15 minutes to go before kick-off, drink around 500 ml of fluid.
- Once the match has started, it is important to consume liquid when you can. If possible, aim for 100 ml–150 ml every 15 minutes.
- After the game, try to drink immediately. This will ensure that you do not dehydrate.

(Adapted from www.bbc.co.uk/sport)

Sports drinks

Isotonic drinks

These are designed to replace quickly the fluids that are lost by sweating. They also boost carbohydrate levels.

Isotonic fluids are the most common drinks for athletes. They are particularly popular for middle- and long-distance runners.

The body prefers to use glucose as its source of energy. Sometimes it is better to consume isotonic drinks where the carbohydrate source is a concentrated form of glucose.

Hypertonic drinks

Hypertonic drinks are used to supplement daily carbohydrate intake. They contain even higher levels of carbohydrates than isotonic and hypotonic drinks. The best time to drink them is after exercise as they help the body to top up on muscle glycogen stores. These are valuable energy stores. High levels of energy are required in very long-distance events such as marathons.

Hypertonic drinks can also be taken during exercise to meet the energy requirements. However, it is advisable to use them only during exercise alongside isotonic drinks to replace fluids.

Hypotonic drinks

Hypotonic drinks are designed to replace quickly fluids lost through sweating. Unlike isotonic and hypertonic drinks they are low in carbohydrates. They are very popular with athletes who need fluid without the boost of carbohydrate. Jockeys and gymnasts use them regularly.

The best time to drink them is after a tough exercise workout. Hypotonic drinks can directly target the main cause of fatigue in sport – dehydration – by replacing water and energy fast.

A healthy diet

There are no healthy or unhealthy foods; there are only bad uses of food. The right balance in a diet is essential for health and fitness. Enjoyment is an important aspect of eating; a healthy diet does not mean that you have to give up all your favourite foods – it is the overall balance that counts. Balanced meals contain starchy foods with plenty of vegetables, salad and fruit. Your fat content should be kept to a.minimum by using low-fat or lean ingredients.

Factors that also affect choice of foods include:

■ culture, morals, ethics

■ family influences

■ peer group influences

■ lifestyle

■ finance

Eating sufficient fruit and vegetables is important for a healthy diet. It helps to reduce the likelihood of coronary heart disease and some cancers. Government guidelines suggest that you should eat at least five portions of fruit and vegetables each day.

> *remember*
>
> What is a portion of fruit or vegetables?
> - 2 tablespoons of vegetables
> - 1 dessert bowl of salad
> - 1 apple/orange/banana
> - 2 plums
> - 1 cupful of grapes/cherries
> - 2 tablespoons of fresh fruit salad
> - 1 tablespoon dried fruit
> - 1 glass fruit juice
>
> (Adapted from Health Development Agency, 2000)

Most healthy eating guidelines warn against eating too much salt. If your diet contains too much salt then this may lead to high blood pressure, which can cause heart and kidney disease.

Figure 4.11

Food choices

© Crown Copyright

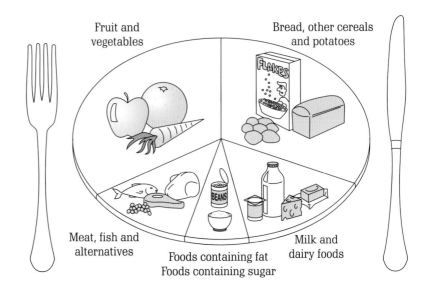

Fruit and vegetables

Bread, other cereals and potatoes

Meat, fish and alternatives

Foods containing fat
Foods containing sugar

Milk and dairy foods

case study 4.5   Diet of a successful Olympic swimmer

The Australian swimmer Ian Thorpe reports about his eating habits:

Ian Thorpe restricts himself to a very precise diet. When he is at home he enjoys a breakfast of cereal, toast with jam and fresh orange juice.

Swimming is a sport in which the athlete expends huge amounts of energy; therefore Ian for the rest of the day restricts himself to low fat foods with a high carbohydrate component. He also ensures that he eats plenty of protein and fresh vegetables and tends to supplement fluids with isotonic drinks.

Ian will stick to this diet for at least six days out of seven. He manages to avoid pleasures such as chocolate, but admits that he is bored with his regular diet. One day a week he treats himself to a restaurant meal, allowing himself to eat whatever takes his fancy. He prefers Japanese food and in particular sashimi.

Ian admits that on his single day off a week he does indulge himself if he needs a snack. His preference is for Caramel Space Food Sticks, which are long, chewy and tasty energy sticks. Despite his dedication, Ian knows that he needs to eat normal foods sometimes in order to ward off the hunger pangs and by doing this one day a week he manages to stick to his diet for the other six.

(Adapted from BBC web site www.bbc.co.uk/sport, 2004)

Nutritional strategies in sport

Glycogen stores

Ensuring that the body has enough glycogen is crucial for optimum energy supply. One method of increasing the glycogen available is through glycogen 'loading', sometimes known as carbo-loading. This process involves depleting one's stores of glycogen by cutting down on carbohydrates and keeping to a diet of protein and fat for 3 days. Light training follows with a high carbohydrate diet for 3 days leading up to the event. This has been shown to significantly increase the stores of glycogen and helps to offset fatigue. When carbo-loading the diet should consist mainly of foods like pasta, bread, rice and fruit. Generally a high carbohydrate diet will ensure that glycogen will be replenished during exercise.

Figure 4.12

Carbohydrate diet graph

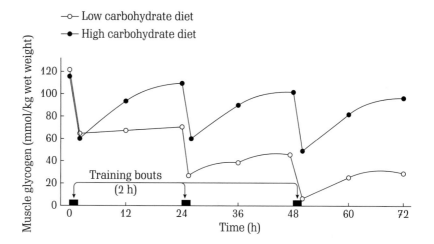

Other energy-giving strategies

- Consume carbohydrates 2 to 4 hours before exercise.
- Consume a small amount of carbohydrates within the first half an hour of exercise to ensure refuelling of glycogen.
- Eat carbohydrates straight after exercise for up to 2 days to replenish stores.

Fluids

The athlete may lose large amounts of water during endurance exercise; therefore rehydration is essential, especially if there are also hot environmental conditions. As we have discovered, thirst is not a good indicator of dehydration therefore the athlete needs to drink plenty during and after exercise even if little thirst is experienced.

Vitamin and mineral supplements

There is an increase in the body's requirements for vitamins and minerals if regular, intensive exercise takes place. This means that the athlete will eat more food because of the need for more energy. This in itself will mean that the body is receiving more vitamins and minerals. As we have already discovered, large quantities of extra vitamins and minerals can damage health. Supplementing the athlete's diet can, in certain circumstances, be beneficial.

Factors to consider with sports performers and nutrition

Sports performers, especially at the top level, have certain aspects to their lifestyles that should be considered when planning nutritional intake:

■ timing of meals to fit around training and events

■ ensuring that there is balance in the diet

■ ensuring that there is adequate fluid intake

■ ensuring adequate iron intake

■ diet should be suitable for a very high workload, depending on the activity

■ psychological wellbeing – if an athlete is unhappy with the diet, then even if physiologically beneficial, it could negatively affect performance because of psychological pressure

■ there should be a sharing of ideas between coach/dietician and the performer to agree the best strategy, depending on an individual's needs and perceptions

■ obsession with food is common with high performance athletes and should be avoided.

Supplements

The use of nutritional supplements in sport is widespread. Ergogenic aids are substances that aim to enhance performance through effects on energy, alertness, or body composition. Sportspeople are always trying to improve performance and give themselves a competitive edge that is not against the rules. Supplements can help but they could still be harmful in the short or long term.

Energy

Several nutritional ergogenic aids are effective at giving an increase in energy. Carbohydrate supplements, whether in the form of powders, gels or sports drinks, are an example. During prolonged exercise, carbohydrates provide extra energy fuel to help prevent fatigue. Sports drinks deliver water and fuel to the body fast, helping to avoid dehydration and fatigue.

Several other ergogenic aids have been shown to be potentially beneficial for certain athletes. However, the long-term effects are still unclear so unless one is competing at the top level they are probably not worth the cost or the risk.

Creatine and bicarbonate supplements have been shown to be useful during high-intensity work. Creatine supplementation can increase muscle creatine phosphate levels for use in the ATP-PC energy system. Alkaline salts, such as sodium bicarbonate (baking soda), can help to neutralise lactic acid and delay fatigue.

Stimulants

Caffeine is performance-enhancing due to being a central nervous system stimulant. However, if you are competing, a caffeine level in the urine above 12 mg/l is not permitted. This level will be achieved by taking about 500 mg caffeine (about seven cups of coffee) in a short time. Caffeine is also a diuretic so make sure you keep hydrated.

Body composition

A variety of supplements, such as protein and amino acid supplements, carnitine, chromium and hydroxymethylbutyrate (HMB), claim to enhance performance by affecting body composition, either by increasing muscle mass and/or reducing body fat. But these have generally been shown to be ineffective.

The Psychological Factors that Affect Sports Training and Performance

> **keyword**
>
> **Motivation**
> A need or drive to do something with determination, for example to keep turning up to hockey practice and hopefully to be picked for the next game.

There is so much information about the way in which the brain affects our performance in sport that there would be more than enough for many books! Unit 4 demands that we explore some of the central areas of psychology and sport, including **motivation**, arousal and anxiety, personality factors and the way in which concentration and self-confidence can affect performance.

Motivation and sports performance

Motivation is important in sport but some sportspeople seem to be better motivated than others. If two athletes of very similar ability race against each other, the one that wins often appears to be better motivated.

There are some people who do not seem at all interested in participating in sport, whereas, at the other end of the scale, some seem to be addicted to playing sport. If we could find out what actually motivates people to participate, we could encourage more to be involved in sport and thus enrich their lives.

When we explore what is meant by the term 'motivation', most psychologists agree that it is to do with a driving force that encourages us towards behaving in a particular way. For example an athlete may be driven to achieve a personal best in throwing the discus. She is driven by the strong desire for self-fulfilment – to feel that she has challenged herself and has won.

Intrinsic or internal motivation

> **keyword**
>
> **Intrinsic motivation**
> This is an inner drive to do well and succeed and to feel good and enjoy the activity.

Intrinsic motivation is the internal drive that people have to participate or to perform well in sport. Intrinsic motives include fun, enjoyment and the satisfaction that is experienced by achieving something. Some athletes describe the intrinsic 'flow' experienced during competition. They speak of high levels of concentration and a feeling that they are in total control.

Figure 4.13

Motivation – she is driven by the strong desire for self-fulfilment – to feel that she has challenged herself and has won

A 40-year-old five-a-side football player who only plays occasionally reports that when he plays he often feels a sense of relief from the day's stresses and strains and that he enjoys the hard physical work and excitement of playing football. This is a typical example of intrinsic motivation.

Extrinsic motivation

Extrinsic motivation involves influences external to the performer. For instance the drive to do well in sport could come from the need to please others or to gain rewards like medals or badges or, in some cases, large amounts of money. Rewards that include badges or prize money are referred to as tangible rewards. Rewards that involve being awarded first place in the league or receiving praise from your parents are known as intangible rewards.

Extrinsic motivation is very useful for encouraging better performance in sport. For instance, if a member of a gymnastics club achieves a badge for reaching a particular standard, the badge is an immediately recognisable sign of that person's standard and can motivate the individual strongly to achieve even higher standards.

keyword

Extrinsic motivation
This is the drive that is caused by motives that are external or environmental. These motives are rewards that can be tangible or intangible.

Arousal
This is a term used for the intensity of the drive that is experienced when an athlete is trying to achieve a goal. High arousal can lead to high levels of stress, both physiologically and psychologically.

Arousal and anxiety

High levels of stress are often caused by over-anxiety to do well. Motivation is important but if personal drive becomes too strong then performance can suffer. Another term for the amount of motivational drive that a sports performer has is called 'arousal'.

Hull (1943) suggested the 'drive theory' to describe the effects of arousal on behaviour. This theory sees the relationship between arousal and performance as being linear:

performance = arousal × skill level

In other words, the higher the arousal, the better the performance. The more emotionally driven you are to achieve a goal; the more likely you are to succeed. Behaviour that is learned is more likely to be repeated, according to Hull, if the stakes are high.

Inverted U hypothesis

This theory has been applied to behaviour in sport. The theory states that as arousal increases so does performance but only up to moderate arousal levels. As arousal becomes even higher then performance starts to decline. At very low levels and very high levels of arousal performance is therefore poor but the optimum level of arousal for the best possible performance is at moderate level. The inverted U hypothesis graph illustrates this theory.

A hockey team player is well motivated and driven to win by her coach, but she keeps relatively calm and concentrates on the skills that she needs to perform. Her arousal level is moderate and therefore she will play at her best level. This is an example of the inverted U theory.

Figure 4.16

Drive theory graph

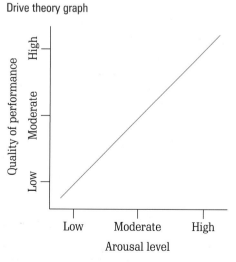

Figure 4.17

Inverted U hypothesis graph

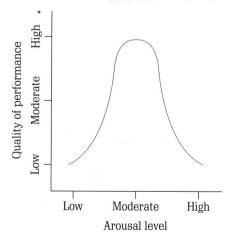

Research reveals that in sport the amount of arousal that is necessary depends on three factors:

- **Types of skill** – the more gross/simple the skill then the higher are the levels of arousal needed. The more fine/complex the skill then the lower are the levels of arousal required.

- **Ability of the performers** – the more expert the performers then the more they need high levels of arousal to reach optimum performance.

- The personality of the performers – the more extrovert the performers then the more arousal they need to perform well. If the performer is introverted then arousal levels are best kept low.

Anxiety

Anxiety involves worry that failure might occur. Of course, the competitive nature of sport means that failure is always a possibility. In sport, winning sometimes assumes gigantic proportions. As Bill Shankly, the inspired Liverpool Football Club's manager, reportedly stated, 'Winning is not like life and death, it is more important than that.'

Some competitors can cope with anxiety and are mainly calm. There are others, including many top performers, who can become extremely anxious. There are two types of anxiety:

- **Trait anxiety** is a personality trait that is enduring in the individual. A performer with high trait anxiety has the predisposition or the potential to react to situations with apprehension.

- **State anxiety** is anxiety in a particular situation. There are two types of state anxiety:
  - somatic: the body's response, such as tension or rapid pulse rate
  - cognitive: the psychological worry over the situation (Honeybourne *et al.*, 2000).

The anxiety experienced in sports competition is often referred to as competitive anxiety.

Competitive anxiety

There are four major factors related to competitive anxiety:

- The interaction between the person and the situation. Some sports performers will be anxious in match situations but not in training.

- Anxiety can be caused by a response that is to do with a personality trait (trait anxiety) or by a response to a specific situation (state anxiety).

- Anxiety levels may vary. Those with high trait anxiety are likely to become anxious in highly stressful situations but they are not equally anxious in all stressful situations.

- Competition factors. This is the interaction between personality factors, trait anxiety and the situation. This interaction will affect behaviour and may cause state anxiety.

Ways to control anxiety and arousal

The management of stress to eliminate anxiety and to control arousal is important, especially to high-level performers

Stress management techniques are widely used by sportsmen and women to cope with high levels of anxiety. Cognitive anxiety management techniques are those that affect the mind and therefore psychological anxiety. Somatic techniques are those, such as relaxation, which affect the body directly. Cognitive techniques can affect the body and somatic techniques can affect the mind. Controlling the heart rate by relaxation methods can make us feel more positive about performing, for example. Positive thinking can, in turn, control our heart rate (Honeybourne et al., 2000).

---

case study 4.6

Jonny Wilkinson's strategies to keep calm

Newcastle Falcons and England

Like many professional sportspeople and athletes, this rugby professional ensures his state of mind is correct and that he has gone through his superstitious rituals before stepping out onto the pitch.

Wilkinson admits that he is both nervous and aggressive, psyching himself up for what he knows he must soon face. Wilkinson's own pre-match superstitions include wearing the same t-shirt under his England shirt. He never puts on his shoulder pads before he has warmed up. He does all of this subconsciously, making sure that he never puts on his England shirt before he has warmed up; feeling that as he has never done this, if he does something will go wrong. His rituals or routines help him control his nerves before a game.

In the dressing room Wilkinson's teammates also show anxiety and are always desperate to begin the game. They are sufficiently psyched up and, for many, even thinking about their state of mind before a match makes them nervous. Nerves are obviously a key feature and one of his unnamed teammates vomits into a bin before every game, due to nerves rather than superstition. Wilkinson admits, 'people like to have their own routines to fight back the nerves to keep them sane.'

(Adapted from www.bbc.co.uk/sport, 2004)

---

keyword

Personality
An individual's behavioural characteristics that make him or her different from others.

Personality and sports performance

Psychologists attempt to see links between certain types of people and success in sport. They also try to find links between types of **personality** and the sports in which they choose to become involved.

Personality profiles

Sports psychologists have put in a great deal of time and effort to build a picture of typical personalities of sports performers. They have attempted to show that there are major differences between successful sportspeople and those who are unsuccessful at sport or who avoid it altogether.

Research has indicated that sports that involve physical contact like wrestling attract people with a different group of personality characteristics than do individual sports such as gymnastics. Team players have also been shown to be more anxious and extroverted but lack the sensitivity and imagination associated with individual sports performers. Links have also been established between player positions and certain personality characteristics, for instance positions which depend on decision making, such as that of a midfield hockey player, will tend to have a personality with more concentration, anxiety control and confidence.

The many personality characteristics are often grouped into two dimensions or scales:

keyword

Extroversion
Seeks social situations and likes excitement. Lacks concentration.

keyword

Introversion
Does not seek social situations and likes peace and quiet. Good at concentrating.

keyword

Stable
Does not swing from one emotion to another.

keyword

Neurotic
Highly anxious and has unpredictable emotions.

Extroversion ◄————————► **Introversion**

Stable ◄————————► **Neurotic**

Each pair should be viewed on a scale or continuum as shown. For instance individuals may have elements of being extrovert and introvert but they are slightly more extroverted than introverted.

There is another trait perspective to personality called the narrow-band approach that states that personality characteristics can be grouped into two main types:

■ **Type A** – these are individuals who are impatient and lack tolerance towards other. They also have high levels of personal anxiety.

■ **Type B** – these are far more relaxed and are more tolerant towards others. They have much lower personal anxiety.

Hinckle *et al.* (1989) researched the link between the narrow-band approach and sports performance. Ninety-six runners, aged between 16 and 66 years, were identified as either Type A or Type B personalities. There was no significant difference between the two groups, except Type A runners ran more when they were not motivated than did Type B.

This research supports the argument that one particular personality type is not preferable to another (Honeybourne *et al.*, 2000).

Different situations often trigger different personality characteristics. For instance a netball player may only show signs of aggression when losing. Research has shown that there is a link between certain personality traits and the sports people choose to participate in but there is little evidence to support the view that knowing whether a performer is extrovert, introvert, type A or type B can predict performance.

Concentration and self-confidence

The ability to concentrate often depends on whether you are able to control the anxiety that you inevitably feel before or during sports competition. The amount of self-confidence that an individual has is also very important in concentration and motivation.

Self-confidence can often be specific to a particular situation – Bandura called this self-efficacy. This specific confidence can vary from situation to situation and, according to Bandura, can affect performance if the individual is skilful enough. People who expect to be confident in a particular situation are more likely to choose that activity. People who expect to have low self-efficacy in a situation will avoid that particular activity.

Our expectations of whether or not self-confidence is going to be high or low may determine the activity we choose, the amount of effort we put into it and whether we stick with the task or give up easily.

Our expectations of self-efficacy depend on four types of information.

- **Performance accomplishments**. These probably have the strongest influence on self-confidence. If success has been experienced in the past, especially if it has been attributed to controllable factors, then feelings of self-confidence are likely to be high.

- **Vicarious experiences**. This refers to what we have observed before. If we watch others perform and be successful, then we are more likely to experience high self-efficacy, as long as the performers we are watching are of a similar standard.

- **Verbal persuasion**. If we are encouraged to try a particular activity, our confidence in that situation may increase. The effectiveness of this encouragement depends upon who is encouraging us and in what ways. Significant others are more likely to persuade us to 'have a go' than strangers.

- **Emotional arousal**. Our perceptions of how aroused we are can affect our confidence in a particular situation. If you have effective strategies to control physiological and psychological arousal levels (perhaps the ability to relax or to use mental rehearsal) then you are more likely to have high self-efficacy.

(Source: adapted from Honeybourne *et al.*, 2004.)

case study 4.7

Strategies that could raise the level of self-efficacy of a high jumper

- Try to give him initial success by lowering the bar to start with, or using some flexi-rope.

- Demonstrate how it can be done or, if you are much better than him, use someone of similar ability to him. An actual demonstration (live modelling) can be more effective in raising self-confidence than a video recording.

- Verbally encourage the athlete. Tell him that he should 'have a go' – that you think that he will succeed – even that the mat is nice and soft!

- Tell him that to be worried is a natural, very positive response because it prepares the body well. Alternatively, teach him some relaxation techniques or how to mentally rehearse the activity (but be aware that this could increase his anxiety).

Figure 4.18

The ability to concentrate often depends on whether you are able to control the anxiety that you inevitably feel before or during sports competition

progress check

1 Name the main components of fitness.

2 Choose two components and describe how you would test the level of fitness for each.

3 Explain how lifestyle factors can affect physical fitness.

4 Give the five main principles of training.

5 What is meant by the interval training method?

6 What are plyometrics?

7 Why is the intake of water so crucial in sport?

8 What is meant by a healthy diet?

9 Give sports examples of intrinsic and extrinsic motivation.

10 Using examples from sport, explain the inverted U hypothesis.

UNIT 5

Planning and Leading Sports Activities

This unit covers:

- skills, qualities and responsibilities associated with successful sports leadership
- planning and leading an activity session
- reviewing the planning and leadership of sports activities and events

This unit provides an introduction to the skills, techniques and knowledge required when leading sports, recreational and play activities. It relates directly to Unit 5 of the BTEC First award and can be adapted to suit work with different groups and activities in the community. The unit will help you to lead practical sessions effectively. It is important to remember that when applying skills related to sports leadership, there should be a suitably qualified member of staff present. It is usual to practise such skills with fellow students before going out into the local community. Health and safety matters will be alluded to but are covered in more detail in Unit 2. The unit will help to prepare students for the Community Sports Leaders Award as well as other related NVQ Level 2 units.

grading criteria

To achieve a **Pass** grade the evidence must show that the learner is able to:	To achieve a **Merit** grade the evidence must show that the learner is able to:	To achieve a **Distinction** grade the evidence must show that the learner is able to:
P1 Describe the skills, qualities and responsibilities associated with successful sports leadership, using two examples of successful sports leaders	**M1** Explain the skills, qualities and responsibilities associated with successful sports leadership, giving comparisons and contrasts between successful sports leaders	**D1** Evaluate the skills and qualities of two contrasting leaders in sport, commenting on their effectiveness
P2 Plan and lead a sports activity with teacher support	**M2** Independently plan and lead a sports activity	**D2** Evaluate own performance in the planning and leading of sports activities and events, commenting on strengths and areas for improvement and further development as a sports leader

grading criteria

To achieve a **Pass** grade the evidence must show that the learner is able to:	To achieve a **Merit** grade the evidence must show that the learner is able to:	To achieve a **Distinction** grade the evidence must show that the learner is able to:
P3 Review their planning and leading of a sports activity, identifying strengths and areas for improvement	**M3** Explain strengths and areas for improvement in the planning and leading of a sports activity, making suggestions relating to improvement	
P4 Assist in the planning and leading of a sports event describing own role within the event, and producing evidence that this has been effective	**M4** Explain stengths and areas for improvement in assisting in the planning and leading of a sports event, making suggestions relating to improvement	
P5 Review their performance in assisting the planning and leading of a sports event, commenting on own effectiveness and identifying strengths and areas for improvement		

Skills, Qualities and Responsibilities Associated with Sports Leadership

Communication

There are many skills associated with being a good coach or leader of a sports activity. The skill of communicating with performers and other coaches, as well as officials, is very important if the leader is going to get the best out of everyone. Communication can be verbal and non-verbal and effective communication does include listening.

Communication skills of the sports leader should include the ability to be:

- **direct** – make instructions brief and easily understood when you can
- **consistent** – avoid double meanings or confusion
- **separate fact from opinion** – be accurate in your analysis rather than an emotional meaningless response
- **focus on one thing at a time** – too much information causes information overload

- **repeat key points** – this reinforces and ensures no misunderstandings
- **have a good 'sense of audience'** – adapt your content and technique depending on the recipient.

Good communication in leading a sports activity should also include the following practical aspects:

- Talk to individuals as they train. Make sure they know that you know them.
- Use positive comments rather than negative ones if at all possible, but do not give praise unless it is deserved.
- Ensure that you can control a group of young people by insisting that they respond to a signal, for example a whistle – stress the health and safety aspect of this.
- Use your voice and vary your tone. Shout if necessary but not too often. Bring the group up to you to give instructions rather than shouting.
- Use questions to try to find out what the group members know and understand.
- Try to make sessions fun so that motivation is high – but do not pick on individuals and embarrass them.

Figure 5.1

Communicating with performers and other coaches, as well as officials is very important if the leader is going to get the best out of everyone

Organisation

An effective coach would be one who is well organised. Good organisation can relieve possible sources of stress and can ultimately help performance. Confidence in the coach is increased if the performer perceives him or her to be organised. Self-confidence on the part of the coach can also be increased if personal organisation is good.

To be well organised make sure that you:

- Plan well in advance and make the necessary arrangements for the activity to go smoothly.
- Prepare and organise the facilities that you will use.
- Prepare the equipment and check it for safety as well as for appropriateness. For example is there enough equipment to go round the group – or is there enough for one between two?
- Work well with others who are sharing the leadership and develop a sense of teamwork. Does each person know what the others are doing?
- Plan your session to take into account time, available facilities and the ability of the learners.
- Can change your plans if things do not go well or circumstances change. For example have you made a plan if the weather is wet and you are outside?

Solving problems

The skills of analysing and problem solving are also important for effective coaching. You need to be able to analyse what exactly is going wrong. Then it is more likely that the problem will be solved. Analysis may be related to the skills that the learners are performing or their behaviour or that the activity needs to be changed because it is unsuitable.

Health and safety

To ensure that you lead a session that is safe and follows health and safety guidelines make sure that you:

- Check all the equipment that you use is safe and in good working condition before, during and after the activity.
- Check that the facilities that you use are safe. The playing surface must be free of dangerous materials such as large stones or broken glass. These checks should also take place before, during and after the activity.
- Check that the learners in your activity are fit and well enough to take part and that you have information about any potential problems. For example, you may have a participant who is diabetic or asthmatic. Ensure you know how to refer any health problems to someone who is qualified to deal with them.
- Always monitor the safety of the participants during the activity. For example a game may be getting too rough and some learners may be vulnerable to injury – you may have to stop or modify the activity to ensure safety for all.

Figure 5.2

If you are not qualified to deal with an injury always get help from someone who is

- Always have or have access to first aid facilities. Make sure that you know exactly what to do if there is an accident and there is an injury. If you are not qualified to deal with an injury always get help from someone who is.

- Have emergency procedures and review them regularly.

See Unit 2 Health Safety and Injury in Sport

Personal qualities of a leader in a sports situation

Coaches also need to be able to educate those they coach regarding:

- **Hydration** – types of hydration, reasons for hydration, hydration recommendations before during and after exercise.

- **Sports psychology** – including basic goal-setting principles and SMART target setting (see below). Basic motivational principles, including what motivates people to exercise and the difference in motivating children and adults.

- **Physiology** – including the principles of warming up and cooling down. Fitness components, strength, speed, flexibility, power, agility and muscular endurance.

- **The principles of training** – overload, progression, specificity, adaptation, variability, reversibility, recovery and over training.

The qualities of a good leader include having good communication skills with other leaders and the participants. A good leader is enthusiastic and well motivated. It is easier to motivate others if you seem to be enjoying your job as leader! Having good sports skills helps, particularly for demonstrations, but is not essential. A good in-depth knowledge of the sport makes it easier to gain respect. One's standard of appearance is also important, especially with young people. If you want the group members to be suitably 'kitted out' for the activity then it is important that you too 'look the part' and are smartly and appropriately dressed. You must always be punctual and reliable. If you wish your participants to turn up on time and to attend regularly then you must too and set a good example for them to follow.

Good leaders are often charismatic. In other words, they naturally command respect because of their personality. A good leader will have a clear vision of what they are trying to achieve, so good planning and organisation is essential for a successful leader in a sports activity.

The leadership style that is adopted by a leader in sport depends on three factors (Honeybourne, 2003):

- **The situation** – for example, is the team winning or losing?
- **The members of the team/group** – for example, are they hostile?
- **The personality of the leader** – for example, is he or she naturally forceful?

There are many different styles of leadership, but the three most common styles are:

- **Authoritarian style**. These leaders just want to get the job or task done. They do not have a particular interest in personal relationships and they gain most from the decisions, rather than other members of the team.
- **Democratic style**. These leaders are concerned with inter-personal relationships. The leader adopting this style would share out the decision-making and ask for advice from other group members.
- **Laissez-faire style**. This type of leader takes very few decisions and gives little direction to the team. The group members choose what they would like to do and how they go about it with little or no input from the leader.

Most leaders who are successful have a mixture of styles to draw from. A good coach may decide to be authoritarian when the team is losing but more democratic in training. In match situations, the leader may decide to let the team 'get on with it' because interference might stifle creativity of team members.

Coaching techniques

Depending on the situation, the coach should be able to incorporate a range of combinations of the following methods:

- **Whole, part, whole** – this is the technique of coaching a complete skill, then splitting it up into parts and then teaching it as a whole again.
- **Shaping** – this is a technique where reward or praise is given when the performer's behaviour/technique is correct. This reinforces the right technique and it is more likely to be repeated. The coach is therefore 'shaping' behaviour (sometimes called operant conditioning).

- **Feedback** – this can be given during the performance or afterwards. Feedback is most effective if it is given close to the performance so the performance is fresh in the participant's mind. Feedback motivates, changes performance or actually reinforces learning. The more precise the feedback then the more beneficial it is. If the feedback involves praise or criticism or involves punishing the individual then this may change the learner's behaviour in the future. This process is called reinforcement.

There are various types of reinforcement:

- **Positive** – this is the giving of a stimulus to ensure repetition of behaviour, for example a badge for swimming.
- **Negative** – this is the taking away of a stimulus to ensure that the right behaviour is repeated, for example not giving any verbal praise if the performer shows the wrong movement.
- **Punishment** – this is the giving of a stimulus to prevent a behaviour occurring, for instance dropping a performer from the squad for not trying hard in training.
- **Modelling** – this is a technique that involves using demonstrations or 'models of performance'. The performer can readily see what is required and then attempt to copy it.

Effective demonstrations

Copying or modelling can affect performance through four processes:

- **Attention**. To be able to imitate a demonstration the performer must pay attention to the demonstration and focus on important cues (this is called 'cueing'). The more that you are looked up to or respected then the more likely it is that the learner will take notice of what you are doing.
- **Retention**. The observer must be able to remember the model or the demonstration. Therefore he or she needs to create a memorable mental picture of the process. So clear demonstrations are important.
- **Motor reproduction**. The observer must be physically able to copy the skill being watched. Demonstrations should therefore be matched to the capabilities of the observer. A demonstration should therefore be very basic for beginners – coaches should resist the temptation to show off their skills!
- **Motivation**. The level of motivation of the observer or learner in your activity is crucial if they are going to want to copy the performance. The use of praise and other rewards may increase motivation. It may also be relevant to insist on their attention and the need for them to watch closely so that they can copy your demonstration effectively (Honeybourne et al., 2004).

Teaching/coaching styles

These are similar to leadership styles, discussed above. They can be adapted depending on the situation, the performer and the coach:

- **Command style (autocratic)** is a technique where the coach makes all the decisions, directs the performer and is authoritarian in approach.
- **Reciprocal style** is a technique that involves group work and performers learn from one another.
- **Discovery style** is when the coach takes a back seat and encourages the performer to discover solutions to problems. This approach by the coach may be termed laissez-faire style.
- The coach may adopt a **democratic style**, which is when the performer participates in decision making.

Learning styles

These are ways in which individual participants prefer to learn; some learn better through instructions and demonstrations, for example; others prefer discovery-learning/problem-solving experiences. Some, for instance, prefer to learn through visual means, some more kinaesthetically or by doing rather than listening.

Guidance

The coach can adopt a variety of different guidance methods:

- **Visual**. For example, demonstration. Demonstrations must be accurate and clear.
- **Verbal**. For example, instructions about technique.
- **Mechanical**. For example, stabilisers on a bike.
- **Manual**. For example, supporting a gymnast for a handspring.

Planning and Leading an Activity Session

For effective planning to take place for a sports activity, the following should be taken into consideration:

- Age of the participants.
- Size of the group/groups.
- Use of other leaders or assistants.
- Skill level of the participants – what can they do already?
- Time – what time do you have for the activity, including the introduction, warm-up and cool-down. Do not forget that the session may have to include time for changing both at the beginning of the activity and at the end.

Do the following:

- Record your session's aims – what are you trying to achieve? Be realistic!
- Identify the facilities that you need as well as the equipment.
- Take health and safety factors into consideration and make a risk assessment.

See Unit 2 Health, Safety and Injury in Sport

> **keyword**
>
> **Target group**
> This represents the type of people on whom one wishes to concentrate for an activity session.

Lesson plan

This must be realistic and be suitable for the level of ability of the participants (often called the **target group**).

The aims and objectives should be made clear at the beginning of the plan. The lesson plan should also record any medical matters related to the participants. They should take into account the numbers of participants, their ages and their gender. There may well be participants who have particular learning needs and a 'learning assistant' may be on hand to help. Resources and equipment should be recorded and the timing of activities.

An effective lesson plan should relate to an overall plan or 'scheme of work'. This scheme of work takes into consideration what is to be taught and what is expected to be learned over a period of time – normally a term or a year. The most important aspect of the plan is to state what you expect to be learned rather than just listing the activities that you wish to teach. Really effective planning also includes 'extension activities', which can be given to those participants who are moving at a faster learning rate than others.

A good plan has a sequence of activities, for example:

> Short introduction/warm up/group activity/individual skills/pair skills/small games/cool down/recap.

In your session ensure that you include at least some of the following activities:

- Warm-up activities, including stretching (always).
- Games such as tag or relay races for fun and as a warm-up and also to satisfy the initial enthusiasm of the participants!
- Pairs activities – to practise skills without too much competition.
- Small group activities – to give some idea of the team game if appropriate and to teach how to work with others effectively.
- Minor games or potted sports – activities that may teach some basic skills related to running jumping and throwing. These activities are also useful to teach the participants how to respond to you – your voice or the whistle.
- Skill circuits and fitness circuits – once skills have been learned you may include circuits to put the skills under some competitive pressure. This activity is also good for fitness.
- Full game activities – these should not dominate a session nor should you get into full games early on in your sessions. Many young people want to 'get into a game', but without the appropriate skills or strategies a game would be dominated by a few and no real learning would take place. There is also a danger that some would never 'get into a game' and so the participants cannot see the relevance of the skills they have learned!

- Cool-down activities (always). As well as the physiological reasons for cooling down (see Unit 4), these can be useful to calm the participants down. If they are school children whose next lesson is classroom based, other teachers will be very grateful!

Characteristics of a good session

- It is lively but controlled.
- It is well planned – it has structure.
- It has variety – try not to do one particular activity for too long.
- It fits well into what has been done before and what is planned for the next session.
- Participants are as active as possible – do not talk too much! Little but often is much better than big speeches.
- Check regularly that the participants understand what is going on.
- A challenging and exciting environment – the facilities are appropriate and the activities are not too difficult and not too easy.

Characteristics of a poor session

- Too much talk from the leader.
- Not enough action for the participants – too much standing around.
- No real purpose to the session – they do not know why they are doing what they are doing and the aims have not been shared with the group.
- The practices are too difficult or too easy.
- Lack of voice projection – the group cannot hear what the leader is saying.
- The leader gives too much information at any one time – this confuses and de-motivates.
- Lack of discipline – misbehaviour by the participants can lead to dangerous situations as well as being a barrier for learning. It is essential for the leader to ensure control early on by insisting that the group listens and that the learners do the activity as requested. If some participants are proving to be too difficult then assistance should be requested from someone in authority!
- Poor facilities/equipment.

Health and safety

It is essential to make a risk assessment of the activity.

See Unit 2 Health, Safety and Injury in Sport

The facility and the equipment should be checked carefully. It is important to be aware of emergency procedures, to look out for any injuries and to act immediately if they occur. First-aid resources should be well stocked and regularly checked. The leader should know who to contact for help and where.

Legal responsibilities

It is essential to be aware of the regulations that are in place to protect both the participants and the group leader. These include the Children Act 1989, the Data Protection Act and the Activity Centre (Young Person's Safety) Act. (More details of these regulations are given in Unit 2.)

Childrens Act 1989

There should be a learner:staff ratio of 8:1 for children under 8 years. Records must be kept of accidents, attendance and the names of all employees and volunteers. There is an increased awareness of child abuse, which is relevant because there are many positions of trust with children associated with the sport and leisure industry. This Act protects not only the children but also employees who can be accused falsely or accidentally of abuse.

- Do not get into isolated situations with children.
- Physical contact must be minimal and involve only non-sensitive areas of the body, such as the hands.
- Use physical restraint only in emergencies.
- Show appropriate role model behaviour, such as not swearing, smoking or drinking alcohol.

See Unit 2 Health, Safety and Injury in Sport

Data Protection Act 1998

This Act makes it illegal to use information about individuals for any purpose other than that for which it was intended. Those who hold information must ensure its security and make sure that only authorised personnel can access it. In the sport and leisure industry computer files often hold personal information on clients. The security of this information comes under this Act. The control of data on such databases would be protected by a password known only by authorised personnel.

Activity Centre (Safety of Young Persons) Act 1995

Clubs and individuals must be aware of the above Act. They may wish to examine the activities that they offer in the context of this Act, particularly in relation to 'taster' sessions with young people under 18.

The Act was passed in 1995. On 16 April 1996 the Regulations to the Act became effective. Since October 1997 it has been a requirement for all centres that want to provide the prescribed activities below, to be registered and licensed with the AALA (Adventure Activities Licensing Authority).

Licenses may be valid for up to 3 years, although most are valid for 1–2 years.

Planning and Leading Sports Activities

The prescribed activities are as follows:

- caving (excluding visits to caves open to the public)

- climbing (including gorge walking, scrambling and sea-level traversing)

- trekking on foot, pony, or mountain bike, on moorland or above 600m where it is more than 30 minutes' travelling time to a road or refuge, and including off-piste skiing in remote country, but not on-piste skiing

- watersports – most activities involving unpowered craft (rowing boats are exempt) on any water where it is possible to be more than 50 m from the nearest perimeter bank, or which is affected by tides or is turbulent.

The Act applies if the provision of the prescribed activities or level of activity involves instruction to those under the age of 18 in return for payment. If any one of those factors does not apply, then the activity – or level of activity – does not come within the scope of the Act and there is no need to register. Neither does the Act apply if the parent or legal guardian of the young person accompanies them throughout their participation.

Other providers must also be aware of the Act:

- Schools are exempt as far as canoeing with their own pupils is concerned.

- Local-authority owned centres: these are not exempt.

- Individuals who offer their services for payment: these are regarded as a 'centre' for the purposed of the scheme. If an individual freelance coach works for another person or organisation and is paid, however, and does not receive payment direction from the candidates, it is that 'centre' which must be registered – should the terms of reference apply – not the freelance coach.

(Adapted from British Canoe Union web site)

Much of this unit has concentrated on the planning and method of delivery. The organisational skills that are needed have been highlighted, including the need to adapt depending on different age groups, resources, facilities and equipment.

Leadership skills have already been covered and good leaders will be flexible in their style of leadership. For example, if the group is a little hostile you might wish to adopt a more 'authoritarian' style to maintain discipline. Later, once the group has settled into the activity, a good leader will then adopt a more 'democratic' style with lots of questions, encouraging the learners to participate in their own learning.

The lesson plans we have identified as being important should include activities such as a warm-up and a cool-down. There must be progression so that there is always something new to learn. Competitive game situations should be avoided until the skills appropriate to the game have been learned. Games, nevertheless, can be conditioned or modified so that only certain skills can be practised. For example the one-touch conditioned game in football or the no-dribbling conditioned game in basketball.

Lesson delivery

The leader should meet the participants punctually and make them feel welcome and at ease. The leader must then explain and agree the aims that are appropriate for participants to achieve.

The leader should check the participants' level of experience, ability and physical readiness to participate effectively and safely. It is very important that the leader makes sure that the participants have the correct equipment and clothing. If any participants are wearing jewellery, for example, it may be necessary to ask them to remove it for health and safety reasons. Remember that personal possessions remain the responsibility of the owner and not you – unless you state that you will look after anything (not usually a good idea).

The leader must include an appropriate warm-up and explain the value and purpose of this. Participants should be reminded regularly about the health benefits of the activities and what is happening to the body when we exercise. The leader must be prepared to revise plans for the session if it is necessary. Flexibility is the sign of a good leader or coach.

For coaching to be effective, explanations and demonstrations need to be technically correct and appropriate to the participants' needs and level of experience. Throughout the session the coach should check the participants' understanding of the activity.

Reviewing the Planning and Leadership of Sports Activities and Events

Review

Good leaders of sports activities will monitor and review or evaluate what they are doing and adjust their plans accordingly.

Evaluation is the process of analysing the sessions you have planned and delivered. This can help leaders to identify what went well and what could have been improved.

Effective evaluation is essential if progress in coaching is to be made. Good sports leaders are always trying to improve what they do. This involves them in thinking about and evaluating the coaching sessions they have planned and delivered, identifying strengths and weaknesses and learning lessons for the future. A technique for this is called the SWOT analysis (strengths, weaknesses, opportunities, threats).

See Unit 9 Psychology for Sports Performance, page 179

The sports leader must also take into account this analysis to modify and develop coaching practice and to set SMART targets.

UNIT 5 — Planning and Leading Sports Activities

link See Unit 7 Practical Outdoor and Adventurous Activities, page 152

Leaders should take part in regular education to develop their coaching practice further and to add to their coaching skills so that lack of knowledge is no longer a threat. This could involve attending courses, conferences, reading journals or other relevant publications, observing and working with other coaches.

When evaluating coaching it is important to review not just the way in which a session is delivered but also the way it was planned. The key to really effective coaching is to plan well. Problems during a coaching session can often be avoided if more thought is put into the planning process.

Figure 5.3
Lesson objectives

Name: _____**Date:**_____

Subject:_____

Group:_____

Activity: _____

Lesson Objectives:

Phase	Learning points / Content	Equipment
Warm Up		
Early Activity		
Focus		
Progression		
Performance / Game / Summary Activity		
Review		
Cool Down		

It is also important to take into account how the participants felt about the coaching session. Their views could be sought via verbal feedback or a written evaluation. It is important to record the evaluations both in terms of self-evaluation by the leader, evaluation by other coaches and supervisors and the participants themselves. The whole process is meaningless if these evaluations are not acted upon. The elements of the coaching that have received favourable evaluations should reinforce good practice and that practice should continue and develop. The issues that arise from poor evaluations should be addressed and become part of an action plan to improve. Progress should be reviewed and there should be a development in coaching practice and updating of the personal action plans accordingly (Honeybourne, 2003).

progress check

1 Give four points for guidance to make a sports leader's communication more effective.

2 Make a list of things you need to organise before teaching a sports activity.

3 What health and safety aspects should be taken into consideration before leading a sports activity?

4 What factors affect the type of leadership style you choose?

5 What is meant by the whole-part-whole method of practice sessions?

6 How can a demonstration be fully effective?

7 Construct a lesson plan for a sports activity of your choice to a group of 11-year-old beginners.

8 What makes a session poor?

9 What is meant by a SWOT analysis?

10 Evaluate any sports activity session that you have experienced or taken yourself. How would you make it even better?

Practical Sport

This unit covers:

■ learning to demonstrate a range of skills, techniques and tactics in selected sports

■ the rules, regulations and scoring systems of selected sports

■ the roles and responsibilities of officials in selected sports

■ analysing the sports performance of an individual or team

This unit supports Unit 6 of the BTEC First Diploma in sport. The focus of the unit is to improve your practical performance in sport as well as analysing the performances of others. This annex is a summary of the BTEC specifications and will give general information to enable you to apply skills, techniques and tactics in a game or individual sport. There is also a requirement to have a good knowledge of rules and regulations and the roles and responsibilities of officials in that sport. A large number of web sites have been provided to help you with your research.

grading criteria

To achieve a **Pass** grade the evidence must show that the learner is able to:	To achieve a **Merit** grade the evidence must show that the learner is able to:	To achieve a **Distinction** grade the evidence must show that the learner is able to:
P1 Demonstrate use of practical skills, techniques and tactics appropriate for one team and one individual sport	**M1** Describe the use of tactics appropriate for one team and one individual sport	**D1** Justify the use of tactics appropriate for one team and one individual sport, identifying areas for improvement
P2 Describe the rules, regulations and scoring systems for one team and one individual sport	**M2** Explain, using appropriate examples, the rules, regulations and scoring systems for one team and one individual sport	**D2** Explain the strengths and weaknesses of an individual, or team, in one individual and one team sport, providing specific recommendations relating to improving upon weaknesses
P3 Describe the main roles and responsibilities of officials in one team and one individual sport	**M3** Independently produce an observation checklist that could be used to review the performance of an individual or a team	
P4 Produce, with teacher support, an observation checklist that could be used to review the sports performance of an individual or a team		

grading criteria

To achieve a **Pass** grade the evidence must show that the learner is able to:	To achieve a **Merit** grade the evidence must show that the learner is able to:	To achieve a **Distinction** grade the evidence must show that the learner is able to:
P5 Use an observation checklist to review the sports performance of an individual, or team, in one individual and one team sport	**M4** Describe the strengths and weaknesses of an individual, or team, in one individual and one team sport, identifying ways to improve upon weaknesses	
P6 Identify the strengths and weaknesses of an individual, or team, in one individual and one team sport		

Learning to Demonstrate a Range of Skills, Techniques and Tactics in Selected Sports

- Select sports that you will enjoy studying as well as playing.
- Choose two different types of sport.

Examples include:

- **Team sports**: association football, basketball, cricket, hockey, lacrosse, netball, rugby league or rugby union, rounders and/or softball, volley ball, water polo; racket games such as badminton, squash, tennis, table tennis.
- **Individual sports**: athletics, golf, gymnastics, trampolining, swimming.

Skills:
applied to a range of sports, e.g. passing, receiving, shooting, serving, starting, striking, tumbling and rotating.

Techniques:
applied to a range of sports, e.g. different techniques of throwing, catching, dribbling, kicking, hitting, bowling and footwork.

Tactics:
including defensive, attacking, fielding, batting, set pieces, possession, penetration, communication, team formations, systems of play and marking systems, strategies, goal setting.

Record:
Including use of diary or logbook, video record, summary sheets, feedback from other participants, coaches, teachers and/or trainers.

The Rules, Regulations and Scoring Systems of Selected Sports

Rules:
related to national governing bodies for team, racket and individual sports.

Regulations:
including player and participant, equipment, playing surfaces, facilities and safe practice, related to umpire/referee, timekeeper, lines person, starter and judge.

Scoring systems:
method of victory, method of scoring in specific team, racket and individual sports.

The Roles and Responsibilities of Officials in Selected Sports

Roles:
as an umpire/referee, scorer, timekeeper, table official lines person, starter and judge.

Responsibilities:
appearance, personal equipment, fitness, knowledge of rules and regulations, use of rules, control of game, safety of players/ individuals, playing equipment, playing surfaces, fair play and spirit of the game.

Communication:
including use of voice, confidence, use of whistle, hand signals, decision making, interpretation of rules, terminology, scoring, starting and judging.

Analysing the Sports Performance of an Individual or Team

Identify:
strengths, weaknesses, skills, techniques, tactical awareness, relevant to team, racket and individual sports.

Performance:
statistical analysis of performance, e.g. shots at goal, number of interceptions, successful passes, misplaced passes, types of shots, number of skills performed and types of defensive or attacking play.

Analyse:
observation, discussion, recording systems, use of charts, tables and graphs, areas for improvement.

To gain a distinction grade for this unit, make sure you can:

- critically analyse own performance and application of different skills, techniques and tactics providing recommendations for changes and/or improvements in two different sports

- evaluate the use and application of the rules, regulations and scoring systems for play and/or performance as detailed in the appropriate National Governing Body guidelines for two contrasting sports

- critically analyse the performance of officials in two contrasting sports drawing valid conclusions and making recommendations for changes and/or improvements

- critically analyse the performance, strengths, weaknesses and tactical awareness of two athletes providing recommendations for changes and/or improvements.

Specific sports web sites

Amateur Athletic Foundation of Los Angeles (AAF). Supports Californian youth sports organisations and conducts youth sports and coaching programmes. Operates the Paul Ziffren Sports Resource Centre. Good sports web links, including SIRC, SportQuest, Yahoo Sport, Sporting News, WSF, BSSH and IOC.
www.aafla.org

BBC Sport. Online programme schedules with links, news, player profiles, audio and video highlights, discussion forums, results and search facility.
www.bbc.co.uk/sport

British Gymnastics Association (BAGA). Founded 1888; based at Lilleshall National Sports Centre. Only recognised governing body for UK gymnastics. Member of FIG.
www.baga.co.uk

BUBL UK Sports Governing Bodies. Provides web addresses for a wide range of UK sports associations and organisations, including: archery, athletics, badminton, baseball, chess, cricket, croquet, cycling, curling, fencing, football, golf, gymnastics, handball, hockey, lacrosse, mini-golf, netball, skiing, orienteering, polo, rugby, table tennis, tennis, volleyball. Also links to BOA, VEFA, FIFA and the Olympic movement.
www.bubl.ac.uk/link

Federation Internationale de Gymnastique (FIG). Part of World Sport.Com. World governing body for gymnastics, and largest international sports federation, founded 1881. Contains Archive of Federation News, 1998 and *World of Gymnastics* magazine.
www.gymnastics.worldsport.com

FIFA.COM. Federation Internationale de Football Association (FIFA). Provides information about FIFA, World Cup, football regulations, associations, laws of football and International Football Hall of Champions archive (IFHOC).
www.fifa.com

Football Association.
www.the-fa.org

Football Task Force. Part of Department of Culture, Media and Sport site. Includes full text of report to Ministry of Sport, 'Football: Commercial Issues', 22 December 1999.
www.culture.gov.uk/sport

International Amateur Athletic Federation (IAAF). World governing body for athletes.
www.iaaf.org

Royal Life Saving Society.
www.lifesavers.org.uk

Rugby Football League.
www.rfl.uk.com

Rugby Football Union.
www.rfu.com

Sportal. Huge European network of sports sites. Football, tennis, Formula 1, horseracing, rugby union, rugby league, cycling etc. covered with reports, live commentary, instantly updated statistics and good photography.
www.sportal.co.uk

Sporting Life. Digital version of print magazine. Information-packed site, including instant news from Reuters, Sportal and other main sites.
www.sporting-life.com

Sports.com. Provides European sports news, results and gossip. Good starting point, but more cluttered than Sportal.
www.sports.com

SwimmersWorld.Com. Provides news, e-mail updates, site of the week, coaching resources, Olympic News and Top 50 swimming sites.
www.swimmersworld.com

Swimming Teachers Association. Founded 1932. Aim 'to preserve lives by teaching swimming, lifesaving and survival techniques'.
www.sta.co.uk

SwimNews Online. Includes full text of *Swim News* magazine and archives from 1995. News, swimming calendar, world rankings, results and photograph library, biographies and links.
www.swimnews.com

Swimming Science journal available online.
www.rohan.sdsu.edu/dept/coachsci/

World of Sport Examined. Part of Granada Learning. Provides full A–Z sports links of major sports organisations and associations, sports media links (BBC World Sport, Sky Sports etc.), and other links (Olympics, wheelchair sport etc.).
www.granada-learning.com/yitm/sport

Yahoo Sports. Links to physical education and world individual sports.
http://dir.yahoo.com/recreation/sports/index.html

Practical Outdoor and Adventurous Activities

This unit covers:

- skills and techniques associated with selected outdoor and adventurous activities
- the organisation and provision of outdoors and adventurous activities
- health and safety considerations and environmental impacts associated with participation in outdoor and adventurous activities
- reviewing your own performance in outdoor and adventurous activities

This unit supports Unit 7 of the BTEC First Diploma in Sport. It gives the necessary background information for you to demonstrate skills and techniques associated with outdoor and adventurous activities. The unit also enables you to gain an understanding of the wider issues associated with outdoor and adventurous activities as demanded by the specifications. Health and safety considerations and environmental impacts are covered and advice is given on reviewing performances and setting targets for future development. Web sites and contact details have been provided to assist you throughout the unit.

grading criteria

To achieve a **Pass** grade the evidence must show that the learner is able to:	To achieve a **Merit** grade the evidence must show that the learner is able to:	To achieve a **Distinction** grade the evidence must show that the learner is able to:
P1 Demonstrate techniques and skills appropriate to two outdoor and adventurous activities	**M1** Review and justify choice of techniques demonstrated in outdoor and adventurous activities	**D1** Explain precautions and actions that can be taken, or used, in relation to health and safety considerations associated with participation in outdoor and adventurous activities
P2 Describe the organisation and provision of two outdoor and adventurous activities	**M2** Compare the organisation and provision of two outdoor and adventurous activities	
P3 Describe health and safety considerations associated with participation in two different outdoor and adventurous activities		**D2** Explain precautions and actions that can be taken, or used, to reduce the environmental impacts associated with participation in outdoor and adventurous activities

grading criteria

To achieve a **Pass** grade the evidence must show that the learner is able to:	To achieve a **Merit** grade the evidence must show that the learner is able to:	To achieve a **Distinction** grade the evidence must show that the learner is able to:
P4 Describe environmental impacts associated with participation in two outdoor and adventurous activities	**M3** Explain health and safety considerations associated with participation in two outdoor and adventurous activities, identifying precautions and actions that can be taken, or used, in relation to them	**D3** Justify recommendations relating to identified areas for improvement, in their performance in outdoor and adventurous activities, and describe specific related activities
P5 Produce a risk assessment for a selected outdoor adventurous activity	**M4** Explain the environmental impacts associated with participation in two outdoor and adventurous activities, identifying precautions and actions that can be taken, or used, to reduce them	
P6 Review their own performance in participating in outdoor and adventurous activities identifying strengths and areas for improvement	**M5** Explain identified strengths and areas for improvement in their performance in outdoor and adventurous activities, making recommendations relating to further development of identified areas for improvement	

Skills and Techniques Associated with Selected Outdoor and Adventurous Activities

Activities

Orienteering

This is normally cross-country running or walking using a map and compass to find the way through a series of control points marked on the map. It is a popular competitive sport. Other forms of orienteering include ski orienteering, mountain bike orienteering and trail orienteering for those with physical disabilities.

 www.britishorienteering.org.uk

Rock climbing

This involves climbing up cliffs, mountainsides or walls with your bare hands, using your legs and with ropes. In a competition, the aim is to climb a set height in the shortest possible time.

 www.UKClimbing.com

Skiing

The aim of skiing is to stand on two thin pieces of wood or man-made materials called skis and to slide down a snow-covered or artificial snow-covered slope. In skiing competitions there are events where you have to avoid obstacles, jump high in the air or perform movements or tricks in the air.

 www.englishski.org

Snowboarding

This is probably closer as a sport to skateboarding and surfing than to skiing. Snowboarding uses a single board and, like skiing, competitions can involve speed, style and jumps.

 www.snowboardinguk.co.uk

Canoeing and kayaking

Canoeing is one of the 'paddlesports' that range from calm steady-paced touring on canals and placid waters to competitive sprint racing and facing the challenge of racing down raging torrents of water. The different disciplines in canoeing include freestyle kayaking, sea kayaking, slalom and sprint racing.

 www.bcu.org.uk

Sailing

This involves competing against others and the elements in a variety of different sailing boats from one man dinghies to ocean going yachts that have a large crew.

 www.sailing.org

Windsurfing

Windsurfing involves riding on a board with a large sail attached to it to catch the wind. Windsurfing takes place on the sea or on a lake. In competition you can do long-distance, fast-turning or freestyle windsurfing with tricks.

 www.ukwindsurfing.com

Mountain biking

Specially built bicycles are used in a variety of different events. There is the downhill race that is against the clock. Another event is the four cross or bicycle supercross, which involves four riders competing against each other on a course and other events, include cross-country and the marathon.

 www.bcf.uk.con

Surfing and body boarding

Surfing involves riding the waves standing on a large board called a surfboard. Competitions involve style and technique in riding the waves. Body boarding involves lying down on the surfboard and competitions again involve freestyle moves and tricks in the surf.

 www.britsurf.co.uk

Techniques and skills

Whatever your selected activity, whether orienteering, rock climbing, skiing or mountain biking, it is important that you are able to demonstrate clearly the main skills and techniques that you use. Demonstrations must be:

- Accurate – make sure that you demonstrate correctly and clearly. For example a handhold in rock climbing must be correctly shown.

- Draw attention to the main points of the demonstration – highlight the cues for success, for example the position of the legs in skiing or the position of the body in mountain biking.

- Repeat the demonstration covering the main points again so that the person watching the demonstration can remember them.

- Make clear and unambiguous verbal points to highlight the important aspects of each movement.

- Limit the information that you give at any one time so that the information can be understood and remembered. Do not talk too much because this may cause confusion.

- Help to develop a mental picture of the movement by keeping each movement simple and clear.

- Always emphasise health and safety aspects. Explain and demonstrate the safe way of performing any skills.

Tactics should be explained clearly and simply. Explain fully any technical words that may be associated with your tactics. Explain why you should use the tactics that you are explaining. There must always be a reason why you are using such tactics. Ask yourself why these tactics are necessary.

For example in orienteering there may be certain tactics that you adopt to conserve your energy and if you use such tactics then you will be able to cover the ground much faster and therefore you are more likely to succeed.

Recording evidence

To show evidence of the development and improvement of skills and techniques related to outdoor and adventurous activities it is important to record such evidence regularly and in an organised manner.

Factors you need to take account of are:

- What level have you reached in your activity?

- Knowledge and skills – what do you know about your sport and what skills have you learned?

- Levels of fitness – what test results do you have (for example, strength/ flexibility)?

- How much effort and commitment do you give to your activity? How many times a week do you practise and for how long?

- What improvements could be made for you to be more effective?

- Methods of assessment. How do you assess your current performance/preparation in your activity? Do you use video for example?

The following are ways in which evidence may be recorded:

- diary
- logbook
- portfolio
- video
- audio
- observation record
- feedback sheets/written feedback about skill learning.

The diary

Use a diary that has enough room for recording progress in your activity. A week-to-view diary should be adequate. Each week record your training and performance activities but also identify the skills and techniques that you have developed or improved. Also record which skills and techniques you wish to develop more over the coming weeks. This diary can form the basis of evidence that you need to show development in your activity.

The logbook

A logbook is another type of record, similar to the diary. Once again you keep a record or a log of the skills and techniques you are working on and what you have mastered and yet to master. This is important evidence to show that you are aware of the skills that need further work and to show which skills and techniques you have learned in your activity.

The portfolio

This is the complete record of all your evidence and assessed pieces of work and should also contain your diary or logbook with a record of the skills and techniques you have mastered. It shows your ability to review, evaluate and to set goals for future development.

Video

Videotape showing the skills and techniques that you have mastered in your outdoor adventurous activities should be an extremely valuable piece of evidence. You can use the video not only to show what aspects of your performance are going wrong but also to highlight what you can do correctly and skilfully. The video should be well shot and clear. It could just show what you can do without sound or a commentary can be included, which helps the viewer put your movements into context. For example if the video shows a particular technique or techniques in surfing the commentary can tell the viewer which techniques you are demonstrating and under what sea/weather conditions.

Audio

An audiotape or dictaphone recording can be used to record your successes as you perform or practise your activity. In rock climbing, for example, when you have completed a climb and have used skills or techniques that have succeeded, a recording of your instructor or climbing partner stating that a particular skill has been demonstrated will be valuable evidence of achievement.

Observation record

Likewise, you could use instructors, teachers or other participants to write a short record of what has been achieved. The sooner this can be written following the success the better. The record should state clearly what has been achieved, with date and contextual information. The name of the observer and the date of the observation must be recorded clearly. Make sure that the person observing you has the experience and/or the qualifications to make an accurate assessment.

Feedback sheets

Written records of what has been observed have been dealt with above but this only forms part of the feedback from someone who has observed your skills and techniques. Other, more detailed feedback can also be given to you from someone who can evaluate and assess your skills and techniques – usually your instructor, teacher or experienced participant. These feedback sheets should include what has been done well and weaknesses for improvement. The feedback should also include ideas to help improve performance. The feedback should be structured, for example: strengths, weaknesses, ideas for improvement with some targets for the future.

The Organisation and Provision of Outdoor and Adventurous Activities

You will need to be able to describe the organisation and provision of two outdoor and adventurous activities. To achieve more than a pass it is important that you can compare the two activities. There is a huge range of activities from which to choose and the governing body web sites or other sites given at the end of this unit should help you to gather the information needed for your activity.

Organisations that are associated with outdoor and adventurous activities in the UK can be divided into: public, private and voluntary. The taxpayer funds the public organisations via the government. The private sector organisations include commercial businesses trying to make a profit and non-profit-making voluntary organisations such as the Youth Hostel Association or amateur activity clubs.

The following gives details of the organisation of some popular activities.

Orienteering

British Orienteering Federation

Support for schools. This organises events and provides help through publications such as *Teaching Orienteering*. It administers a coach award scheme – the Level 1 Certificate in Coaching.

The British Orienteering Federation (BOF) is the officially recognised national governing body for the sport of orienteering in the United Kingdom. It was formed in June 1967 and is a federation of 13 constituent associations – Scotland, Wales, Northern Ireland, nine English regions – each responsible for orienteering within its area – plus the British Schools Orienteering Association (BSOA). The BOF is a member of the International Orienteering Federation (IOF) based in Helsinki, Finland.

BOF has about 130 member clubs in its 12 regional association areas. About half of these are closed, for example, university clubs, while the other half have open membership and, in addition, there are over 200 BSOA member schools. The total membership is approximately 9000 individuals, classified as senior, junior or family units.

The BOF is a company limited by guarantee, which means it has members instead of shareholders.

The BOF currently manages a budget of just less than £1 million a year. Over three-quarters of this is either via the government or lottery grants from UK Sport or Sport England. The lottery money funds the three world-class (international elite) programmes – Performance, Potential and Start. Money also comes from membership fees (around £85 000 a year).

Email: bof@britishorienteering.org.uk
Web site: www.britishorienteering.org.uk

British Schools Orienteering Association

Promotes and develops schools orienteering by providing coaching for teachers through the Teacher Leader course and by organising events. Provides advice and information on getting orienteering started in your school or college.

Email: info@bsoa.org
Web site: www.bsoa.org

Duke of Edinburgh's Awards

Email: info@theaward.org
Web site: www.theaward.org

Northern Ireland Orienteering Association

Email: h.sav.glassoasis@dnet.co.uk
Web site: www.niorienteering.org.uk

Ramblers Association

Email: ramblers@london.ramblers.org.uk
Web site: www.ramblers.org.uk

Scottish Orienteering Association

Web site: www.scottish-orienteering.org

Welsh Orienteering Association

Email: pseward@tinyworld.co.uk
Web site: www.woa.org.uk

Canoeing

British Canoe Union

The British Canoe Union (BCU) was set up in 1936 to send a team to the Berlin Olympics; the BCU is the leading body for canoeing and kayaking in the UK. Since its foundation the organisation has grown considerably and the range of canoeing opportunities have increased tremendously. It is the most popular and fastest growing water sport. The British Canoe Union is the governing body for the sport and recreation of canoeing in the UK. It represents the interests of canoeists at local, national and international level, and is a member of the International Canoe Federation.

It supports schools and colleges through the Paddlepower scheme, which includes skills awards, activity cards and booklets covering the curriculum at Key Stage 2.

The coaching for teachers scheme includes Placid Water Level 1 and the Canoe Safety Award.

Email: paddlesport4all@bcu.org.uk
Web site: www.bcu.org.uk

Scottish Canoe Association

Email: enquiry@scot-canoe.org
Web site: www.scot-canoe.org

Welsh Canoeing Association

Email: welsh.canoeing@virgin.net
Web site: www.welsh-canoeing.org.uk

Skiing and snowboarding

Snowsport England

Formerly the English Ski Council, this is the governing body of the sport for English skiers. It is recognised and directly grant-aided by Sport England and has responsibility for fostering, promoting and developing the interests of English skiers and all aspects of their sports. Membership is open to individuals and to organisations with a commitment to skiing. There is a regional structure for clubs. Most of Snowsport England's activities are organised by volunteers. There is a small professional staff that co-ordinates activities and handles all central administration. Snowsport England is managed by a board and a council.

Recognised and directly grant aided by Sport England, Snowsport England has responsibility for fostering, promoting and developing the interests of English skiers and all aspects of their sport.

The clubs and regional ski associations put on race leagues, specialist training and coaching, skiing proficiency tests, holidays and social events. Much of this activity takes place on local dry ski slopes and local snow. People also travel to Scottish and Alpine ski resorts for many events.

The National Coaching Award Scheme is open to coaches, instructors, performers and officials and it covers participation in Alpine, Freestyle, Nordic and Grass skiing.

Any English skiers wanting to take part in competitions or to train as instructors, coaches or officials can register with Snowsport England National Coaching Award Scheme.

Snowsport England administers several award schemes, catering for people of different ages and levels of ability and also for the different skiing disciplines.

The Snowlife Snowsport award scheme replaced the previous British Alpine Ski awards, the new Snowlife Snowsport award scheme is a fun set of nine levels that can be achieved by participation, awareness and safety in your chosen snowsport. The aim of this award system is to build snowsport skills by introducing developmental activities to help the participant explore the possibilities available in all environments.

Competitions take place all around the country at all different standards in Alpine, Freestyle, Nordic and Grass disciplines. Participation in a club or regionally organised competition can lead on to a higher level of competition, organised nationally. Dry slope racing and freestyle competitions take place throughout the summer and there are also roller ski races on appropriate terrain. Snow competitions take over in winter, with one of the major national events sited in Europe and other races and contests running in Scotland and the north of England.

Practical Outdoor and Adventurous Activities

The Ski Course Leader scheme is primarily for teachers or lecturers, and provides basic training in how to set about taking groups away for a skiing holiday or course. The syllabus covers all the essential information such as safety, equipment travel arrangements, programme planning and so on, and provides valuable background for the inexperienced group leader.

A five-day Ski Leader training course for the most experienced, which takes place on snow, provides a higher level of training and information including recognition of snow conditions, avalanche precautions and practical work on snow.

The Ski Course Leader award is achieved after completing a training 'log' and three-day assessment. Ski Course Leaders are considered able to lead and supervise their youth or school group within recognised skiing areas.

The national squads are the major goal for club skiers and provide the vital link with international competition providing the focus of excellence in performance and coaching for all members of the National Coaching and Performance Development Scheme. The squads are selected annually from the nation's best skiers in the Alpine and Freestyle disciplines.

British Ski Club for the Disabled

Email: bscdweb@hotmail.com
Web site: www.bscd.org.uk

British Snowboarding Association

Email: info@thebsa.org
Web site: www.thebsa.org

Northern Ireland Ski Council

Web site: www.niweb.com/niid/sport/skiing

Ski Club of Great Britain

Email: skiers@skiclub.co.uk
Web site: www.skiclub.co.uk

Snowsport England

Email: web@snowsportengland.org.uk
Web site: www.snowsportengland.org.uk

Snowsport GB

Email: info@snowsportgb.com
Web site: www.snowsportgb.com

Snowsport Scotland

Email: info@snowsportscotland.org
Web site: www.snowsportscotland.org

Snowsport Wales

Email: admin.snowsportwales@virgin.net
Web site: homepage.ntlworld.com/natjax

Provision of outdoor and adventurous activities
The following shows the main providers and their locations:

British Canoe Union
John Dudderidge House
Adbolton Lane
West Bridgford
Nottingham
NG2 5AS
Tel: 0115 982 1100
Email info@bcu.org.uk
Web site: www.bcu.org.uk
Offers courses for canoe coaches.

British Mountaineering Council
177–179 Burton Road
West Didsbury
Manchester
M20 2BB
Tel: 0161 445 4747
Email: office@thebmc.co.uk
Web site: www.thebmc.co.uk
*Offers courses for mountaineering instructors,
mountain walking leaders and rock climbing
(including abseiling).*

British Orienteering Federation
Riversdale
Dale Road North
Matlock
DE4 2HX
Tel: 01629 734042
Fax: 01629 733769
Email: bof@bof.cix.co.uk
Web site: www.britishorienteering.org.uk
*Offers certificates for orienteering instructors and
coaches.*

Central Council of Physical Recreation (CCPR)
Francis House
Francis Street
London
SW1P 1DE
Tel: 0207 854 8500
Fax:0207 630 7046
Email: admin@ccpr.org.uk
Web site: www.ccpr.org.uk
Offers the Basic Expedition Training Award (BETA).

Duke of Edinburgh's Award
Gulliver House
Maderia Walk
Windsor
SL4 1EU
Tel: 01753 810753
Fax: 01753 810566
Email: info@theaward.org
Web site: www.theaward.org

The Open University Business School
PO Box 481
Walton Hall
Milton Keynes
MK7 6AA
Tel: 01908 274066
Fax: 01908 653744
Web site: www.open.ac.uk
Offers course details in outdoor management.

Royal Yachting Association
RYA House
Romsey Road
Eastleigh
SO50 9YA
Tel: 02380 629924
Fax: 02380 629924
Email: admin@rya.org.uk
Web site: www.rya.org.uk
Offers courses for sailing, windsurfing and yachting instructors.

Adventure Education/Outdoor Learning
12 St Andrews
Penrith
Cumbria
CA11 7YE
Tel: 01768 891065
Fax: 01768 891914
Email: horizons@adventure-ed.edi.co.uk
Web site: www.adventure-ed.co.uk
Publish Horizons *magazine.*

Bisham Abbey National Centre
Near Marlow
Buckinghamshire
SL7 1RT
Tel: 01628 476911
Fax: 01628 472410

Crystal Palace National Sports Centre
Ledrington Road
London
SE19 2BB
Tel: 0208 778 0131

Sports Coach UK Information Service
114 Cardigan Road
Headingley
Leeds
LS6 3BJ
Tel: 0113 274 4802
Fax: 0113 275 5019
Email coaching@sportscoachuk.org
Web site: www.sportscoachuk.org

Glenmore Lodge National Outdoor Training Centre
Aviemore
Inverness-shire
PH22 1QU
Tel: 01479 861256
Fax: 01479 861212
Email: enquiries@glenmorelodge.org.uk
Web site: www.glenmorelodge.org.uk

National Water Sports Centre
Adbolton Lane
Holme Pierreport
Nottingham
NG12 2LU
Tel: 0115 982 1212
Fax: 0115 945 5213
Web site: www.nationalwatersports.co.uk

Lilleshall National Sports Centre
Nr Newport
Shropshire
TF10 9AT
Tel: 01952 603003
Fax: 01952 814423
Email: enquiries@lilleshall.co.uk
Web site: www.lilleshall.co.uk

National Cycling Centre
Stuart Street
Manchester
M11 4DQ
Tel: 0161 233 2244
Fax: 0161 230 2309
Email: admin@manchestervelodrome.com
Web site: www.manchestervelodrome.com

The Northern Ireland Mountain Centre
Tollymore
Bryansford
County Down
BT33 0PT
Tel: 028 437 22158
Plas y Brenin

National Mountain Centre
Capel Curig
Conwy
Gwynedd
LL24 0ET
Tel: 01690 720214
Fax: 01690 720394
Email: Infor@pyb.co.uk
Web site: www.pyb.co.uk

Plas Menai National Water Sports Centre
Llanfairisgaer
Cearnarfon
Gwynedd
LL55 1UE
Tel: 01248 670964
Fax: 01248 673939
Email: plas.menai@scw.co.uk
Web site: www.plasmandi.co.uk

Scottish National Sports Training Centre
Burnside Road
Largs
Ayrshire
KA30 8RW
Tel: 01475 674666
Fax: 01475 530013
Email: johnken@sportscotland.org.uk
Web site: www.sportscotland.org.uk

Scottish National Water Sports Training Centre
Cumbrae
Isle of Cumbrae
Ayrshire
KA28 0HE
Tel: 01475 530757
Fax: 01475 674720
Email: carol.benson@sportscotland.org.uk
Web site: www.sportscotland.org.uk

YMCA National Centre Lakeside (Outdoor Activities, Education and Training)
Ulverston
LA12 8BD
Tel: 015395 31758
Fax: 015395 30015
Web site: www.londoncityymca.free-online.co.uk
Offers a full range of outdoor activity courses.

Health and Safety Considerations and Environmental Impacts Associated with Participation in Outdoor and Adventurous Activities

Health and safety

Many outdoor and adventurous activities are by nature demanding, challenging and at times dangerous unless suitable precautions are taken following realistic risk assessments (dealt with later in this unit). There are three major bodies that deal with health and safety related to these activities:

- Health and Safety Executive
- Adventurous Activities Licensing Authority
- national governing body for each activity.

Health and Safety Executive

Britain's Health and Safety Commission (HSC) and the Health and Safety Executive (HSE) are responsible for the regulation of almost all the risks to health and safety arising from work activity in Britain. They exist to protect people's health and safety by ensuring risks in the workplace are properly controlled.

They look after health and safety in the work of outdoor and adventurous activities. Other areas that they oversee include:

- nuclear installations and mines
- factories and farms
- hospitals and schools
- offshore gas and oil installations and the safety of the gas grid
- the movement of dangerous goods and substances
- railway safety
- many other aspects of the protection both of workers and the public.

Adventurous Activities Licensing Authority

The Adventurous Activities Licensing Authority (AALA) inspects activity centres and other activity providers on behalf of the Department for Education and Skills (DfES). The Licensing Authority issues a licence if it is satisfied that the provider complies with nationally accepted standards of good practice.

The Adventure Activities Licensing Authority is an independent authority, funded by the Department for Education and Skills and operating under the written guidance of the Health and Safety Commission. In effect it is an independent watchdog on the delivery of outdoor adventure activities for young people.

The aim of the licensing scheme is to provide assurances to the public about the safety of those activity providers who have been granted a licence. In this way young people can enjoy adventurous and stimulating activities outdoors without being exposed to avoidable risks of death or injury.

A licence indicates that the authority has inspected the provider. The AALA looks carefully at the management of safety. Providers must be able to demonstrate that their standards reach nationally accepted levels and that they follow proper procedures in the delivery of adventure activities to young people. The licensable activities include the following:

Climbing	Watersports	Trekking	Caving
Rock climbing	Canoeing	Hillwalking	Caving
Abseiling	Kayaking	Mountaineering	Potholing
Ice climbing	Dragon boating	Fell running	Mine exploration
Gorge walking	Wave skiing	Orienteering	
Ghyll scrambling	White-water rafting	Pony trekking	
Seal-level traversing	Improvised rafting	Off-road cycling	
	Sailing	Off-piste skiing	
	Sailboarding		
	Windsurfing		

National governing bodies

The majority of sports and some outdoor activities that we know today were developed and organised in the late nineteenth century. The majority of outdoor and adventurous activities have been developed through the organisation of governing bodies only comparatively recently. The participants in adventurous and outdoor activities needed to agree rules and regulations and so formed their own committees called governing bodies. Examples are the British Canoe Union (BCU), formed 1936, the British Orienteering Federation (BOF), formed 1967, and the British Surfing Association (BSA), formed in 1966. There are over 265 governing bodies for sport and outdoor activities in the UK. The clubs and societies then pay a subscription to the governing body. They, in turn, administer the sport nationally, organise competitions and organise the national team. There are still many amateur positions within each governing body but, increasingly, more salaried staff are involved.

One of the most important aspects of the role of governing bodies is to ensure that there are health and safety guidelines in place for all those involved in the sport. All governing bodies have health and safety policies, which are statements and procedures designed to ensure that all participants and coaches/instructors practise their activity safely.

There is a responsibility in law for organisers of activities to see that reasonable precautions are undertaken to ensure the safety of participants. Where obvious hazards exist, therefore, it is expected that organisers will undertake to identify and take such precautions as seem appropriate and reasonable in the circumstances to provide for the safety of event organisers, volunteers and participants. These could include:

case study 7.1

The British Canoe Union (BCU)

Health and safety policy for the BCU

As a national governing body the BCU has a responsibility for health and safety. The policy provides coaches, clubs and centres operating and running activities in the name of the BCU with guidelines to support and ensure that the safety of BCU members and members of the public with whom they come into contact receives appropriate attention and consideration in all circumstances.

Safety Principles (British Canoe Union, 2005, from their web site, www.bcu.org.uk

---

keyword

Risk assessment
Risk assessment is the technique by which you measure up the chances of an accident happening, anticipate what the consequences would be and plan what actions to prevent it.
(Source: British Safety Council, 2002)

- Ensuring that a **risk assessment** of the event or activity has taken place to establish that any planned activity or event is indeed safe and reasonable.

- Ensuring that any identified hazard can be controlled, that monitoring activities for the event or activity are in place and that established cutoff procedures are in place.

- Giving factual information to participants concerning the particular nature of any hazards that may exist. This could be by way of ensuring access to, and knowledge of, the BCU Statement of Participation.

- Ensuring that each participant has signed an acknowledgement of risk. These actions do not absolve organisers from their responsibility to undertake reasonable precautions, nor does it remove the participant's right in law to sue for damages should negligence be involved. It does, however, affirm that the attention of the person has been drawn to the hazardous nature of the activity, if such is involved.

- Ensuring safe codes of practice that cover all reasonable measures to protect all those taking part in canoeing activities, keeping them safe from unhealthy and unwanted advances and role modelling.

- Where 'open water' is involved in a competitive event or rally (other than tours by groups of paddlers trained and equipped for the venture or under the leadership of suitably qualified current BCU Coaching Scheme members) sufficient safety craft should be provided for any situation that could develop in the conditions in which the event, held in part or in whole on open water, is to be run.

- Where 'white water' or the shooting of weirs is involved, the wearing of buoyancy aids and crash helmets is mandatory for slalom and wild-water racing, and is strongly advised for other events where an obvious risk is present.

- Participation should be limited to those who declare themselves competent to handle the conditions, taking into account the type and amount of safety cover it is practical to provide at sites of particular difficulty.

- Suitable safety-cover for events involving weirs or rapids of particular difficulty could range from having reliable, competent canoeists strategically placed, to having trained bank-side rescue parties or divers on hand.

Risk assessments

Unit 2 Health, Safety and Injury in Sport, page 50, for a risk assessment pro-forma.

case study

7.2

Examples of deaths and injuries related to outdoor activities

'A man died when his jet ski collided with a similar water craft piloted by a friend. The jet skis had been inspected and serviced by the proprietor of the Jet Ski centre. Observers said the two men were not observing sufficient caution while piloting the craft. The coroner reported a verdict of accidental death. No blame was attached to the proprietors. An engineer found the craft to be in perfect working order.'

'A member of the public was killed when he crashed at a motor racing circuit. The man had been taking part in a motorcycle "experience" activity. The rider died as a result of head injuries sustained in the accident. The investigation revealed that there was no obvious cause of the accident.'

Of the 999 major injuries:

- 349 (35%) injuries resulted from a slip or trip (106 involved slipping on a slippery surface);

- 75 involved lost footing (62 involved falling over an obstruction and 60 involved slipping whilst playing sports);

- 227 (23%) injuries resulted from fall from a height (97 involved a fall from an animal, 30 involved a fall down stairs and 25 resulted from a fall from another object);

- 95 (10%) injuries resulted from being struck by a moving or falling object (17 involved being struck by an object falling from a shelf, table or stack, 15 were struck by a door or ramp, 11 involved being struck by a falling piece of structure and 11 involved being struck by flying chips or nails);

- 79 (8%) injuries resulted from handling, lifting or carrying a load (of which 39 involved an awkward or sharp object and 24 involved a heavy object):

- 68 (7%) injuries resulted from being injured by an animal.

(Source: Health and Safety Executive)

When assessing the risk of your outdoor adventurous activity it is important to identify the risk to health and safety of an actual situation. This includes identifying possible faults with equipment (for example ropes and harnesses in climbing).

The purpose of a risk assessment is to identify the level of risk of your activity. The assessment is designed mostly to minimise injury to participants and workers. It is also designed to ensure that the activity involved can be successful with no injury or accident but hopefully keeping the excitement and thrill of the outdoor and adventurous activity. A safe environment is crucial if the activity is to be successful.

Participants, coaches, instructors and supervisors must all be aware of their responsibilities in limiting the risks in any sports activity. The risks should be calculated, specialist equipment used and record sheets and other documents kept up to date.

There must be appropriate procedures for monitoring or checking that risks are kept to a minimum. If there are any changes to the planning of an activity these should be reviewed to identify their levels of success. There may be other equipment to buy to make the environment safe or new procedures to be used. All this must be planned within an identified time cycle.

Identifying hazards

The area in which the activity takes place must be looked at carefully to recognise hazards that may be present. The facilities and equipment that are used in outdoor and adventurous activities often carry warnings of possible injuries and these must be taken into account.

It is also important to identify who might be harmed. Care must be taken for those who may not be aware of risks – for instance young children or those with learning difficulties, or those new to a job in an activity centre or a beginner. Safety procedures should be put into place to make sure that those involved are protected from harm.

Evaluation of safety measures

There should be regular evaluations of whether existing safety measures are adequate.

There must be an assessment of how dangerous a particular hazard is and then whether the risks associated with that hazard are high, moderate or low. If the hazard is particularly dangerous and the risks are high, then clearly the more serious the situation is and the more care has to be taken.

See Unit 2 Health, Safety and Injury in Sport

case study 7.3

Hazards

Hazards for surfers include unpredictable sea currents; for skiers hazards include snow-covered rocks or the artificial slopes' tendency to give friction burns.

Legal requirement for risk assessment

It is a legal requirement for an organisation that has five or more employees to record risk assessments. Assessments are often quickly out of date, so it is important that assessments are reviewed regularly. Procedures should also be reviewed after any incident that may have caused or nearly caused injury. If there was any aspect of risk assessment that was not accurate or realistic then there should be a reassessment and procedures reviewed and changed if necessary (Honeybourne, 2003).

See Unit 2 Health, Safety and Injury in Sport, page 49

Environmental impacts

Outdoor and adventurous activities often take place in the natural environment and therefore have an impact on that environment. Some aspects of this impact may be undesirable, for example a climber disturbing the nesting of birds or a mountain biker causing erosion to a forest floor.

The present by-laws applying to the Norfolk Broads, adopted in 1992, which preceded the development of **wakeboarding**, prohibit the skier from leaving the water or creating a sustained wake against the bank of more than one foot.

The Broads Authority has received complaints from boat owners and birdwatchers who believe there has been a big increase in wakeboarding, that a number of ski boats have been modified for wakeboarding and that by-laws are being contravened.

case study 7.4

The Norfolk Broads and impact of waterskiing on the environment

The Broads is more than a collection of important sites and species. The different landscapes, land-use, habitats and the wildlife they support make up an internationally renowned wetland ecosystem. The potential for recreation on land and water in the Broads is immense. Sailing, motor boating, rowing, canoeing, fishing, walking, sight-seeing and bird watching are just some of the ways people enjoy the area.

(Source: adapted from Norfolk Broads Authority web site: www.broads-authority.gov.uk)

As a result of the management plan:

■ all waterskiers and wakeboarders on the Broads have to be members of the ERSC, which is affiliated to British WaterSki, providing public indemnity

■ all boat drivers have to pass the British Waterski Ski Boat Driver Award, which is recognised by the Royal Yachting Association, and have the option of taking the International Certificate of Competence

■ unlike other boat owners, ski-boat owners must take out boat insurance

■ all members of ERSC pay a £25 fixed charge to help with the administration of managing waterskiing on the Broads

■ waterskiing is limited to 3% of the Broads area with restricted time zones.

All participants should be aware of the environmental impacts of their outdoor and adventurous activities. The land, the air and water can all be affected by our activities, as can wildlife and plant life.

Whenever a person engages in an oudoor sport or adventurous activity there is an impact on the environment. Equipment, clothing and facilities all have an **ecological footprint**.

Building and managing a sport or adventure facility and running an event uses energy and can contribute to air pollution, greenhouse gas emissions and the generation of waste, as well as to ozone layer depletion, habitat and biodiversity loss, soil erosion and water pollution.

keyword
Ecological footprint
This is the impact or effects that man has on our natural environment, some of which may last for a very long time.

Some common ways in which sport affects the environment

■ Limiting the amount of land available for ecosystems to exist naturally.

■ Noise and light pollution from activities.

■ Using non-renewable resources (such as fuel and metals), for example the fuel used by motor boats in waterskiing.

■ Consumption of natural resources (such as water and wood).

■ Emission of greenhouse gases by consuming electricity and fuel.

■ Ozone layer depletion (from refrigerants).

■ Soil and water pollution from pesticide use or from the discarding of rubbish.

■ Soil erosion during construction of facilities, from spectators and from the competitors themselves, for example runners in orienteering or mountain bikes eroding forest trails.

■ Waste generation from construction of facilities, from spectators and from competitors.

> **remember**
>
> An important aspect of limiting the negative impact on the environment is firstly recognising that you are having such an impact. Once this has been realised and the manner in which the activity is affecting the environment has been noted then strategies can be adopted to try to minimise the effects of the outdoor and adventurous activity on the environment.

Limiting the environmental impact

Examples of limiting the impact of activities on the environment include:

■ making all participants and spectators of outdoor and adventurous activities aware of their impact via educational material

■ ensuring that governing bodies of outdoor and adventurous activities have codes of conduct related to the environment

■ ensuring that all participants agree to leave the environment in the state in which they found it – for example, taking away all litter

■ setting aside separate areas away from areas that may have a delicate eco-balance so that the environment is protected

■ building indoor facilities to be used if outdoor areas are in danger of becoming damaged, for example in the winter months

■ ensuring that any motorised machinery has equipment that limits the discharge of potentially dangerous gases.

Positive impacts of sport on the environment

1 In Sydney, Australia a place called Homebush Bay was a toxic waste dump for decades. It was restored as a safe recreational site because it was chosen as the main site for the Olympic Games.

2 The 2008 Olympics to take place in Beijing have been the cause of a massive air quality campaign that has seen a significant reduction in air pollution.

3 The United Nations Environment Programme (UNEP) and the Global Sports Alliance (GSA) launched a Nature and Sport Training Camp in Nairobi in August 2001. The camp provided leadership training on the environment, culture and sport to children from the biggest slum in Kenya (Kibera). Since 2001, over 6000 children have been involved in basic training on the development of community environmental activities (such as recycling and cleanups) and on various sports activities (such as soccer, tennis and basketball).

Reviewing Your Own Performance in Outdoor and Adventurous Activities

Reviewing or evaluating is the process of analysing your performance in your activity. This can help in identifying what went well and what could have been improved.

Effective review is essential if progress in an activity is to be made. Good performers are always trying to improve what they do. This involves them in thinking about and evaluating the activities they have planned and performed, identifying strengths and weaknesses and learning lessons for the future. You must also take into account developments in your activity by keeping in touch with developing equipment or techniques. This could include attending courses, conferences, reading journals or other relevant publications, and observing and working with others on your outdoor or adventurous activity.

It is also important to take into account how your coach or instructor felt about the session or activity. Their views are important and probably more objective than your own. Their views could be sought via verbal feedback or a written evaluation.

It is important to record your evaluations and reviews and those of others. The whole process is meaningless if your review leads to little action. Those aspects of the review that are positive should reinforce your good practice and that practice should continue and develop. The issues that arise from poor evaluations should be addressed and become part of an action plan to improve. Progress should be reviewed and there should be a development in practice and updating of personal action plans accordingly.

Assessment of current performance

Factors that you need to take into account are:

- Previous experience – what level have you reached in your activity?
- Technical knowledge and skills – what do you know about your activity and what skills have you mastered?
- Technical ability – what underlying abilities do you have?
- Levels of fitness – what test results have you had related to all aspects of your fitness (for example, cardiovascular/flexibility)?
- Commitment, training attendance and effort. How much time and effort do you give to your activity? How many times a week do you train and for how long? Do you keep a training diary?
- Access to equipment and facilities – Do you have your own equipment for your activity? What facilities do you use? How easy is it to access training equipment and facilities?
- Access to effective coaching or instruction. Who coaches you? How is this funded? How many coaches/instructors do you have?
- Diet. Do you keep a food diary? Are there any foods you have to avoid? Does your diet vary depending on the stage of the season or leading up to a competition/expedition?
- Areas for improvement. Having taken into account all of the above, what improvements could be made to enable you to be more effective in your activity?
- Methods of assessment. How do you assess your current performance/preparation in your sport? Do you use the assessments of others? Do you use video analysis? Do you use a SWOT (strengths, weaknesses, opportunities, threats) analysis? Do you use objective tests such as a recognised fitness test or a psychometric test?

Targets for future performance

Targets should be based on the SMARTER principle. Targets should be divided into short, medium and long term and seasonal.

SMARTER goal setting

S – **Specific**　　If goals are clear and unambiguous they are more likely to be reached.

M – **Measurable**　This is important for monitoring and makes you accountable.

A – **Agreed**　　The sharing of goal-setting between coach/instructor and performer can give a sense of teamwork.

R – **Realistic**　　Motivation will improve if goals can actually be reached.

T – **Timed**　　An effective approach is to split goals up into short-term goals that are planned and progressive.

E – **Exciting**　　The more stimulating the activities can be the more motivating is their effect.

R – **Recorded**　　Recording is crucial for monitoring and, once achieved, can be deleted or checked-off, thus improving motivation.

Performance plan

This should involve:

- aims and objectives
- recognition of resources required
- set and agreed goals
- training details and competitions
- diet details
- use of any technical equipment
- recognition of the barriers that need to be overcome, for example:
  - injury and illness
  - weather
  - travel and travel costs
  - team selection
  - lack of equipment/facilities
  - lack of coaching expertise
  - financial implications to live and train
  - the expectations and demands of others, for example personal relationships/family
  - monitor and evaluate performance
  - assess performance against SMARTER targets
  - peer and teacher assessments
  - feedback from coaches and training results
  - acquisition of new skills
  - recommendations for future plans/aims
  - identify support needed, for example training courses, NVQs or other qualifications.

Self-review in rock climbing

Improving your climbing begins with getting to know yourself whether on the rock or in the gym preparing. You must become aware of your climbing-related strengths and weaknesses in each area of the performance triad – technical, mental and physical.

Too many climbers have wasted their time practising and training the things at which they already excel, while the 'ball and chain' of their weaknesses unknowingly holds them back. For instance, many climbers think 'more strength' is important whereas physical strength only makes up about one-third of climbing performance with strategies, other aspects of fitness and mental preparation being other major contributors.

---

case study 7.6

Surfing

Surf awareness in self-rescue skills

Observation checklist for applying surf awareness and self-rescue skills

Name:

Venue:

Date of assessment:

Element

1. **Demonstrate knowledge of the surf environment.**

   1. Potential hazards and environmental conditions of the surf environment are identified.

   2. Characteristics of different types of waves and their impact on surf safety are used to identify safe surfing locations.

   3. Distinguishing features of rips, gutters and sweeps are identified and used to determine the most suitable surfing venue.

   4. Different types of beaches and the safety aspects of the beach structure is identified.

2. **Apply surf skills and techniques.**

   1. Techniques for survival in the water are demonstrated.

   2. Ability to avoid personal safety and environmental hazards while in the water is demonstrated.

3. **Demonstrate self-rescue techniques.**

   1. Ability to negotiate the surf in the prevailing conditions is demonstrated using craft and without craft.

   2. Ability to get back to the shore in the prevailing conditions is demonstrated, using craft and without craft.

   3. Strategies to implement when not able to self-rescue or return to shore unassisted are identified and applied.

   (Adapted from Surf Life Saving Australia Ltd web site, www.slsa.asn.au)

progress check

1. Name four adventurous outdoor activities.

2. For one of your chosen activities describe how you would demonstrate a specific skill or technique.

3. How would you record evidence that you have mastered the above skill or technique?

4. Describe the diary method or recording evidence of performance in your activity.

5. Describe the organisation of a chosen outdoor and adventurous activity.

6. Identify the providers of your activity locally and nationally.

7. Explain how the Adventurous Activities Licensing Authority ensures health and safety in outdoor and adventurous activities.

8. Write a risk assessment for an aspect of your chosen activity.

9. Name two ways in which your activity affects the environment. How would you limit these effects?

10. Identify strengths and weaknesses in your own performance in a chosen outdoor adventurous activity.

UNIT 8

Technical Skills and Tactical Awareness for Sport

This unit covers:

- the technical and tactical demands of a selected sport
- assessing technical skills and tactical awareness in a selected sport
- completing a programme to develop technical skills and tactical awareness
- monitoring and evaluating technical and tactical development and setting goals for further development

This unit covers material to support Unit 8 of the BTEC First Diploma in Sport. The general technical aspects of fundamental skills, as well as more specific techniques related to a number of different sports, are explored. The ways in which we can identify the tactical demands of chosen sports are also covered. When following this unit you will be required to assess technical and tactical aspects and this unit will help you to prepare for such assessments. Information important for the design of a programme of skills and tactics development is also covered as well as ways of monitoring development and setting targets for improvement.

<table>
<tr><th>grading criteria</th><th>To achieve a Pass grade the evidence must show that the learner is able to:</th><th>To achieve a Merit grade the evidence must show that the learner is able to:</th><th>To achieve a Distinction grade the evidence must show that the learner is able to:</th></tr>
<tr><td></td><td>P1
Describe the technical and tactical demands of a chosen sport</td><td>M1
Explain the technical and tactical demands of a chosen sport</td><td>D1
Compare and contrast their own technical skills and tactical awareness with those of an elite performer and the demands of a chosen sport</td></tr>
<tr><td></td><td>P2
Assess the technical skills of an elite performer, identifying strengths and weaknesses</td><td>M2
Assess the technical skills and tactical awareness of an elite performer, explaining strengths and weaknesses</td><td>D2
Evaluate the training programme, justifying suggestions made regarding improvement</td></tr>
</table>

grading criteria

To achieve a **Pass** grade the evidence must show that the learner is able to:	To achieve a **Merit** grade the evidence must show that the learner is able to:	To achieve a **Distinction** grade the evidence must show that the learner is able to:
P3 Assess the tactical awareness of an elite performer, identifying strengths and weaknesses	**M3** Assess their own technical skills and tactical awareness, in a chosen sport, explaining strengths and weaknesses	**D3** Analyse their goals for technical and tactical development, suggesting how these goals could be achieved, recommending specific activities
P4 Assess the technical skills, in a chosen sport, identifying strengths and weaknesses	**M4** Independently produce a six-week training programme to develop their own technical skills and tactical awareness, describing strengths and areas for improvement, and suggesting ways in which it could be improved	
P5 Assess their own tactical awareness, in a chosen sport, identifying strengths and weaknesses	**M5** Independently describe their own development, explaining their goals and technical and tactical development	
P6 Produce a six-week training programme, with teacher support, to develop their own technical skills and tactical awareness		
P7 Undertake a six-week training programme to develop their own technical skills and tactical awareness, commenting on strengths and areas for improvement in the programme		
P8 Monitor and review their own development, identifying goals for further technical and tactical development, with teacher support		

The Technical and Tactical Demands of Sport

Technical demands

Whatever the sport you select to study, the technical demands relate to skills. There are a number of different types of skills:

- **Fundamental motor skills**. These are very basic skills like jumping, kicking and throwing. We learn these skills at a young age, usually through play. If these fundamental motor skills are learned thoroughly the more complex actions required in sport can then be built upon them.

- **Motor skill**. A motor skill is an action or task that has a goal and that requires voluntary body and/or limb movement to achieve the goal, for example, a forehand in tennis.

- **Cognitive skills**. These are skills that involve the mind and the intellectual ability of the performer. These skills help us to make sense of what is required in any given situation. They are essential if the performer is to make correct and effective decisions.

- **Psychomotor ability**. This is our ability to process information regarding movement and then to put our decisions into action. Psychomotor abilities include reaction time and limb co-ordination. For example, in responding to the gun in a 100 m race.

- **Gross motor ability**. Ability involving actual movement – for example, strength, flexibility, speed.

Classification of skills

Figure 8.1
A basketball player

It is helpful to classify skills if their nature is to be understood fully by those who teach and learn skills in sport. Classification makes it clearer what is required in order to learn and perform a particular skill.

If, for instance, you wish to coach a performer to shoot the ball in basketball, it would be useful to know that the skill is not affected much by the environment and that the shooter has complete control over how the technique is executed. The coach can then train the performer to shut out many of the external stimuli and to concentrate on a smooth and fluent technique.

keyword

Complex skills
These include slip catch in cricket, or a pass by a midfield player in hockey who has to make lots of decisions before she passes.

keyword

Simple skills
These include a sprint start in swimming, for example, where there are very few decisions – other than to dive – that have to be made.

If a skill is affected by the surrounding environment and requires the performer to make perceptual decisions, it is called an open skill. If a skill at the other extreme is not affected at all by the environment then it is called a closed skill.

Skills can be classified according to the types of judgements and decisions that you have to make to perform them. If there are many decisions to make, then the skill is known as a **complex skill** and may have to be learned in stages. If the skill is a straightforward one with hardly any judgements and decisions to make then it is known as a **simple skill** and can be taught as a whole and in a fairly repetitive way.

The type of skill and the way in which it is made up or organised can also be classified so that effective teaching and learning can take place. If a skill has elements or subroutines that are very difficult to separate then it is known as a highly organised skill, such as dribbling the ball in basketball. If a skill has subroutines that are easily identified as separate movements then it said to have low organisation, such as a tennis serve.

Figure 8.2

A tennis serve is a skill with low organisation

Skills that have a definite beginning and end are called discrete skills, such as passing in netball.

Figure 8.3

Passing in netball is a discrete skill

Some of these discrete skills may have some separate elements to them, which makes them more like serial skills – in other words a small collection of separate skills rolled into one, such as the triple jump in athletics.

Figure 8.4

The triple jump is a serial skill

There are other skills in which it is very difficult to separate out the subroutines because the elements of the skill are highly organised. These are called continuous skills, such as the leg action in cycling.

Figure 8.5

The leg action in cycling is a continuous skill

The discrete – serial – continuous continuum

Discrete--1----------2--Serial------------3---- Continuous

1   skill such as shot put

2   skill such as high jump

3   skill such as flutter kick leg action in swimming

Implications for training and coaching

If a coach and the performer are familiar with and understand the nature of the task or skill that has to be learned and performed, then training techniques can be adapted depending on these requirements.

If a closed skill is to be coached, then it is going to be more effective if it is practised repetitively so that the skill is 'grooved'. It is also unnecessary to vary the situation because its closed skills remain mainly constant.

If an open skill were learned then a variety of situations would be effective because the performer would build up a repertoire of strategies due to the ever-changing circumstances.

If a discrete skill is to be coached effectively then it is probably more effective to teach it as a whole rather than artificially try to split it up into parts.

If a serial skill were coached, then clearly it would be more effective to learn and practise each element separately but then to string the subroutines together and practise as a whole entity.

If a continuous skill is to be coached, it is difficult to split into subroutines because the 'flow' of the skill may be disturbed. It is probably more effective to practise the skill as a whole so that the **kinaesthetic sense** of the skill is not lost.

The tactical demands in sport

This includes positioning (for example in a football match) and the choice of appropriate strokes (for example in badminton).

In order for you to do well or win the game you need to plan, often in advance of the competition. You will beat your opponent or do well depending on a number of factors:

- **Environment** – take note of where you are and what the conditions are like.

- **How good your opponent is** – your tactics will take into account the ability of your opponent. If for example your opponent is highly skilled then your tactics may be more defensive.

- **Your own feelings on the day**. You may feel under the weather and so would be more careful in your approach – for example you may stay on the base line in tennis to try and avoid too much running.

- **Your coach/captain** – they may have already decided the tactics and you may have to follow what has been dictated, although you may find that tactics can change as the activity or game develops.

Whatever your tactics, you must be prepared to practise them so that you are ready to adapt if the situation changes. For example you may go all out to score a goal in football and once you have scored you may decide to increase safe short passing near the end of the game and not give the opponents the ball.

There are also tactics for set plays, for example corners in hockey. It is important in many such situations that players are aware of what other players are doing. This can prevent confusion.

For most activities in sport attack and defence are the main tactics. For each sport there are basic principles for attack and defence.

Assessing Technical Skills and Tactical Awareness in Sport

Performance analysis

When you analyse your selected sport you may wish to use some form of performance analysis. This can include observing other players or yourself with the possible use of a video recorder. The analysis can be quite a simple one that

keyword

Notational analysis
This involves taking notes about a person's or group of people's performance during the activity. The notes serve as important information to use to assess what went well and to identify areas for improvement.

involves highlighting main strengths and weaknesses or it can be more in-depth involving **notational analysis**. Obviously the greater the depth often the more reliable your analysis becomes.

Notational analysis may take into consideration statistics related to the activity or game – for example how many shots were on target or how many passes a player successfully completed. In tennis, for example, the number of aces, double faults and forehand winners may be recorded. The results of these analyses can highlight areas of concern or may give important information about a player, which you can use to develop your own tactics. For example, if you know your opponent hits all his successful shots in tennis on the forehand then you would try to avoid playing the ball onto his forehand. A coach may use such analyses to work on strengthening a particular skill. For example, in hockey the coach might find, through analysis, that one of her players is failing to pass successfully. The coach can then work on passing practices to improve her game.

Analysis model

For any analysis to be successful there needs to be a sequence of events.

Figure 8.6

Analysis model flow diagram

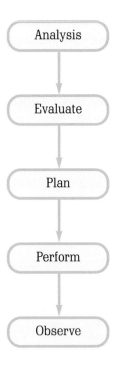

```
Analysis
   ↓
Evaluate
   ↓
Plan
   ↓
Perform
   ↓
Observe
```

Whatever the form of your analysis, this must lead to an evaluation – what is going wrong and what is going well? What needs to be praised and what needs to be developed? Following this evaluation a plan must be formulated, setting realistic goals. For example, to work on shooting technique in netball. Following the plan of action there needs to be practice or performance – the player then has to work on her shooting skills. Her performance in the next match is again observed and there is again a cycle of analyses as the diagram above suggests.

Performance profiling

This involves gathering together information about a performance to give a profile or picture of someone's strengths and weaknesses. The profile shown is an example of how you can assess performance. It includes what is expected, what is currently being seen and then the difference between the two. The higher the number for the area for improvement the more work has to be done in that area. This is an excellent way to prioritise skill and tactical development.

Figure 8.7

Performance profile
(Source: Mawdsley and Howes (2004) *BTEC National Sport Teacher Support Pack*, Nelson Thornes)

Name _____ Sport/activity _____

Position _____

Player characteristic	Ideal player (1–10) (A)	Player assessment (1–10) (B)	Area for improvement (A–B=C)
Psychological e.g. confidence	8	4	4
Physical e.g. strength	6	6	0
Technical e.g. penalty flick	10	10	10
Tactical e.g. awareness	10	6	4
Other			

Completing a Programme to Develop Technical Skills and Tactical Awareness

To develop your own technical skills and tactical awareness you should firstly be able to describe your strengths and areas for improvement and suggest what could be improved and how. The more you can justify your decisions, the more marks you will attract for your programme. The aims of your programme will arise from your analyses of your own performance. So if you find that your tackling skills in rugby need to be improved then your programme should include tackling practice and coaching. Your programme should also involve the principles of training.

 See Unit 4 Preparation for Sport

When you are constructing your training programme you should seek the help of a 'mentor' or someone who will give you advice. Usually your mentor will be your coach, instructor or trainer. Mentors can assist you in your programme and will check that you have completed your programme. You should set specific targets for your programme over six weeks that are based on the technical and tactical development of performance.

Your programme should be recorded in a diary or training log and should include comments on developments or problems that have occurred during the training programme.

Aims and objectives

These should be based on the strengths and weaknesses identified from your analysis. For example, technical weaknesses might include jump shots in basketball from outside the key or drop shots in front of the net in badminton. Tactical weaknesses may include marking players in basketball or front and back play in badminton doubles.

Targets

These are more specific objectives and should be SMART:

S – **Specific** – to improve successful short drop shots in badminton to 70%.

M – **Measurable** – to assess how many shots out of ten in a match situation are successful.

A – **Achievable** – the target must be within the capability of the performer but not so that it is too easy.

R – **Realistic** – in a six-week programme it must be possible to improve the drop shot in badminton.

T – **Timed** – the target of seven out of ten shots should be achieved within six weeks.

Training

The training programme that is planned should be set out week-by-week, session-by-session. Each training session should also be planned and structured to take into account the development of specific techniques and tactics. Each training session should also involve a warm-up and a cool-down appropriate to the activity. All this should be written clearly as part of the programme.

Technical development

Practices in each training session should include specific activities to improve the targeted technique or skill. For example if the target is to improve shooting in netball then each session should have an element of shooting with specific practices – such as shooting with and without pressure.

Tactical development

Practices in each training session should also include tactical development. Techniques could be practised against different levels of performer – from the less skilled to the very skilled. Practices could also be varied in nature to emulate 'real game' situations. Tactics can be developed as an individual, then in small groups, then in a full game situation if appropriate.

Recording documentation

The programme must be planned and recorded but the development of the programme should also be recorded – what happens in each session and what adaptations can be brought into the next training session. It might be, for example, that dribbling in basketball was planned to be non-opposed in the first two sessions, but after one session it was found that you are now ready for opponents to put you under pressure in a variety of different situations and so you adapt your programme accordingly.

Recording documents include:

- diary
- logbook
- portfolio
- video
- audio
- observation record
- feedback sheets/written feedback about skill learning.

See Unit 7 Practical Outdoor and Adventurous Activities

Monitoring and Evaluating Technical and Tactical Development and Setting Goals for Further Development

Monitor
This involves taking notes of developments as they happen. It is an ongoing record of progress or lack of progress.

Evaluation
This follows monitoring and usually occurs at the end of a process. An evaluation takes into account the overall strengths and weaknesses of the programme and factors that have affected the results.

To be able to **monitor** your own performance during your training programme it is important to keep a record of your progress as described above. Regular short-term assessments could also be included and recorded so that monitoring is continuous.

Evaluation takes place by comparing the outcomes of your training to your targets. So if your target was 70% of drop shots in badminton to be achieved after six weeks of training and only 60% of successful drops are now on average being achieved then in your evaluation you can state that you have not been fully successful. Remember that the outcome of the development programme is not assessed; it is how you have constructed the programme and how you monitor and evaluate that are important. In your evaluation you must include factors that have affected your technical and tactical development. For example, you may have missed some training due to illness or because the coach was unavailable or the facilities were not up to scratch.

Goal setting

This is the identification of objectives and can be short term, medium term or long term. Goal setting is a useful strategy and one that is widely used in sport for training and performance. Coaches can set goals or performers and they tend to more effective if they are set together. Goal setting has been a proven way of increasing motivation and confidence and controlling anxiety.

There are two types of goal that can be recognised and set in sport. Performance goals are related directly to the performance or technique of the activity. Outcome goals are concerned with the end result – whether you win or lose for instance.

Goal setting following evaluation is important if you wish to continue to develop technical and tactical skills. Goals should include both long-term and short-term elements. For example, suppose that after achieving only 60% of successful drops in badminton after your training programme you have evaluated your programme and have decided that your training sessions should involve more practices under pressure in a realistic environment. A short-term goal would be to spend ten minutes of every session practising the drop. A medium-term goal would be that after six weeks 70% of drops will be successful and by the end of the season 80% of drops will be successful in a competitive situation. When goals are set they are more effective if they have been worked out with all interested parties agreeing on the way forward. For example, if appropriate you should get your coach or instructor to agree your goals and write a joint statement. Remember that all goals should follow the SMART principle.

progress check

1   Identify three technical demands for your selected sport.

2   Name a continuous skill, a serial skill and a discrete skill in your sport.

3   Describe a tactic that you use regularly in your sport – when do you use it?

4   Set up a notational analysis that someone else can use to analyse your performance.

5   Explain the analysis model.

6   What should you take into account when designing a training programme for techniques and tactics?

7   Describe two different recording documents.

8   What do the terms monitor, evaluate and goal setting mean?

9   Give a performance goal and an outcome goal for your sport.

10   What is the SMART goal-setting principle?

UNIT 9

Psychology for Sports Performance

This unit covers:

- the psychological demands of a selected sport
- the impact motivation can have on sports performance
- the effects of personality and aggression on sports performance
- assessing your own attitudes and mental skills, and planning a programme to enhance them in relation to sports performance

This unit is linked directly to the requirements of Unit 9 for the BTEC First Diploma in Sport. It introduces the concept of sport psychology and will enable the development of appropriate attitudes and mental skills for effective sports performance. The unit will enable you to apply psychological principles to practical performance and will develop your understanding of how personality and motivation influence sports performance. It will also develop your awareness of how aggression affects performance in sport.

<table>
<tr>
<th>To achieve a Pass grade the evidence must show that the learner is able to:</th>
<th>To achieve a Merit grade the evidence must show that the learner is able to:</th>
<th>To achieve a Distinction grade the evidence must show that the learner is able to:</th>
</tr>
<tr>
<td>

P1

Describe the psychological demands of a selected sport

</td>
<td>

M1

Explain the psychological demands of a selected sport

</td>
<td>

D1

Analyse strategies used to maintain and increase motivation for sports performance

</td>
</tr>
<tr>
<td>

P2

Describe the impact of motivation on sports performance, and identify strategies that can be used to maintain and increase motivation

</td>
<td>

M2

Explain the impact of motivation on sports performance and the strategies that can be used to maintain and increase motivation

</td>
<td>

D2

Evaluate the strategies that can be adopted to control aggression

</td>
</tr>
<tr>
<td>

P3

Describe personality and identify how it affects sports performance

</td>
<td>

M3

Explain strategies that can be adopted to control aggression

</td>
<td>

D3

Evaluate the training programme, justifying suggestions relating to improvement, including specific activities in relation to their own attitudes and mental skills in a selected sport

</td>
</tr>
</table>

grading criteria

grading criteria

To achieve a **Pass** grade the evidence must show that the learner is able to:	To achieve a **Merit** grade the evidence must show that the learner is able to:	To achieve a **Distinction** grade the evidence must show that the learner is able to:
P4 Describe aggression and identify strategies that can be adopted to control it	**M4** Independently assess their own attitudes and mental skills in a selected sport, explaining areas for improvement	
P5 Assess their own attitudes and mental skills, with teacher support, in a selected sport, identifying areas for improvement	**M5** Independently plan and carry out six-week training programme, to improve attitudes and mental skills in a selected sport	
P6 Plan, and carry out, a six-week training programme, with teacher support, to improve attitudes and mental skills in a selected sport	**M6** Evaluate the training programme, explaining areas for improvement, and making suggestions in relation to how improvements could be achieved	
P7 Evaluate the training programme, identifying areas for improvement		

The Psychological Demands of a Selected Sport

To perform at the top level in sport it is now agreed that you need to adopt the right attitude and mental skills such as the ability to concentrate under pressure. The football player who is asked to take a penalty needs a positive attitude to scoring but also needs to be able to shut out the noise of the crowd and keep emotions under control.

Figure 9.1
A penalty in football

Psychology for Sports Performance

There are numerous research studies that link attitudes to sports performance in sport. In psychology it is very difficult to link cause and effect. In other words did a player miss a penalty because that player had the wrong attitude, was unable to concentrate or was simply not good enough to kick the ball effectively? How do you find out which one applies? For instance you could ask the player why the penalty was missed but the reply might be biased and inaccurate.

case study 9.1 — Mental toughness in rugby players

Jim Golby and Michael Sheard (University of Teesside, Middlesbrough) investigated whether elite rugby league players in the UK showed higher levels of mental toughness and hardiness than their less elite counterparts.

They asked 115 professional rugby league players from three standards of the game – International, Super League and Division One – to fill out two questionnaires:

- the Personal Views Survey III-R – a measure of mental hardiness

- the Psychological Performance Inventory – a measure of mental toughness.

On the mental hardiness questionnaire, International players scored significantly higher on items measuring 'control' than Division One players. This suggests that they feel more able to influence matches. They scored higher on measures of 'commitment' and 'challenge' than both the Division One and Super League players. This suggests that they have higher levels of organisation and commitment to the sport and an ability to view difficult situations as opportunities for personal growth, rather than as a threat.

On the mental toughness questionnaire, International players scored significantly higher than the Division One players on 'negative energy control' and 'attention control', showing that they were better able to remain calm and relaxed under pressure, and also to maintain intense concentration for long periods.

keyword

Attitudes
These are thoughts that we have towards something or somebody. These thoughts include beliefs, feelings and how we behave towards something or somebody.

Types of attitudes and mental skills needed to perform at the highest level

To perform effectively in sport, whether you play for your school, college, club or for your national team, you need to have positive **attitudes** to winning, playing well and playing fairly and negative attitudes towards losing, playing poorly and cheating or against the spirit of the game.

Attitudes in sport

For example in sport a top netball player will probably have a positive attitude to training hard, including the belief that training is good for her. She will also enjoy training and will probably train regularly and for long periods of time. Her beliefs, feelings and behaviour all add up to her positive attitude to training.

There are many mental demands on a sports performer. There is a need to concentrate fully and be able to focus on what is important. For example, a golfer needs to concentrate on where the hole is in relation to the ball as well as blocking out any other distractions such as noise around him.

Figure 9.2

Sports performers often need to concentrate fully on the task in hand

Other demands include having to lower your anxiety and stress levels when you are about to perform. This is especially important if the skill you are performing is one that demands precision and complex movements. It is also important that the performer can react quickly – this is another reason for total concentration on the task in hand. If performers can make the right decision or solve the problem quickly then they are more likely to react quickly.

The mental skills that are important to succeed in any sport, then, include:

- **Concentration and focus**. A batsman or batswoman in cricket must concentrate on the flight of the ball as well as the position of the fielders.

- **Quick decision making**. A hockey goalkeeper trying to save a penalty has to assess where the ball is going and make a very quick decision so that she can save the ball.

- **Ability to control anxiety or worry**. A gymnast just before competition must try to be calm and controlled so that her balance and concentration are not affected.

- **Thinking positively with positive attitudes**. A rugby player tackling must believe that he will be successful.

- **Being confident in one's own ability**. A basketball player must believe that she will score the free shot at the basket.

- **Determination in sticking to the task**. An athlete on the final bend of a 400 m race must be determined to win the race.

The Impact Motivation can have on Sports Performance

Motivation

<table>
<tr><td>**keyword**

Motivation
A need or drive to do something with determination. For example to keep turning up to hockey practice and hopefully to be picked for the next game.</td></tr>
</table>

It is obviously important for sports performers to be well motivated, but some seem to be better motivated than others. You can watch two athletes of very similar ability race against each other, but the one who invariably wins will appear to have better **motivation**.

There are some people who do not seem at all interested in participating in sport whereas, at the other end of the scale, others seem to be addicted to playing sport. It is important to find out what actually motivates people to participate and to do well in sport because we could then encourage more to be involved in sport and performing at a higher level.

An athlete may be driven to achieve a personal best in throwing the discus. She is driven by the strong desire for self-fulfilment – to feel that she has challenged herself and has won.

Intrinsic or internal motivation

<table>
<tr><td>**keyword**

Intrinsic motivation
This is an inner drive or need to want to do well and succeed and to feel good and enjoy the activity.</td></tr>
</table>

Intrinsic motivation is the internal drive that people have to participate or to perform well in sport. Intrinsic motives include fun, enjoyment and the satisfaction that is experienced by achieving something. Some athletes describe the intrinsic 'flow' experienced during competition. They speak of high levels of concentration and a feeling that they are in total control.

An example of intrinsic motivation could be the club tennis player who is 50 years of age and reports that when he plays he often feels a sense of relief from the day's stresses and strains, and that he enjoys the hard physical work of playing tennis.

External or extrinsic motivation

Extrinsic motivation involves influences external to the performer. For instance the drive to do well in sport could come from the need to please others or to gain rewards like medals or badges or in some cases large amounts of money. Rewards that include badges or prize money are referred to as tangible rewards. Rewards that involve attaining first place in the league or receiving praise from your parents are known as intangible rewards.

Extrinsic motivation is very useful to encourage better performance in sport.

Extrinsic motivation can increase levels of intrinsic motivation. If, for example, you win the cup in boxing this will probably result in you feeling good about the activity and enjoying boxing in future bouts.

> **keyword**
>
> **Extrinsic motivation**
> This is the drive or need that is caused by motives that are external or environmental. These motives are rewards that can be tangible or intangible.

---

case study 9.2

Extrinsic motivation

A young girl is just starting to learn to swim. After much effort she achieves a width of the pool without any help and without armbands. She is given a badge, which clearly shows everyone else that she has achieved success. This reward is pleasurable to the girl and her interest and determination in swimming increases. The reward has reinforced the correct behaviour.

Coaches like Sven-Goran Eriksson and Alex Ferguson know that being motivated is important in helping players to be the best.

Another way of describing intrinsic and extrinsic motivation is identifying sports performers as having:

- **Ego orientation**. Playing sport because you want to win (mostly extrinsic).
- **Task orientation**. Playing sport because you enjoy improving your own personal best performances (mostly intrinsic).

You can have both kinds of motivation but it is best to be high in both ego and task orientation or low in ego and high in task orientation. People with these types of motivation try hard in sport and do not give up when things are not going well. People who are high in ego orientation and low in task orientation may give up when they are no longer winning.

Goal setting and motivation

By setting goals you can:

- achieve more
- improve your performance
- improve your training

- increase your motivation
- increase your pride and satisfaction.

Goal setting is a very powerful technique that can lead to high rewards and increase your motivation levels.

By knowing what you want to achieve, you know what you need to concentrate on and improve and what to ignore because these aspects may be distracting.

Achieving goals

When you have achieved a goal, enjoy the satisfaction of having done it – pat yourself on the back. Plan to achieve even greater or higher goals.

If you have failed to reach a goal, make sure that you have learned lessons from it.

Reasons for not attaining your goals:

- you did not try hard enough
- poor technique, which needs to be adjusted
- the goal you set was unrealistic at this time.

Use this information to adjust your goals or to set different goals to learn new skills or build to improve fitness. Turn everything into a positive learning experience. Failing to meet a goal is a step forward towards success.

When you have achieved a goal:

- if it was achieved easily make your next goals harder
- if the goal took too long to achieve, make the next goals a little easier
- if you learned something that would lead you to change future goals, then change them.

Goal setting is a useful strategy and one that is widely used in sport for training and performance. Goal setting is a proven way of increasing motivation and confidence and controlling anxiety.

There are two types of goal that can be recognised and set in sport:

- **performance goals** – these are directly related to the performance or technique of the activity
- **outcome goals** – these are concerned with the end result, whether you win or lose for instance.

A golfer is trying to improve his driving swing and to improve his timing – these are performance goals. A tennis player is trying to win the grand slam by winning each open tournament – these are outcome goals.

Outcome goals tend to be medium to long term and performance goals tend to be short term.

Goals can affect performance in a number of ways, the main ones being:

- they focus your attention and concentration
- they direct your efforts in a particular way
- they increase the amount of effort
- they are motivating to the performer who often wants to develop a variety of strategies to be successful.

Effective goal setting

For goal setting to be effective there must be short-term goals leading to longer term goals. For example to win the league cup, the netball team may have to concentrate on winning more games away from home. For this to be achieved, there may be short-term goals of improving the defending strategies of the team.

Motivation can be increased by splitting long-term goals into medium-term and short-term goals, which are more specific and manageable over a short period of time.

SMARTER goal setting

S – **Specific**. If goals are clear and unambiguous they are more likely to be reached.

M – **Measurable**. This is important for monitoring and makes you accountable.

A – **Agreed**. The sharing of goal-setting between coach/instructor and performer can give a sense of teamwork.

R – **Realistic**. Motivation will improve if goals can actually be reached.

T – **Timed**. An effective approach is to split goals up into short-term goals that are planned and progressive.

E – **Exciting**. The more stimulating the activities can be the more motivating is their effect.

R – **Recorded**. Recording is crucial for monitoring and, once achieved, can be deleted or checked-off, thus improving motivation.

The Effects of Personality and Aggression on Sports Performance

Personality

Sports psychologists do not agree about where we get our **personalities** and how they affect performance in sport.

Personality profiles

Sports psychologists have attempted to show that there are major differences between successful sports people and those who are unsuccessful or avoid sport altogether.

keyword

Personality
An individual's behavioural characteristics that make him or her different from others.

Psychology for Sports Performance

Sports that involve physical contact like wrestling attract people with a different group of personality characteristics than do individual sports such as gymnastics. Team players have also been shown to be more anxious and extroverted but lack the sensitivity and imagination associated with individual sports performers. Links have also been established between player positions and certain personality characteristics, for instance positions which depend on decision making, such as that of a midfield hockey player, will tend to have a personality with more concentration, anxiety control and confidence. Many of these assumptions are only partly backed up with valid research. There are too many other factors that affect performance. The effects of personality characteristics are therefore difficult to prove.

Trait theory of personality

Trait theory states that we inherit our personality characteristics or traits and that these may appear depending on the situation. We have certain personality characteristics that we are born with and these characteristics influence the way in which we behave, whether in sport or in everyday life. Personality traits are stable and therefore do not change much over time.

The many personality characteristics are often grouped into two dimensions or scales:

Extroversion ◄————————► Introversion

Stable ◄————————► Neurotic

Many individuals in sport may have elements of being extrovert and introvert but they are slightly more extroverted than introverted.

There is another trait approach to personality called the 'narrow band' approach that states that personality characteristics can be grouped into two main types: Type A and Type B.

- **Type A** – these are individuals who are impatient and lack tolerance towards other. They also have high levels of personal anxiety.

- **Type B** – these are far more relaxed and are more tolerant towards others. They have much lower personal anxiety.

Hinckle *et al.* (1989) researched the link between the narrow-band approach and sports performance. Ninety-six runners, aged between 16 and 66 years, were identified as either Type A or Type B personalities. There was no significant difference between the two groups, except Type A runners ran more when they were not motivated than did Type B.

This research supports the argument that one particular personality type is not preferable to another. (Source: Honeybourne, Hill and Moors (2000) *Advanced PE and Sport*, Nelson Thornes).

keyword

Extroversion
Seeks social situations and likes excitement. Lacks concentration.

keyword

Introversion
Does not seek social situations and likes peace and quiet. Good at concentrating.

keyword

Stable
Does not swing from one emotion to another.

keyword

Neurotic
Highly anxious and has unpredictable emotions.

It is important that when teaching and coaching sports performers, to take into account the different feelings, concentration levels, motives and other personality characteristics of each individual. We can then get the most out of them.

Aggression

The word 'aggression' is often used in sport, either to encourage players to foul or show other unfair play or to encourage more forceful play. A coach may shout 'Come on, be more aggressive' – meaning to encourage players to put maximum effort into the task and to be more forceful without breaking any rules. It is therefore important to distinguish between the aggression that is useful and fair and what is unacceptable and against the rules and spirit of fair play.

Aggression in sport is often defined as behaviour that is intent to harm others outside the rules of the game or activity. In sport it is often very difficult to distinguish between what is aggressive behaviour and what is not. A foul in rugby may well look aggressive but it may well have been unintentional or an accident. On the other hand, what is seemingly accidental on the surface may well have the intent to harm and therefore is aggression.

Aggressive behaviour that is controlled within the laws of the game is seen as assertion rather than aggression. Assertion in sport is sometimes called instrumental or channelled aggression. Assertion is preferable in sport because a player who is aggressive is likely to play poorly, to get injured themselves or to be removed or sent off from the game.

Controlling aggression in sport

To explore ways in which we can control our own aggression in sport or the aggression of others we must firstly identify what causes aggression.

Figure 9.3

In sport we may have the instinctive urge to strike out and protect ourselves or to defend our terriotory

Possible causes of aggression

■ We can't help it – it is an instinctive response. This is known as the instinct theory. In sport we may have the instinctive urge to strike out and protect ourselves or to defend our territory. For example in rugby a player in an offside position may well cause an opponent to be aggressive.

■ We become frustrated. Again, this is a type of instinct that we have so that if we feel frustrated we may well lash out and be aggressive to get rid of the frustration. Such things as playing poorly and what we feel are poor referees' decisions can cause frustration.

■ We copy others. To fit into a group and be accepted and to behave in a way our role models behave, we may become aggressive. If those you look up to behave aggressively you are more likely to imitate or copy their behaviour because you think that this must be the right thing to do.

■ We simply become angry. This might be caused through frustration as we have already explored, or we might have seen someone else get away with aggressive behaviour without being punished. When we become angry our heart rate increases as well as our blood pressure and the hormone adrenaline is released more readily into the bloodstream. We therefore become agitated and we want to show that we are angry and therefore aggressive.

Strategies to control aggression

The following strategies could be employed to control aggression.

■ Calm down by relaxing or by concentrating on your own performance in the game or activity. Focusing attention on the job in hand – this is sometimes called 'channelling aggression'.

■ Avoid situations that might make you angry or aggressive – for example by walking away from trouble or trying a new position on the field of play.

■ Remove yourself completely from the situation – for instance, a basketball coach may replace an aggressive player with a substitute to calm him down.

■ Enjoy praise for not being aggressive.

■ Recognise others who are successful (role models) but who do not resort to aggression. Most successful sportspeople are not aggressive but are assertive.

■ Punishment or fear of being punished may well control aggression. Often fines are used or a player may be dropped from the team.

■ Recognise that you have a position of responsibility. Aggression could let the rest of the team down.

■ Anger management. Try to identify what makes you angry and try to avoid the triggers to anger. You may learn to deal with your feelings early on rather than waiting for your anger to build up out of control.

■ Breathing exercises. Relax in your mind and body by deep, controlled and slow breathing. This can affect your heart rate, which will decrease as your breathing becomes steadier – and then you will be able to feel calmer.

Assessing your Own Attitudes and Mental Skills, and Planning a Programme to Enhance them in Relation to Sports Performance

To be able to develop your own programme of mental skills training and to enhance your own performance you need to be able to make a self-assessment. Once you know what skills you have and what further skills you need to develop, you can construct a meaningful and helpful programme. As you follow your programme you will need to record your progress and after the completion of your programme you will be required to evaluate its effectiveness and to plan for future development.

Assessment of your attitudes and mental skills

Your assessment can be carried out by your coach, teacher or friend or can be a self-assessment. Some of the more reliable assessments include a combination of these people. Your strengths, weaknesses, opportunities and threats can be analysed. We call this the SWOT analysis.

S – Strengths. What goes well in your sport? What positive attitudes do you have? What positive mental skills do you have? For example, can you concentrate and can you control your anger? Can you handle defeat well?

W – Weaknesses. What does not go so well when you are participating in sport? Do you misbehave in training or show negative attitudes to fitness or fair play? Do you lack concentration? How do you handle defeat?

O – Opportunities. What can you do next time to improve? Will you try to enjoy your play more? Can you watch others who have more positive attitudes or better mental skills and learn from them? Are you now ready for some more advanced coaching related to mental skills training?

T – Threats. What barriers are getting in the way of taking up these opportunities? You may not know how to obtain help, whom to turn to or what books to read. You may not have enough time to develop your mental skills.

Assessment of current performance

The following should be taken into consideration when monitoring and evaluating performance:

- **Previous experience** – what level have you reached in your sport?
- **Technical knowledge and skills** – what do you know about your sport and what skills have you mastered?
- **Technical ability** – what underlying abilities do you have?
- **Levels of fitness** – what test results have you had related to all aspects of your fitness, for example cardiovascular/flexibility?

- **Commitment, training attendance and effort**. How much time and effort do you give to your sport – how many times a week do you train and for how long? Do you keep a training diary?

- **Access to equipment and facilities**. Do you have your own equipment for your sport? What facilities do you use? How easy is it to access training equipment and facilities?

- **Access to effective coaching**. Who coaches you? How is this funded? How many coaches do you have?

- **Diet**. Do you keep a food diary? Are there any foods you have to avoid? Does your diet vary depending on the stage of the season or leading up to a competition/match?

- **Areas for improvement** – having taken into account all of the above, what improvements could be made to enable you to be more effective in your sport?

- **Methods of assessment**. How do you assess your current performance/preparation in your sport? Do you use the assessments of others? Do you use video analysis or a coach's match analysis? Do you use a SWOT analysis? Do you use objective tests such as a recognised fitness test or a psychometric test?

Your programme for development

Any programme should include targets for future performance. Targets should be based on the SMART principle.

S – **Specific**. Have definite, clear targets, such as increasing concentration during the game.

M – **Measurable**. For example an increase in your concentration could be seen by your fellow players because you make fewer mistakes during a game.

A – **Achievable**. For example, your target of better concentration is within your capabilities.

R – **Realistic**. For example, you have given yourself enough time and you have obtained enough help towards reaching your target.

T – **Timebound or time phased**. For example, your target of better concentration is split into smaller short-term goals.

Targets should be divided into short term, medium term and long term.

Performance plan

This should involve:

- Aims and objectives.
- Recognition of resources required.

- Set and agreed goals.

- Training details and competitions.

- Use of any resources/books/tapes/technical equipment.

- Recognition of the barriers that need to be overcome. For example:
  - injury and illness
  - weather
  - travel and travel costs
  - team selection
  - lack of equipment/facilities
  - lack of coaching expertise
  - the expectations and demands of others, e.g. personal relationships/family.

Recording and evaluation of performance

- Assess performance against SMART targets.

- Peer and teacher assessments.

- Feedback from coaches and training results.

- Learning new mental skills.

- Recommendations for future plans/aims.

- Identify support needed, for example training courses, stress management courses, NVQs or other qualifications.

Recording can take place using the following methods:

- diary or logbook

- portfolio

- video/DVD

- audiotap

- observation of record – from someone else watching and recording your attitudes and behaviour during your sports activity.

Evaluation of your programme must assess whether you have reached your goals and should also contain strategies for the future. Identify what you can do to improve and to develop.

Imagery

A Winter Olympic athlete who is responsible for steering the team's bobsleigh visualises or uses imagery to picture the track, with all its bends, twists and turns. He goes through the movements he has to perform when he pictures each aspect of the run in his mind. This is an example of imagery or mental rehearsal.

Figure 9.4
Bobsleigh athletes

To be effective in using imagery the following points should be taken into consideration (Source: Honeybourne, Hill and Moors (2000) *Advanced PE and Sport*, Nelson Thornes)

- Relax in a comfortable, warm setting before you attempt to practise imagery.
- If you want to improve skill by using imagery then practise in a real-life situation.
- Imagery exercises should be short but frequent.
- Set goals for each session – for instance, concentrate on imagining the feel of a tennis serve in one short session.
- Construct a programme for your training in imagery.
- Evaluate your programme at regular intervals.

Self-talk

This technique involves sports performers being positive about past performances and future efforts by talking to themselves. This technique has been shown to help with self-confidence and to raise the levels of aspiration. Unfortunately self-talk for many performers in sport can be negative. It is very common for sports performers to 'talk themselves out of winning' – for instance a penalty taker saying 'I will probably miss this'. This negative self-talk should be

Figure 9.5

Positive thinking can help self-confidence

minimised if performance is to be good. High-level performers cannot afford to be negative and they must develop strategies to change these negative thoughts into positive ones.

Using progressive relaxation training:

1   Sit on the floor with your legs out straight in front of you.

2   Now with your right leg, tense the muscles by pulling your toes up towards your knee by using your leg and foot muscles.

3   Develop as much tension as possible and hold for about 5 seconds and concentrate on what it feels like.

4   Now completely relax your leg muscles and let your foot go floppy and now concentrate on what the relaxed muscles feel like.

5   Now try to relax your muscles even more.

Your leg should feel far more relaxed.

progress check

1   Identify three attitudes that are positive in sport and three attitudes that are negative.

2   What are the main mental skills that are important for success in sport?

3   Choose one mental skill that you have in sport and describe how you use it.

4   Give examples of extrinsic and intrinsic motivation in sport.

5   How does goal setting help in motivating a sports performer?

6   What is meant by SMART goal setting?

7   Describe the following personality types:

    – Introvert

    – Extrovert

    – Type A

    – Type B

8   What causes aggression in sport?

9   How can aggression be controlled in sport?

10 How can you assess your attitudes and mental skills in sport?

Nutrition for Sports Performance

This unit covers:

- the nutritional demands of a selected sport
- assessing your diet
- planning your nutritional strategy
- implementing and evaluating your personal nutritional strategy

This unit covers the information required by the BTEC specifications for Unit 10, related to nutrition and sports performance. It enables you and specialist staff to plan, implement and evaluate a personal nutritional strategy specific to their goals in sport. Energy demands and nutritional needs will be explored to enable you to assess your own diet. The unit aims to develop an understanding of the nutrients essential to health. The importance of a healthy diet is investigated and also the links between diet and health. You will be able to evaluate the effectiveness of sports people's diets after considering the information in this unit.

grading criteria

To achieve a **Pass** grade the evidence must show that the learner is able to:	To achieve a **Merit** grade the evidence must show that the learner is able to:	To achieve a **Distinction** grade the evidence must show that the learner is able to:
P1 Describe the nutritional requirements of a selected sport	**M1** Explain the nutritional requirements of a selected sport	**D1** Evaluate the nutritional requirements of a selected sport describing suitable meal plans
P2 Collect and collate information on their own diet for two weeks	**M2** Explain the strengths of their diet and make recommendations as to how it could be improved, in relation to sports performance and training	**D2** Justify recommendations made regarding improving their own diet, in relation to sports performance and training
P3 Describe the strengths of their own diet and identify areas for improvement, in relation to sports performance and training	**M3** Contribute own ideas to the design of a personal nutritional strategy	**D3** Justify recommendations made regarding improving the personal nutritional strategy

To achieve a **Pass** grade the evidence must show that the learner is able to:	To achieve a **Merit** grade the evidence must show that the learner is able to:	To achieve a **Distinction** grade the evidence must show that the learner is able to:
P4 Describe a personal nutritional strategy, designed and agreed with an advisor	**M4** Explain the strengths of the personal nutritional strategy, and make recommendations as to how it could be improved	
P5 Implement a personal nutritional strategy		
P6 Describe the strengths of the nutritional strategy and identify areas for improvement		

The Nutritional Demands of a Selected Sport

Macronutrients

The following are the main nutrients the body requires, sometimes called macronutrients.

Carbohydrates

These are made up of the chemical elements carbon, hydrogen and oxygen. Carbohydrates are primarily involved in energy production. There are two forms of carbohydrate:

- **Simple sugars**. These provide a quick energy source and include glucose and fructose.
- **Complex starches**. These have many sugar units and are much slower in releasing energy.

Carbohydrates are very important to the athlete, especially in very intense exercise. They are also essential to the nervous system and determine fat metabolism.

Carbohydrates are stored in the muscles and the liver as glycogen but in limited amounts that need to be replenished.

If exercise levels are below 95% of the athlete's VO_2 max, both carbohydrates and fats are used as fuels. Above this intensity, carbohydrates appear to be used exclusively; thus a fast pace in early stages of exercise may lead to glycogen depletion and premature exhaustion.

Examples of sources of carbohydrates include:

- **Complex**. Cereal, pasta, potatoes, bread, fruit.
- **Simple**. Sugar, jam, confectionery, fruit juices.

When exercise takes place, glycogen is broken down to glucose, which supplies muscles with energy. When glycogen stores are depleted, there is less energy available and the athlete will become fatigued. It is recommended that about 60% of a sportsperson's diet should consist of carbohydrates.

Fats

These are also very important and are a major source of energy, especially for athletes performing low intensity endurance exercise. Fats or lipids are made up of carbon, hydrogen and oxygen but in different proportions to carbohydrates. There are two types:

- Triglycerides, which are stored in the form of body fat.
- Fatty acids, which are used mainly as fuel for energy production. These are either **saturated** or **unsaturated fats**.

When muscle cells are readily supplied with oxygen, then fat is the usual fuel for energy production. This is because the body is trying to save the limited stores of glycogen for high-intensity exercise and therefore delays the onset of fatigue. The body cannot solely use fat for energy and so the muscle is fuelled by a combination of fat and glycogen.

In practice

One explanation for marathon runners 'hitting the wall' is that there is a complete depletion of their glycogen stores and the body attempts to metabolise fat, which is a slower way of producing energy. Therefore extreme fatigue is experienced and muscles struggle to contract.

Fat consumption should be carefully monitored and can cause obesity, which will be dealt with later on in this unit. Fat is very important to protect vital organs and is crucial for cell production and the control of heat loss. It is generally accepted that a maximum of 30% of total calories consumed should be from fatty foods.

Examples of sources of fats include:

- **Saturated fats**. Meat products, dairy products, cakes, confectionery.
- **Unsaturated fats**. Oily fish, nuts, margarine, olive oil.

Proteins

Proteins are composed of carbon, hydrogen, oxygen and nitrogen and some contain minerals such as zinc. Proteins are known as the building blocks for body tissue. They are essential for repair. They are also necessary for the production of haemoglobin, enzymes and hormones. Proteins are also potential sources of energy but are not used in this way if fats and carbohydrates are in plentiful supply.

keyword

Saturated fats
A saturated fat is a solid, such as lard, and is primarily from animal sources.

keyword

Unsaturated fats
An unsaturated fat is liquid, such as vegetable oil, and is from plant sources.

Protein should account for approximately 15% of total calorie intake. If protein is taken excessively then there are some health risks such as kidney damage due to the excretion of so many unused amino acids.

Examples of sources of protein:

- Meat, fish and poultry are the three primary complete proteins.
- Vegetables and grains are called incomplete proteins because they do not supply all the essential amino acids.

Protein breaks down more readily during and immediately after exercise. The amount of protein broken down depends upon how long and how hard you exercise. Increased protein intake may be important during the early stages of training to support increases in muscle mass and myoglobin.

Micronutrients

The following nutrients are essential but are only needed in small quantities and are often referred to as micronutrients.

Vitamins

Vitamins are non-caloric chemical compounds that are needed by the body in small quantities. They are an essential component of our diet because they are vital in the production of energy, prevention of disease and our metabolism. With the exception of vitamin D the body cannot produce vitamins. Vitamins A, D, E and K are fat soluble. Vitamins B and C are water soluble.

A well-balanced diet will ensure sufficient vitamin intake. Vitamins can be found in fresh fruit and vegetables.

> **remember**
> To ensure you do not destroy the vitamins in your food:
> - buy good-quality, fresh fruit and vegetables
> - wash/scrub food rather than peeling it because vitamins are often found just below the skin
> - prepare just before cooking and boil in as little water as possible; steaming or microwave cooking is even better
> - eat soon after cooking.

Extremely large doses of vitamins can be dangerous. An overdose of vitamin A can cause hair loss and enlargement of the liver. There is little evidence to suggest that supplementary vitamin pills can enhance performance and most excess vitamins are simply excreted via urine.

Minerals

These are non-caloric, inorganic elements essential for our health. There are two types:

- **Macro-minerals**. These are needed in large amounts, for example, calcium, potassium and sodium.
- **Trace elements**. These are needed in very small amounts, for example, iron, zinc, and manganese.

The major vitamins and their functions

Vitamin	RDA for healthy adult (milligrams)	Dietary sources	Major body functions	Deficiency disease	Symptoms of excess
Water-soluble vitamins					
B1 (thiamine)	1.4–1.5 (M), 1.0–1.1 (F)	Pork, organ meats, whole grains, legumes	Coenzyme in reactions involving the removal of carbon dioxide	Beri beri (peripheral nerve changes, oedema, heart failure)	None reported
B2 (riboflavin)	1.6–1.7 (M), 1.2–1.3 (F)	Widely distributed in foods	Constituent of two coenzymes involved in energy metabolism	Reddened lips, cracks at corner of mouth, lesions of eye	None reported
Niacin	18–19 (M), 13–14 (F)	Liver, lean meats, grains, legumes (can be formed from tryptophan)	Constituent of two coenzymes involved in oxidation-reduction reactions	Pellagra (skin and gastrointestinal lesions, nervous and mental disorders)	Flushing, burning and tingling around neck, face and hands
B6 (pyridoxine)	2.2 (M), 2.0 (F)	Meats, vegetables, whole-grain cereals	Coenzyme involved in amino acid metabolism	Irritability, convulsions, muscular twitching, dermatitis near eyes, kidney stones	None reported
Pantothenic acid	4–7 (M, F)	Widely distributed in foods	Constituent of coenzyme A, which plays a central role in energy metabolism	Fatigue, sleep disturbances, impaired co-ordination, nausea (rare in humans)	None reported
Folic acid	0.4 (M, F)	Legumes, green vegetables, whole-wheat products	Coenzyme involved in transfer of single-carbon units in nucleic acid and amino acid metabolism	Anaemia, gastrointestinal disturbances, diarrhoea, red tongue	None reported
B12	0.003 (M, F)	Muscle meats, eggs, dairy products (not present in plant foods)	Coenzyme involved in transfer of single-carbon units in nucleic acid metabolism	Pernicious anaemia, neurological disorders	None reported
Biotin	0.1–0.2 (M, F)	Legumes, vegetables, meats	Coenzyme required for fat synthesis, amino acid metabolism and glycogen formation	Fatigue, depression, nausea, dermatitis, muscle pains	None reported
C (ascorbic acid)	60 (M, F)	Citrus fruits, tomatoes, green peppers, salad greens	Maintains intercellular matrix of cartilage, bone and dentine. Important in collagen synthesis	Scurvy (degeneration of skin, teeth, blood vessels, epithelial haemorrhages)	Relatively non-toxic. Possibility of kidney stones
Fat-soluble vitamins					
A (retinol)	1.0 (M), 0.8 (F)	Provitamin A (beta carotene) widely distributed in green vegetables. Retinol present in milk, butter, cheese, fortified margarine	Constituent of rhodopsin (visual pigment). Maintenance of epithelial role in mucopolysaccharide synthesis	Xerophthalmia (keratinisation of ocular tissue), night blindness, permanent blindness	Headache, vomiting, peeling of skin, anorexia, swelling of long bones
D	0.075 (M, F)	Cod-liver oil, eggs, dairy products, fortified milk and margarine	Promotes growth and mineralisation of bones. Increases absorption of calcium	Rickets (bone deformities) in children. Osteomalacia in adults	Vomiting, diarrhoea, loss of weight, kidney damage
E (tocopherol)	10 (M), 8 (F)	Seeds, green leafy vegetables, margarines, shortenings	Functions as an antioxidant to prevent cell membrane damage	Possibly anaemia	Relatively non-toxic
K (phylloquinone)	0.07–0.14 (M, F)	Green leafy vegetables. Small amount in cereals, fruit and meats	Important in blood clotting (involved in formation of active prothrombin)	Conditioned deficiencies associated with severe bleeding; internal haemorrhages	Relatively non-toxic. Synthetic forms at high doses may cause jaundice

RDA = recommended daily amount; M = male; f = female

The major minerals

Mineral	Amount in body (g)	RDA for healthy adult (milligrams)	Dietary sources	Major body functions	Deficiency disease	Symptoms of excess
Calcium	1500	800 (M, F)	Milk, cheese, dark green vegetables, dried legumes	Bone and tooth formation, blood clotting, nerve transmission	Stunted growth, rickets, osteoporosis, convulsions	Not reported in humans
Phosphorus	860	800 (M, F)	Milk, cheese, meat, poultry, grains	Bone and tooth formation, acid–base balance	Weakness, demineralisation of bone, loss of calcium	Erosion of bone (fossy jaw)
Sulphur	300	Provided by sulphur amino acids	Sulphur amino acids (methionine and cystine) in dietary proteins	Constituent of active tissue compounds, cartilage and tendon	Related to intake and deficiency of sulphur amino acids	Excess sulphur amino acid intake leads to poor growth
Potassium	180	1875–5625	Meats, milk, many fruits	Acid–base balance, body water balance, nerve function	Muscular weakness, paralysis	Muscular weakness, death
Chlorine	74	1700–5100	Common salt	Formation of gastric juice, acid–base balance	Muscle cramps, mental apathy, reduced appetite	Vomiting
Sodium	64	1100–3300	Common salt	Acid–base balance, body water balance, nerve function	Muscle cramps, mental apathy, reduced appetite	High blood pressure
Magnesium	25	350 (M), 300 (F)	Whole grains, green leafy vegetables	Activates enzymes involved in protein synthesis	Growth failure, behavioural disturbances, weakness, spasms	Diarrhoea
Iron	4.5	10 (M), 18 (F)	Eggs, lean meat, legumes, whole grains, green leafy vegetables	Constituent of haemoglobin and enzymes involved in energy metabolism	Iron-deficiency anaemia (weakness, reduces resistance to infection)	Siderosis, cirrhosis of liver
Fluorine	2.6	1.5–4.0	Drinking water, tea, seafood	May be important in maintenance of bone structure	Higher frequency of tooth decay	Mottling of teeth, increased bone density, neurological disturbances
Zinc	2	15	Widely distributed in foods	Constituent of enzymes involved in digestion	Growth failure, small sex glands	Fever, nausea, vomiting, diarrhoea
Copper	0.1	2	Meats, drinking water	Constituent of enzymes associated with iron	Anaemia, bone changes (rare in humans)	Rare metabolic condition (Wilson's disease)
Silicon, vanadium, tin, nickel	0.024, 0.018, 0.17, 0.010	Not established	Widely distributed in foods	Function unknown (essential for animals)	Not reported in humans	Industrial exposures: silicon – silicosis, vanadium – lung irritation, tin – vomiting, nickel – acute pneumonitis
Selenium	0.013	0.02–0.05	Seafood, meat, grains	Functions in close association with vitamin E	Anaemia (rare)	Gastrointestinal disorders, lung irritation
Manganese	0.012	Not established (diet provides 6–8 g per day)	Widely distributed in foods	Constituent of enzymes involved in fat synthesis	In animals: poor growth, disturbances of nervous system, reproductive abnormalities	Poisoning in manganese mines: generalised disease of nervous system
Iodine	0.011	0.15	Marine fish and shellfish, dairy products, many vegetables	Constituent of thyroid hormones	Goitre (enlarged thyroid)	Very high intakes depress thyroid activity
Molybdenum	0.009	Not established (diet provides 0.4 g per day)	Legumes, cereals, organ meats	Constituent of some enzymes	Impaired ability to metabolise glucose	Occupational exposures: skin and kidney damage
Cobalt	0.0015	(Required as vitamin B12)	Organ and muscle meats, milk	Constituent of vitamin B12	Not reported in humans	Industrial exposure: dermatitis and diseases of red blood cells
Water	40 000 (60% of body weight)	1.5 litres per day	Solid foods, liquids, drinking water	Transport of nutrients, temperature regulation, participates in metabolic reactions	Thirst, dehydration	Headaches, nausea, oedema, high blood pressure

RDA = recommended daily amount; M = male; F = female; g = grams

Minerals can be lost through sweating and so there are implications for those who exercise. Minerals should be replaced quickly to ensure good health.

Examples of important minerals

- **Iron**. This is an essential component of haemoglobin, which carries oxygen in the blood. Iron-deficiency anaemia can impair performance in endurance events. Research has shown that 36 to 82% of female runners are anaemic and therefore should seek iron rich foods in their diets. It should be noted that only a qualified medical doctor should prescribe iron supplements because too much iron can be dangerous. Iron can be found in meat, fish, dairy produce and vegetables. Main sources are from red meat and offal.

- **Calcium**. This mineral is essential for healthy bones and teeth. If there is a deficiency of calcium then there is an increased likelihood of osteoporosis and bone fractures. For calcium to be absorbed, there needs to be sufficient vitamin D, which is found in sunlight. Calcium is found in milk and dairy products, green vegetables and nuts.

- **Calcium deficiency**. Calcium deficiency can be found in females who are underweight, smokers, alcoholics, vegetarians and those who overdo training in sport.

Water

This is also a nutrient and is crucial for good health and in particular for those who participate in sport. It carries nutrients in the body and helps with the removal of waste products. It is also very important in the regulation of body temperature. The body readily loses water through urine and sweat for instance. This water loss accelerates depending on the environment and the duration and intensity of any exercise that is being undertaken. On average, daily consumption of an individual should be about 2 litres. Those involved in exercise should take more to ensure a good state of hydration.

Studies show that individuals who are dehydrated become intolerant to exercise and heat stress. The cardiovascular system becomes inefficient if there is dehydration and there is an inability to provide adequate blood flow to the skin – which may lead to heat exhaustion.

Fluids must be taken in during prolonged exercise. This will minimise dehydration and slow the rise in body temperature.

There are a number of sports drinks available commercially that contain electrolytes and carbohydrates. Some of the claims that are made about these drinks have been misinterpreted. A single meal, for instance, can replace the minerals lost during exercise. Water is the primary need in any drink taken before, during and after exercise because it empties from the stomach extremely quickly and reduces dehydration associated with sweating. Thirst is not a reliable indicator for fluid intake; therefore it is best to drink small amounts regularly even if you are not thirsty. Under cooler conditions a carbohydrate drink may give the extra energy needed in events lasting over an hour.

Healthy diets

Healthy eating involves a daily calorie intake in the following proportions:

- 50% carbohydrate
- 30% to 35% fat
- 15% to 20% protein.

The principles that should govern your food choice include:

- enjoyment
- not too much fat
- not too many sugary foods
- include vitamins and minerals
- eat plenty of fibre
- keep alcohol within prescribed limits
- maintain balance of intake and output
- eat plenty of fruit and vegetables.

Unit 12 The Influence of Lifestyle on Physical Fitness, page 215

The right balance in a diet is essential for health and fitness. Enjoyment is an important aspect of eating. A healthy diet does not mean that you have to give up all your favourite foods that are considered 'bad' foods – it is the overall balance that counts. Balanced meals contain starchy foods with plenty of vegetables, salad and fruit. Your fat content should be kept to a minimum by using low fat or lean ingredients.

Factors that also affect choice of foods include:

- culture; morals; ethics
- family influences
- peer group influences
- lifestyle
- finance.

In practice

The balance of good health model

This is a model that shows what healthy eating means.

Eating sufficient fruit and vegetables is important for a healthy diet. It helps to reduce the likelihood of coronary heart disease and some cancers. Government guidelines suggest that you should eat at least five portions of fruit and vegetables each day.

Figure 10.3

The balance of good health model

© Crown Copyright

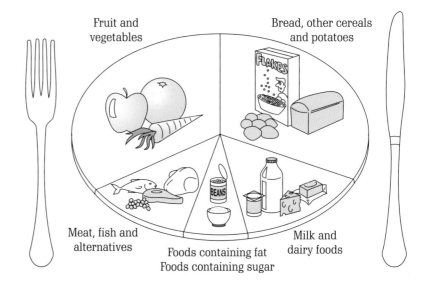

Most healthy eating guidelines warn against eating too much salt. If your diet contains too much salt then this may lead to high blood pressure, which can cause heart and kidney disease. There are dietary values that are widely recognised as recommended nutrient intake (RNI).

> **remember**
>
> What is a portion of fruit or vegetables?
> - 2 tablespoons of vegetables
> - 1 dessert bowlful of salad
> - 1 apple/orange/banana
> - 2 plums
> - 1 cupful of grapes/cherries
> - 2 tablespoons of fresh fruit salad
> - 1 tablespoon dried fruit
> - 1 glass fruit juice
>
> (Source: adapted from Health Development Agency, 2000)

Energy requirements for sport

We need to eat enough for our energy whether we participate in sport or not. The body's metabolism is often mentioned. The basal metabolic rate (BMR) is a measure of the amount of energy we need at rest. Therefore our food intake needs to take into account our BMR in addition to the energy to participate in sport. Men can consume 2800–3000 kcal a day and women 2000–2200 kcal a day without putting on weight. Metabolic rates vary between individuals and it also becomes slower with age.

Energy is measured in kilocalories and kilojoules. 1 kcal = 4.2 kJ.

Factors that affect energy expenditure include:

- frequency of exercise
- intensity of exercise
- type and duration of exercise
- age, gender, body composition of individual
- fuels available.

Recommended daily nutritional intakes		
	Male	**Female**
Calories	2550 kcal	1940 kcal
Chloride	2500 mg	2500 mg
Copper	1.2 mg	1.2 mg
Folate	200 mg	200 mg
Iodine	140 mg	140 mg
Iron	8.7 mg	14.8 mg
Magnesium	300 mg	270 mg
Niacin	17 mg	13 mg
Phosphorus	550 mg	550 mg
Potassium	3.5 g	3.5 g
Protein	55.5 g	45 g
Selenium	75 mg	60 mg
Sodium	1.6 g	1.6 g
Vitamin A	700 mg	600 mg
Vitamin B	1.0 mg	0.8 mg
Vitamin B1	1.0 mg	0.8 mg
Vitamin B2	1.3 mg	1.1 mg
Vitamin B6	1.4 mg	1.2 mg
Vitamin B12	1.5 mg	1.5 mg
Vitamin C	40 mg	40 mg
Zinc	9.5 mg	7.0 mg

© Crown copyright

Fuels available include:

- protein – used during prolonged exercise
- alcohol – unable to be metabolised by working muscles
- glycogen – stored in the liver used to top up glucose levels in the blood
- glycogen in the muscles from fat and carbohydrates
- water.

The intensity of exercise dictates the use of energy by the muscles. This energy needs to be replaced because otherwise the muscles would not be able to continue to function and the exercise would have to terminate.

Nutritional strategies in sport

Glycogen stores

Ensuring that the body has enough glycogen is crucial for optimum energy supply. Ensuring that the body has enough glycogen is crucial for optimum energy supply. One method of increasing the glycogen available is through glycogen 'loading', sometimes known as carbo-loading. This process involves

Figure 10.4
An exhausted athlete

depleting one's stores of glycogen by cutting down on carbohydrates and keeping to a diet of protein and fat for 3 days. Light training follows with a high carbohydrate diet for 3 days leading up to the event. This has been shown to significantly increase the stores of glycogen and helps to offset fatigue. When carbo-loading the diet should consist mainly of foods like pasta, bread, rice and fruit. Generally a high carbohydrate diet will ensure that glycogen will be replenished during exercise.

Other energy-giving strategies include:

- consuming carbohydrates 2 to 4 hours before exercise
- consuming a small amount of carbohydrates within the first half-hour of exercise to ensure refuelling of glycogen
- eating carbohydrates straight after exercise for up to 2 days to replenish stores.

Fluids

The athlete may lose up to 1 litre of water per hour during endurance exercise, so rehydration is essential, especially if there are also hot environmental conditions. As we have discovered, thirst is not a good indicator of dehydration, therefore the athlete needs to drink plenty during and after exercise even if little thirst is experienced.

Taking fluids

- Take fluids, preferably water, before exercise to ensure full hydration.
- Take fluids continuously during exercise even if not thirsty.
- Small amounts are often best.
- Take fluids straight after exercise before alcohol is consumed.
- Some sports-specific drinks may be useful for high-intensity and long-duration exercise.

Vitamin and mineral supplements

There is an increase in the body's requirements for vitamins and minerals if regular, intensive exercise takes place. This means that the athlete will eat more food because of the need for more energy. This in itself will mean that the body

Figure 10.5

An athlete should drink plenty of water to ensure full hydration

is receiving more vitamins and minerals. As we have already discovered, large quantities of extra vitamins and minerals can damage health. Supplementing the athlete's diet can be beneficial in certain circumstances.

Supplements

■ Smokers should consider extra vitamin C.

■ If planning to become pregnant it is recommended that folic acid is taken.

■ If you are on a diet and consuming less than 1200 calories per day, supplements in low doses have been found to be beneficial.

■ If vegan or vegetarian and the diet is limited then multivitamins and mineral supplements could be useful.

Please note that supplementation is best considered under medical supervision.

Factors to consider with sports performers and nutrition

Sports performers, especially at the top level, have certain aspects to their lifestyles that should be considered when planning nutritional intake:

■ timing of meals should fit around training and events

■ ensure that there is balance in the diet

■ ensure that there is adequate fluid intake

■ ensure adequate iron intake

■ diet should be suitable for very high workload, depending on the activity

■ psychological wellbeing – if an athlete is unhappy with the diet, then even if physiologically beneficial, it could negatively affect performance because of psychological pressure

- there should be a sharing of ideas between coach/dietician and the performer to agree the best strategy, depending on an individual's needs and perceptions

- obsession with food is common with high performance athletes and should be avoided.

---

case study 10.1

Diet of Mark Foster – Olympic and Commonwealth Games sprint swimmer

I weigh about 14 stone, but when it comes to competition, I aim to have lost half a stone. I eat a lot of protein food. Two hours of work in the gym burns off anything, but while I watch my diet, I have a lot of protein drinks after weight sessions and take supplements to make sure my body does not become broken down.

(Source www.bbc.co.uk/sport)

Assessing your Diet

Collecting information about your diet

- Keep a food diary or logbook detailing what you eat each day over a 1- or 2-week period.

- Compare your diary entries with the requirements stated earlier in this unit.

- Write a report and identify the strengths of your diet, for example good water intake, and identify your weaknesses, for example excessive levels of fat.

- Identify what you would do to improve your diet, for example eating more fruit and vegetables, eating at different times of the day or drinking more fluid.

Planning your Nutritional Strategy

Your nutritional strategy or your future diet should take into account the necessary food groups that we have identified:

- Ensure that you have the right balance of foods.

- Ensure regular rehydration.

- Take into account the way you cook food – for example, overboiling vegetables destroys all the important vitamins.

- Take into account the timing of your eating.

- Review whether it is important to take supplements such as vitamins, minerals, creatine and protein powders.

Daily food recommendations table

Record your daily intake for each meal and using the website (www.dietclub.com) work out the percentage intake of each food group.

Meal	Food	Quantity	Carbo-hydrate	Fat	Protein	Energy
Breakfast						
Lunch						
Dinner						
Snacks						
Total						
%						

Critically analyse the diet and give recommendations (you may need to continue on a separate sheet).

....

....

Please note that any significant change in your diet or any use of nutritional supplements must be approved by a qualified nutritionist or doctor.

Implementing and Evaluating your Personal Nutritional Strategy

Take into account when you are going to eat. This depends on when you need immediate energy, for example, or when you need a rest between eating and exercise. Your diet should take into account what you need before, during and after training or competition. A food diary should also be continued.

Your nutritional strategy should be monitored and evaluated. Assess whether your diet is meeting your needs and fitting in well with your lifestyle. For example how does your eating strategy take into account the rest of the family or friends?

You may find that there is an increase in cost in buying good-quality food – assess:

■ the financial implications

■ whether you feel better/well

■ whether you have a lot of energy

■ whether you feel tired and 'under the weather'.

Take the results of your nutritional strategy and then modify or replan your diet for the future.

progress check

1 Name the main macronutrients required by the body.

2 Choose one macronutrient and identify some foods that contain it.

3 Why is water so valuable as part of a balanced diet?

4 Name three different vitamins and state why each should be part of a diet.

5 Why are minerals important in a diet?

6 Explain what carbo-loading means?

7 Give four guidelines for healthy eating.

8 What must you take into consideration when planning a nutritional strategy in sport?

9 How can you assess the effectiveness of your diet over a 2-week period?

10 What advice would you give yourself about future eating habits?

UNIT 11

Fitness for Sports Performance

This unit covers:

- the fitness requirements necessary to achieve excellence in a selected sport
- assessing your own level of fitness
- planning a personal fitness training programme
- implementing and evaluate a personal fitness training programme

This unit covers the fitness theories and practices that are essential for preparing effectively for sports performance in Unit 11 of the BTEC First Diploma in Sport. The unit explores the physical requirements for excellence in sport. It then enables you to assess your own fitness levels and to compare these with the demands of sport at the desired level. It provides essential information for planning a personal fitness training programme and for implementing and evaluating such a programme.

grading criteria

To achieve a **Pass** grade the evidence must show that the learner is able to:	To achieve a **Merit** grade the evidence must show that the learner is able to:	To achieve a **Distinction** grade the evidence must show that the learner is able to:
P1 Describe the fitness requirements for achieving excellence in a selected sport	**M1** Explain the fitness requirements for achieving excellence in a selected sport	**D1** Evaluate their personal level of fitness, considering the level required to achieve excellence in a selected sport
P2 Describe their personal level of fitness, by aministering four different tests for different components of fitness	**M2** Explain their personal level of fitness, identifying strengths and areas for improvement	**D2** Justify suggestions related to identified areas for improvement in the personal fitness training programme
P3 Plan, and agree, a six-week personal fitness training programme with a coach	**M3** Contribute own ideas to the design of a six-week personal fitness training programme	

To achieve a **Pass** grade the evidence must show that the learner is able to:	To achieve a **Merit** grade the evidence must show that the learner is able to:	To achieve a **Distinction** grade the evidence must show that the learner is able to:
P4 Implement a six-week personal fitness training programme, maintaining a training diary	**M4** Explain the strengths of the personal fitness training programme, making suggestions for improvement	
P5 Describe the strengths of the personal fitness training programme and identify areas for improvement		

The Fitness Requirements Necessary to Achieve Excellence in a Selected Sport

Components of physical fitness

The term 'fitness' is used very loosely and often refers to aerobic endurance or how far you can run without becoming too much out of breath. Fitness is more complex than that. It involves many different components or parts. Depending on the type of sport you are involved with you might be very fit in one component but not another. For example, strength and power is very important to the discus thrower in athletics but is less important in archery. All sports activities, however, require a good general level of fitness for all components. In some team games, for example, all components of fitness are equally important, although this may vary depending on what position you play. The following are recognised as the main components of physical fitness:

Figure 11.1

Strength is in the ability of a muscle to exert force for a short period

- **Strength** – this is the ability of a muscle to exert force for a short period of time. The amount of force that can be exerted by a muscle depends on the size of the muscles and the number of muscles involved, as well as the type of muscle fibres used and the coordination of the muscle involved.

- **Muscular endurance** – this is the ability of a muscle or group of muscles to repeatedly contract or keep going without rest.

- **Aerobic endurance** – this is the ability to exercise continuously without growing tired. The more the oxygen can be transported around the body and the more the muscles can use this oxygen then the greater will be the level of aerobic endurance you have.

- **Flexibility** – this is the amount or range of movement that can occur around a joint. The structure of the joint restricts movement as well as the muscles, tendons and ligaments.

- **Power** – this is often referred to as fast strength. Power is a combination of strength and speed.

- **Speed** – this is the ability of the body to move quickly. The movements may be the whole body or parts of the body, for example arm speed in cricket bowling.

- **Body composition** – this refers to the way in which the body is made up. The percentage of muscle, fat, bone and internal organs is taken into consideration. There are two main components: body fat and lean body mass, which is body mass without the fat.

Other components are also important in determining how fit you are for sport. They include:

- **Agility** – how quickly you can change direction under control.

- **Co-ordination** – ability to perform tasks in sport, for example running and then passing a ball in rugby.

Figure 11.2

Speed is important for a squash player

- **Balance** – the ability to keep your body mass over a base of support – for example, a gymnast performing a handstand on a balance beam.

- **Reaction time** – this is the time it takes someone to make a decision to move. For example how quickly a sprinter reacts the gun and decides to drive off the blocks.

Figure 11.3

Good reaction time is important for a swimmer to get a good start

Assessing Your Own Level of Fitness

Fitness tests

Fitness testing is important for discovering the present fitness level of a performer. It also serves as a basis for progress. In other words a training programme may be followed after testing and then, after a few weeks, another fitness test will reveal how effective the training has been and whether the performer has increased his or her fitness. As we have discovered, physical fitness involves a number of different components, therefore fitness tests must be designed to test a specific component.

It is important that individuals view the tests as benchmarks for their own improvements instead of against the results of others.

To assess your own fitness:

- Identify exactly what you want to assess and choose the fitness tests accordingly.

- If a specific type of fitness needs to be assessed then only use the tests that are required.

- Make sure that you are medically fit to take a test (see a doctor if you are at all unsure about your capability of performing a test). A common practice in health clubs is to complete a Physical Activity Readiness questionnaire (PAR-Q).

- Make sure you feel well enough for the test.
- Make sure that you have not eaten a heavy meal for approximately 3 hours before the test.
- Do not consume alcohol the day before the test and on the day of the test.
- Make sure that you have had enough water to drink.
- Do not smoke for at least 2 hours before the tests.

Strength tests

An objective measure of strength can be via the use of dynamometers such as the handgrip dynamometer, which measures the strength of the handgrip.

Make sure that the handgrip is adjusted to fit the subject's hand. The subject should stand, holding the dynamometer parallel to the side of the body, with the dial facing away from the body. The handle should be squeezed as hard as possible without moving the arm. Three trials are recommended with a one-minute rest between each trial.

Speed

This can be measured by the 30 m sprint test. This should be on a flat non-slippy surface to prevent accidents. The sprint should be from a flying start back from the beginning of the marked out stretch. The time is taken from the beginning of the 30 m stretch to the end.

Figure 11.4

Speed can be measured by the 30 m sprint test

Cardiovascular endurance

The level of endurance fitness is indicated by an individual's VO_2 max – that is the maximum amount of oxygen an individual can take in and use in one minute.

VO_2 max

Top endurance athletes such as marathon runners usually have a very high VO_2 max – approximately 70 ml/kg/min. The average performer is about 35 ml/kg/min. A low VO_2 max of 25 or less would probably indicate that you are not going to be an endurance athlete. The more endurance training you do, however, generally the higher your VO_2 max scores will become.

The potential VO_2 max of an individual can be predicted via the multistage fitness test (sometimes called the 'bleep' test). This test involves a shuttle run that becomes progressively more difficult.

The test is in the form of a cassette tape. Subjects run a 20 m shuttle as many times as possible but ensure that they turn at each end of the run in time with the 'bleep' on the tape. The time lapse between each bleep sound on the tape becomes progressively smaller and so the shuttle run has to be completed progressively more quickly. At the point when subjects cannot keep up with the bleeps, they are deemed to have reached their optimum level. The level reached by the subject is recorded and used as a baseline for future tests or can be compared to national norms.

case study 11.1   The 'bleep test'

The test usually consists of 23 levels. Only the very top or elite athletes can get into the top three levels. Cyclist Lance Armstrong and footballer David Beckham are two such examples.

The test is often recommended for players of sports that involve a lot of stop–start sprinting, such as tennis, rugby, football or hockey.

Muscular endurance

Testing the endurance of one particular muscle group can assess an individual's muscular endurance. One such test is called the abdominal conditioning test. This tests the endurance of the abdominal muscle group by measuring the number of sit-ups an individual can perform by again keeping to a 'bleep' indicated on the cassette tape. When individuals cannot complete any more sit-ups in time with the bleep, then it is deemed that they have reached their optimum level. Again, this test can be used as a benchmark for training or used for comparison with national norms.

Flexibility

This can be tested via the sit and reach test. The subject sits on the floor with legs outstretched in a straight position. The subject reaches as far forward as possible but keeping the legs straight and in contact with the floor. The distance that the ends of the fingers are from the feet (pointing upwards) is measured. Using a 'sit-and-reach' box ensures more accurate measurements. Once again this test can provide measurements that can be used in assessing any future training and also for the subject to compare performance with national norms.

Power

An individual's power can be measured by using the vertical jump test. There are commercial jump test boards that can be fixed to the wall. The subject jumps vertically, using both feet, then touches the calibrated scale on the board with one hand. The position of the touch is noted; the test is completed three times and the maximum height attained is recorded.

Body composition

This can be assessed in a number of different ways:

- **Skinfold measurement of body fat**. Completed using a skinfold calliper. Measurements of body fat are taken from the areas around the biceps, triceps, subscapular and supra iliac. The total measurements are added together and recorded to compare with national averages (called norms) or more importantly to assess training or weight management programmes.

- **Hydrostatic weighing**. Completed by measuring the water displacement when the subject is submerged in water.

- **Bioelectrical impedance**. A small electric current is passed through the body from the wrist to the ankle. Fat is known to restrict the flow of the electrical current, therefore the greater the current needed, the greater the percentage of body fat (adapted from Honeybourne, 2003).

Planning a Personal Fitness Training Programme

For an effective training programme, it is important to understand the theory on which that training is based. Useful training is based on what are called 'principles of training'. It is also important to set personal goals towards fitness training. Any effective training programme must take the following into consideration:

- **Lifestyle** – the training needs to fit around your work and studies and family responsibilities.

- **Medical history** – take into account any medical conditions that you have, such as diabetes.

- **Activity history** – take into account what sort and how much training you have done in the past.

■ **Dietary history/habits** – what are your eating habits and do they fit into your intended fitness routine?

■ **Your motivation/attitudes** – are you determined and committed enough for your intended fitness routine?

 Unit 8 Technical Skills and Tactical Awareness for Sport

Principles of training

Training programmes must take into account the needs and personality of the particular individual. The aims or goals of the training should be agreed – what are you trying to do? Are you wishing to prepare over a short or long time? An individual's goals must be understood. Does the performer want to become generally fit or fit for a particular sport? The individual's current activity level must be assessed by doing an initial fitness test (see above in this unit). The age, time available, equipment available and skill level must all be taken into consideration before the following principles of training are applied.

The principles of training include specificity, overload, progression, reversibility and variance. The following are more detailed explanations.

Specificity

This principle indicates that the training should be specific and therefore relevant to the appropriate needs of the activity or the type of sport involved. For example a marathon runner would carry out more aerobic or stamina training because the event is mostly aerobic in nature. It is not just energy systems that have to match the training; muscle groups and actions involved in the training also have to be as specific as possible. For example, a high jumper would work on power in the legs. There is, however, a general consensus that a good general fitness is required before any high degree of specificity can be applied.

Figure 11.5

Good, general fitness is required before specificity can be applied

keyword

FITT

F = frequency of training (number of training sessions each week)

I = intensity of the exercise undertaken

T = time or duration that the training takes up

T = type of training to be considered that fulfils specific needs

Overload

This principle states that you need to work the body harder than normal, so that there is some stress and discomfort on the body's systems and parts. The body will become fitter and physical progress will follow overload because the body will respond by coping or adapting to the stress experienced. For example, in weight training the lifter will eventually attempt heavier weights or an increase in repetitions, thus overloading the body. The weightlifter will then in the future adapt to this stress and be able to lift heavier weights.

Overload can be achieved by a combination of increasing the frequency (how many times), the intensity (how hard you train) and the duration (how long each session is) of the activity. These aspects are important if the **FITT** programme is to be followed.

Progression

The work done in training should progressively become more difficult so that progress can be made. If the same level of exercise is attempted week in and week out then the athlete will only reach a certain level of fitness and then stay there. Once adaptations or changes to the body's fitness have occurred then the performer should make even more demands on the body and do more strenuous work. It is important not to make too many demands of the body too early. Training must be sensibly progressive and realistic if it is to be effective, otherwise injury may occur and there would be a fall in fitness levels instead of progression.

Figure 11.6

If training becomes more difficult, athletes will often achieve more

Reversibility

This principle states that fitness can deteriorate if training stops or decreases in intensity for any length of time. If training is stopped, then the fitness gained will be largely lost. For instance VO_2 max and muscle strength can decrease. Therefore it is important to 'keep going' with your training. It is better to have days of light training rather than no training at all if you wish to improve your fitness significantly.

Variance

This principle states that there should be variety in training methods. A lot of different types of training or different activities will make training interesting and exciting. If training is too predictable then performers can become demotivated and bored. Overuse injuries such as muscle strains are also common when training is too repetitive with one muscle group or part of the body. Variance in training can therefore be motivating and also helps to prevent injury.

Training methods

Warm-ups and cool-downs

The warm-up enables the body to prepare for exercise. It reduces the likelihood of injury and muscle soreness. There is also a release of adrenaline that will start the process of speeding up the delivery of oxygen to the working muscles. An increase in muscle temperature will help to ensure that there is a ready supply of energy and that the muscle becomes more flexible to prevent injury.

The cool-down is also important for effective training. If light exercise follows training then the oxygen can more effectively be flushed through the muscle tissue, oxidising lactic acid. Cool-downs also prevents blood pooling in the veins, which can cause dizziness.

Figure 11.7

The warm-up enables the body to prepare for the onset of exercise

Aerobic and anaerobic fitness training

Aerobic capacity can be improved through continuous, steady state (submaximal) training. The rhythmic exercise of aerobics, or continuous swimming or jogging, are good for aerobic fitness.

This low-intensity exercise must take place over a long period of time from 20 minutes to 2 hours. The intensity of this exercise should be 60% to 80% of your maximum heart rate.

Anaerobic training involves high intensity work that may be less frequent, although elite athletes will frequently train both aerobically and anaerobically.

Interval training is one of the most popular types of training. It is adaptable to individual needs and sports. Interval training can improve both aerobic and anaerobic fitness. It is called interval training because there are intervals of work and intervals of rest. For training the aerobic system, there should be slower intervals. This is suitable for sports like athletics and swimming and for team games like hockey or football. For training the anaerobic system, there should be shorter, more intense intervals of training.

The following factors have to be taken into account before the design of a training session:

- **Duration of the work interval**. The work interval should be between 3 seconds and 10 seconds at high intensity for anaerobic training and 7 minutes to 8 minutes for aerobic training.
- **Speed** (intensity) of the work interval. This should be between 90% and 100% intensity for anaerobic training and moderate for aerobic training.
- **Number of repetitions**. This depends on the length of the work period but if repetitions are short, then up to 50 repetitions are appropriate for anaerobic training. For aerobic training, 3 or 4 are more appropriate.
- **Number of sets** of repetitions. Repetitions can be divided into sets. If 50 repetitions are to be used then these could be divided into sets of 5.
- **Duration of the rest interval**. This is the length of time that the heart rate falls to about 150 bpm. Aerobic training will require a shorter rest interval for effective training.
- **Type of activity during the rest interval**. If the energy system is anaerobic, then only light stretching might be used. If it is aerobic then some light jogging may help to disperse lactic acid.

Fartlek training

This is also known as 'speedplay' training. This training is good for aerobic fitness because it is an endurance activity. It is good for anaerobic fitness because of the speed activities over a short period of time. Throughout the exercise, the speed and intensity of the training are varied. In an hour session, for instance, there may be walking activity, which is low in intensity, or very fast sprinting, which is high intensity. Cross-country running with sprint activities every now and again is a simplistic but reasonable way of describing fartlek.

Muscular strength, muscular endurance and power training

For strength and power training the performer needs to work against resistance. The training is effective only if it is specific enough. In other words the training needs to be targeted depending on the type of strength that needs to be developed, for instance, explosive strength for a thrower in athletics or strength endurance for a gymnast.

Circuit training

This involves a series of exercises that are arranged in a particular way called a circuit because the training involves repetition of each activity. The resistance that is used in circuits relates mainly to body weight and each exercise in the circuit is designed to work on a particular muscle group. For effective training different muscle groups should be worked on, with no two muscle groups being worked on one after the other. For instance, an activity that uses the main muscle groups in the arms should be followed, for example, by an exercise involving the muscle groups in the legs.

The types of exercises that are involved in circuit training are press-ups, star jumps, dips and squat thrusts.

Circuit training can also incorporate skills in the activities. For example hockey players may include dribbling activities, flicking the ball, shuttle runs and shooting activities.

Figure 11.8

Training needs to be targeted depending on the type of strength that needs to be developed, such as strength endurance for rugby players

The duration and intensity depends on the type of activities that have been used. An example would be a circuit with one minute's worth of activity, followed by one minute's worth of rest. The whole circuit could then be repeated three times. Scores at the end of the circuit may be related to time or repetitions and are a good way of motivating in training. It is also easy to see progression in fitness as the weeks go by when more repetitions can be attempted or when times are improved.

Weight and resistance training methods

For strength to be developed more resistance can be used in the form of weight training or against other types of resistance such as the use of pulleys. Weight training involves a number of repetitions and sets, depending on the type of strength that needs to be developed. For throwing events in athletics, for example, training methods must involve very high resistance and low repetition. For strength endurance that you may need in swimming or cycling then more repetitions need to be involved with less resistance or lighter weights.

Plyometrics

Plyometrics involve bounding, hopping and jumping. This type of training is designed to improve dynamic strength. Plyometrics improves the speed in which muscles shorten. If muscles have previously been stretched, then they tend to generate more force when contracted. Any sport that involves sprinting, throwing and jumping will benefit from this type of training, as will players of many team sports like netball or rugby.

One type of jumping used in this training method is called in-depth jumping, which is when the athlete jumps onto and off raised platforms or boxes. This type of training is very strenuous on the muscles and joints and a reasonable amount of fitness must be present before this training is attempted. As usual it is important that there is sufficient stretching of the muscle before attempting this type of training. It is also important to have the right sort of footwear so that impact injuries do not occur.

Flexibility training

This is sometimes called mobility training. It involves stretching exercises of the muscles and this can help with performance and to avoid injury. There are two types of flexibility exercises.

Active stretching is when there are voluntary muscular contractions that are held by the performer for 30 seconds to one minute. When the muscle is relaxed at the limit of the stretching range, muscle elongation may occur if this practice is repeated regularly. The stretching must be under control and muscles should be suitably warmed-up before stretching begins.

One method of active stretching is called the ballistic method. In ballistic stretching the subject actively uses the momentum or movement of the limb to propel the body. This is achieved through a bouncing-type movement and should only be attempted by those who are extremely flexible such as gymnasts or certain athletes because muscle tissue damage is easily experienced with such active stretching.

Passive stretching incorporates an external 'helper' who pushes or pulls the limb to stretch the appropriate muscles. This is obviously potentially dangerous, so the subject must be thoroughly warmed up and should go through some active stretching to begin with. Gymnasts often favour this particular type of stretching.

Figure 11.9

Flexibility training involves stretching the muscles to help with performance and avoid injury

One type of passive stretching is called proprioceptive neuromuscular facilitation (PNF). This method tries to decrease the reflex shortening of the muscle when the muscle is fully stretched:

■ the limb is moved to its limit by the subject

■ the limb is then taken to its passive limit by the partner

■ just before the point of real discomfort, the muscle is contracted isometrically for a few seconds, then relaxed

■ it will be possible to stretch the muscle a little more during the next stretch.

Implementing and Evaluating a Personal Fitness Training Programme

- Your training session must be planned, taking into consideration all the information already covered in this unit.

- You must train regularly and show commitment with any missed training recorded with the reason for missing.

- You must train to the best of your ability and show good motivation to progress.

- Recording what you do in training is important. This can take the form of a training log or diary that also records achievements such as personal bests or results of team games.

- Your training diary must also record the progression in your training, such as more repetitions or higher resistance in weight training.

- Evaluate during the programme and after the programme has been completed by reading through your diary or log along with someone else such as your coach or parents. Write down what you have achieved and what has gone wrong.

- Use your evaluation to plan for the next training phase. You might wish to modify your training by making it more difficult or easier. You might need to modify your planned goals because you might have become fitter quicker than you thought or you may have been slower than you thought in building up your fitness. It is important that, whatever your evaluation, you concentrate on the successes and you are realistic about your future goals.

progress check

1 Name the main components of fitness.

2 Choose two components and describe how you would test the level of fitness for each.

3 What are the typical fitness levels for an excellent performer in your sport?

4 Give the five main principles of training.

5 What is meant by the interval training method?

6 What are plyometrics?

7 Describe two fitness tests.

8 How do you ensure that fitness testing is as accurate as possible?

9 Construct a physical fitness session for strength. Explain the reasons for the activities you have chosen.

10 How can you evaluate your fitness training programme?

Lifestyle and Sports Performance

This unit covers:

- planning and managing work commitments and leisure time
- appropriate behaviour for an elite athlete
- the factors that influence the effective planning of a career
- being able to communicate effectively with the media and significant others

This unit gives the essential information needed to complete Unit 12 of the BTEC First Diploma in Sport. Elite athletes are required not only to be very physically fit and skilful but also to be professional in all aspects of their lives. They must be reliable and must be able to plan other commitments carefully so that they can train and perform at the highest level. Good communication skills and the ability to manage time effectively are necessary for success in sport. This unit helps to give you the knowledge to develop skills to adopt an appropriate lifestyle.

grading criteria

To achieve a **Pass** grade the evidence must show that the learner is able to:	To achieve a **Merit** grade the evidence must show that the learner is able to:	To achieve a **Distinction** grade the evidence must show that the learner is able to:
P1 Produce a realistic plan for work commitments and leisure time, for one month	**M1** Explain the way work commitments and leisure activities have been planned	**D1** Evaluate the effects and consequences of behaviour of elite athletes
P2 Describe three different pressures on elite athletes and identify strategies that can be used to deal with these pressures	**M2** Explain three different pressures on elite athletes and describe suitable strategies that can be used to deal with these pressures	**D2** Justify goals, in personal career plan, and second, career choices
P3 Describe appropriate behaviour for elite athletes in three different situations	**M3** Explain appropriate behaviour for elite athletes in three different situations	**D3** Present recommendations on how to improve their media interview skills

grading criteria

To achieve a **Pass** grade the evidence must show that the learner is able to:	To achieve a **Merit** grade the evidence must show that the learner is able to:	To achieve a **Distinction** grade the evidence must show that the learner is able to:
P4 Describe realistic goals in a personal career plan, including second career choices	**M4** Explain goals, in personal athletic career plan, and second career choices	
P5 Describe three financial issues elite athletes need to consider	**M5** Explain the skills required to communicate and work effectively with others	
P6 Describe the skills required to communicate and work effectively with others	**M6** Explain their strengths and areas for improvement when participating in a media interview	
P7 Plan for, and be the subject of, a media interview, describing own strengths and areas for improvement		

Planning and Managing Work Commitments and Leisure Time

Work commitments can affect the time spent on training and preparing. Competitions also take up time and other aspects of your life may well restrict the amount of time you have to spend on preparation and sports competition. There is a need to prioritise time and so time management skills are essential. Diaries, lists and help from others such as personal assistants can improve time management. Leisure time activities such as socialising, although important for the athlete's wellbeing, should be managed effectively. Inappropriate activities, such as alcohol consumption, smoking and taking drugs, must be prohibited or at least restricted to ensure peak mental and physical fitness. The following sections deal with the main influences of lifestyle on physical fitness.

The influence of lifestyle on physical fitness

Training for fitness is only one, albeit very important, aspect of getting and keeping physically fit. Our lifestyle – in other words the way in which we conduct our everyday lives – can affect significantly our overall fitness for sport. There is an increase in people being overweight and, when extreme, this is called obesity. Many of us now live more sedentary lives. In other words we are less active. We use the car more for getting from A to B even if B is just up the road to the local shop! There are more instances of diabetes and coronary heart disease, which is affected by the food we eat.

Unit 10 Nutrition for Sports Performance

The main 'lifestyle' factors that can affect our physical fitness are given below.

Stress levels

There is now an increase in stress-related ailments. These are often due to our hectic lives, which leave little room for relaxation. Modern life is very competitive and, for many, becoming involved in competitive sport is the last thing people wish to do. Many, however, find that sport is a great release from everyday life and they find participating or watching sport refreshing and relaxing.

Alcohol consumption

Alcohol is a concentrated source of energy but cannot be available during exercise for our working muscles. Therefore many elite performers in sport do not drink alcohol and most drink very little.

The Health Development Agency recommends for adults (not necessarily sporting adults):

■ males: 3–4 units per day

■ females: 2–3 units per day.

A unit is half a pint of 'ordinary strength' beer (3.0%–3.5% alcohol = 90 calories), or one standard glass of wine (11% alcohol = 90 calories), or a single measure of spirits (38% alcohol = 50 calories).

'Binge drinking', which is a growing habit amongst teenagers and young adults, is particularly bad for health. It is better to spread alcohol consumption across the week and to leave some alcohol-free days.

Smoking

Few serious sportspeople smoke. There is overwhelming evidence that health and fitness are affected adversely by smoking, whatever age you are. Cigarettes contain tar, nicotine, carbon monoxide and other irritants that cause coughing for instance. Normally haemoglobin in the blood carries oxygen. Haemoglobin seems to prefer carbon monoxide when it is present in the body and once it has taken up carbon monoxide it is unable to take up oxygen again, therefore less oxygen is available for the body to work effectively. Up to 10% of the oxygen-carrying capacity can be lost in this way.

Drugs

The use of drugs whether they be recreational (for example cannabis) or performance-enhancing drugs (for example anabolic steroids) is widespread and can seriously affect the health and wellbeing of a sports performer.

case study 12.1

Smoking and sport

- The time needed to complete exercise trials increases after smoking.

- Endurance and capacity for exercise is reduced in proportion to the cigarettes smoked – the more you smoke the less fit you will be.

- Training has less effect on smokers – so you can train really hard but smoking can undo all the good work.

Smoking is the biggest cause of preventable death in the Western world. It kills more than 120 000 in the UK every year, with most dying from three main diseases: cancer, chronic obstructive lung disease (bronchitis and emphysema) and coronary heart disease. Around 29% of men and 25% of women in Great Britain smoke. However, these figures are an average for the population as a whole – the figures for those on low incomes and from poor backgrounds are much higher. One in two regular cigarette smokers will be killed by their habit.

Drug taking involves the use of chemicals that alter the way we feel and see things and is one of the oldest activities of the human race.

Even when there are serious consequences to their use – of tobacco, alcohol, cannabis, heroin or performance enhancing drugs in sport – those consequences will not always make people wish to stop using their drug of choice. If and when they do decide to give up they may find that this is harder than they thought.

There is often more to an addiction than the physical withdrawal symptoms. Addiction includes anxiety, depression and lowering of self-esteem. The pattern of these symptoms will depend not only on the drug used but also on the psychological makeup of the person and the circumstances in which that individual is attempting to remain drug free.

UK Sport has been designated by the government to deliver its policy objectives as the national anti-doping organisation, to represent government in international meetings and to coordinate the national anti-doping programme of testing and education and information for sport throughout the UK.

The core aim of anti-doping policy in the UK is the planning and delivery of an effective programme that:

- protects athletes' rights to participate in drug-free sport
- actively encourages the support of medical professionals and administrators
- is publicly accountable for its plans and outcomes.

A major landmark in the fight for drug-free sport was achieved in January 2002 when UK Sport published its Statement of Anti-Doping Policy. This was the result of widespread consultation both nationally and internationally and took over two years to develop. The policy set out the requirements of governing bodies and sports councils to deliver effective anti-doping systems. It brought the UK in line with all phases of the International Standard for Doping Control.

(Adapted from www.uksport.gov.uk)

Athletes are advised to check all medications and substances with their doctor or governing body medical officer. All substances should be checked carefully when travelling abroad as many products can, and do, contain different substances from those found in the UK.

Substances and methods are prohibited in sport for various reasons including:

- **Performance-enhancing effects**, which contravene the ethics of sport and undermine the principles of fair participation.

- **The health and safety of the athlete**. Some drug misuse may cause serious side effects, which can compromise an athlete's health. Using substances to mask pain/injury could make an injury worse or cause permanent damage. Some drug misuse may be harmful to other athletes participating in the sport.

- **Illegality**. It is forbidden by law to possess or supply some substances

Most sporting federations have anti-doping regulations to ensure that all athletes compete by the same principle of being drug free. The regulations aim to achieve drug-free sport through clearly stated policies, testing and sanctions. They are also intended to raise the awareness of drug misuse and to deter athletes from misusing prohibited drugs and methods.

Prohibited classes of substances include:

- stimulants
- narcotic analgesics
- anabolic agents
- anabolic androgenic steroids

case study 12.2 — Prohibited substances in sport

Prohibited substances may vary from sport to sport. It is the athlete's responsibility to know their sport's anti-doping regulations. In cases of uncertainty, it is important to check with the appropriate governing body or UK Sport and be sure to read carefully the anti-doping rules adopted by the relevant governing body and international sports federations.

(Adapted from www.uksport.gov.uk)

- other anabolic agents
- diuretics
- peptide hormones, mimetics and analogues
- substances with anti-oestrogenic activity
- masking agents.

Prohibited methods include:

- enhancement of oxygen transfer
- blood doping
- administration of products that enhance the uptake, transport and delivery of oxygen
- pharmacological, chemical and physical manipulation
- gene doping.

Classes of substances prohibited in certain circumstances:

- alcohol
- cannabinoids
- local anaesthetics
- glucocorticosteroids
- beta blockers.

See Unit 4 Preparation for Sport, page 80

Financial considerations

Many part-time sportspeople as well as full-time professionals now receive sponsorship, grants, appearance money and prize money. If you are serious about committing a large slice of your life to sport it is important, as you prepare for it, that you also take all the financial implications into consideration.

The influence of sponsorship on the development of sport has been enormous. Sport is now big business, with large amounts of money being spent by commercial companies on sports participants and events. For example a company such as Adidas might sponsor a top class tennis player to wear a particular style of training shoe. At the other end of the scale, a local hockey club might attract a small amount of money to go towards the first team kit.

There has also been a significant increase in sponsorship due to sports clothing being fashionable. There has been a huge increase in sales for instance in training shoes. Many people wear 'trainers' who would never dream of participating in sport! Nevertheless commercial companies recognise that top sports stars can be fashion role models for the young and therefore use them in advertising campaigns (Honeybourne, 2003).

For instance David Beckham and many other top football stars were featured heavily in an advertising campaign during the Euro 2004 championships.

case study 12.3 — Funding young athletes

There are some funds available but they are limited. For example you can apply to the Ron Pickering Fund, which was set up by the wife of the late Sports Commentator Ron Pickering to help up-and-coming young athletes. The telephone number to ring for an application form is 01438 715814.

There are some competitions that offer prize money but not very many for people of school age. For example if you were a national class junior cross-country runner taking part in the Reebok Challenge series of races you would be competing for the following prize money:

- 1st place: £100
- 2nd place: £75
- 3rd place: £50

If you won the series, of which there are six races, you would win an additional prize of £250.

Therefore if you were the best runner in the country you could win a total of £850!

case study 12.4 — Lottery money reduction for sport

Britain's aspiring Olympians have been warned to expect cuts in their funding in the wake of falling Lottery sales. The government has pledged to provide £14.1 million to cover UK Sport's programme for elite competitors until the Athens Olympics. While funding for the current crop of athletes should be unaffected in the short term, the development of new talent could suffer given anticipated falls in Lottery cash. Sport England, which allocates around £200 million of funds each year, is already warning organisations to look at ways of making savings ahead of expected cuts. Sport England has seen the Lottery money it allocates fall from a high of £268 million in 1997/98 to £170 million for 2002/03.

That figure is set to decline further if the current trend in Lottery sales continues. While UK Sport handles around £23 million of Lottery funding for elite competitors based on performance, Sport England deals largely with talent identification at grass-roots level.

Figure 12.1

Money allocated to some athletes has fallen over the last ten years

Sport England funding for world-class plans: 1997–2005

Athletics: £10.5 million

Boxing: £7.3 million

Canoeing: £6.5 million

Cycling: £10.9 million

Gymnastics: £8 million

Netball: £7.3 million

Rowing: £11.6 million

Rugby Union: £8 million

Sailing: £12.2 million

Swimming: £10.2 million

(Source: adapted from Sport England, 2005)

case study 12.5 — Rugby sponsorship

O_2 extends England deal

The mobile phone network operator, O_2, entered into a sponsorship deal with the rugby world champions, England. The deal lasts for four years, beginning in 2004, costing the business £3 million each year. O_2 already had an ongoing relationship with the Rugby Football Union, which it has been supporting since 1995.

The deal secures sponsorship of the England official shirt until 2008 and the funds will also filter down to the grass roots, where the money will be used to develop young players. Former England coach, Sir Clive Woodward, said of the deal 'O_2 has been a longstanding supporter of the England rugby team and has made a great contribution to the sport.'

case study 12.6 Turning professional as a surfer

The fact that Britain's top male surfer, Sam Lamiroy, comes from Newcastle just goes to prove that with dedication you don't have to have sports facilities on the doorstep to succeed. Most British surfers come from Devon or Cornwall.

Sam took up surfing at the age of 11 and most of what he learned in those early days was from watching good surfers. In fact no one told him how to paddle or perform on a board. After three years of self-training with friends, he became proficient and did not consider turning professional until he was around 20 years old.

Sam entered his first competitions at the age of 17 and to his astonishment he was ranked fifth in the world in the World Junior Championships. Sam lacked funding and despite the opportunity to turn professional opted to go to university for three years. This bought him valuable time to take a long, hard look at the sport and, above all, to make initial contact with sponsors.

Sam was under no illusion that any sponsor providing money or equipment would want something in return for their investment. Sponsors tend to want a sportsperson or athlete to have attained a notable level of success, or it may be that the individual represents the type of lifestyle associated with their products or services. Sam quickly realised that he had to be a good surfer to attract sponsorship. He slowly built up his sponsorship, firstly at a local level and then at a national level.

Businesses such as those providing surfing products have sponsorship budgets. Sam prepared a brief background on himself and his competition results and sent it to all potential sponsors. He briefly outlined what he could offer and what he expected in return. Sam recognised the fact that he could not expect huge amounts of money or lavish gifts and began with t-shirts, watches, wetsuits and other surfing related equipment.

Sam adopted the gradual approach and over time he could ask for more sponsorship and get it. Once he began competing abroad he began to ask for a travel budget.

Sam recognises that any press coverage has a value. If a photograph or a feature about him appears in a newspaper or magazine he finds out how much that amount of space would be worth if he had to pay for it by placing an advertisement. He then gets a firm idea as to the value of the coverage he has achieved. He can then approach a sponsor and say that he has had £5,000 worth of coverage and ask for £2,000 worth of sponsorship. That way the sponsoring business feels that they are getting a good deal out of the sponsorship.

(Adapted from www.bbc.co.uk/sport, 2004)

Travel

As a sportsperson now or in the future you have to deal with increased travelling. Some individual sportspeople on the professional tennis circuit are always travelling and flying around the world. Although this sounds glamorous and exciting it can be extremely stressful and can harm personal relationships with your friends, partner or family. When you find yourself in a different culture and climate you need to adapt to it so that your sports performance does not suffer.

---

case study

12.7

Dealing with heat – Athens Olympics, 2004

The Athens Olympic Games were held under very hot conditions. The heat hugely affected performances. Athletes who had prepared thoroughly were less affected. The English Institute of Sport (EIS) researched the Greek conditions for over 6 years. The average temperature in Athens was 34°C. To prepare athletes for the Olympics, they built a room to recreate the Athens environment – the Heat Chamber.

It replicates temperatures from 4°C to 34°C with air conditioning and heaters, and altitude conditions from sea level up to 3000 m by extracting oxygen from the air.

A 10-minute session is enough for many of the athletes. Rehydration was crucial in Athens with athletes losing 10–15 litre of fluid a day. And every litre lost should be replaced by 1.5 times that amount.

It is vital to bring down core body temperature before, during and after exercise or competing. Ice jackets, cooling wrists and feet in tanks of cold water, and applying ice towels to the head and neck were all used. Pinsent and Cracknell and the other rowers all did it, as well as the cyclists and even the hockey team. The EIS researches other environmental factors such as pollution and the cold of Winter Olympics. And they've already started looking ahead to Beijing. The humidity will be about 95% for the 2008 Chinese Olympics so the heat chamber will be soon be brought into use again by the British athletes.

Ice Jackets

The ice jacket slows the rise of an athlete's body temperature by approximately 19%, reducing the risk of overheating and heat stroke and allowing the athlete a higher level of performance. Only 25% of our total body's energy goes into moving muscle while 75% is used to regulate heat.

Medical support

All sports people at the top level and many below have medical support for their training and competitions. Professional footballers have in-house physiotherapists and masseurs and the weekend footballer may well visit a physiotherapist because of an injury. There is a wide range of medical support now for sportspeople:

- chartered physiotherapy
- sports therapy
- sports massage
- osteopathy
- chiropractic
- doctors
- surgeons
- podiatry
- chiropody
- complementary therapy.

Sports medicine

Exercise and sports medicine practitioners look after the medical care of illness in sport, giving advice about exercise programmes and also dealing with injuries caused by exercise and sport. Sports medicine is not, at the moment, part of the NHS, so there is a limited amount of expertise available.

See Unit 2 Health, Safety and Injury in Sport, page 34

---

case study

12.8

A typical day in the life of a sports therapist who works for the English Institute of Sport

A sports therapist often works as a part of a multidisciplinary team to provide a quality service to the athletes. During the course of a typical day about six athletes are seen during the morning for consultations and more in the afternoon. There are meetings with other staff during the day, such as physiotherapists and strength-and-conditioning staff, to review the progress of particular rehabilitation cases. Their must be excellence in communication with other members of the multidisciplinary team; otherwise the team will not be effective in the treatment of the athletes.

There are nine sports represented, including track and field. About 70% of the cases are injuries, about 20% are medical problems in sport and about 10% are underperformance issues – people not performing to their potential and wanting to find out if there a medical reason for it.

Pressure and demands

There are many different pressures and demands on sportsmen and women, whatever their level of performance. Factors that can affect sports performance include family commitments and expectations. Training for sport can be a very selfish activity because you need to train mostly on your own in individual sports or with the rest of a team in team sports. This often means being away from home – an hour or two per week for the casual sportsperson and several weeks if you are an Olympic athlete preparing for a major competition.

Other team members can be very demanding, not only with their expectations of you but also as competitors for places. If you are in a large premiership football squad you may be friends with other players but you often have to compete with them for a place in the team and this can cause friction and disagreement among people who have been close friends.

Coaches and managers can also be very demanding and they may be unrealistic at times. It is important that you share your goals with your coach so that you agree what is expected from you.

In the world of sponsorship and business, with the media becoming involved in sport, there are many commercial pressures. Many top professional sportspeople can often be distracted by the demands of commercial companies, so much so that their own sports performance may suffer.

case study 12.9

In it for the money – the pressures on a tennis star?

Anna Kournikova achieved fame by reaching the Wimbledon semi-finals in 1996. Since then she has given relatively poor performances on court, but nonetheless sponsors, the public and the media seem to have been obsessed with her. In 2002 she was knocked out in the first round of Wimbledon and it seemed for many that the world's love affair with the tennis player had come to an end. Her critics describe her as being arrogant, disinterested in tennis and sulky. She was interviewed on the day that she was knocked out by Tatiana Panova. It was a revealing interview. Garry Richardson asked the question whether she would consider stepping down to challenger tournaments in order to regain her confidence. Kournikova simply wanted to talk about the match and not the future. She was asked how she could regain her confidence, to which she replied that she would work hard to do that. She agreed that she needed to concentrate and that despite her game not being as successful as it had been, she refused to give up tennis.

Before the interview she was asked at a news conference whether her media career got in the way of her tennis career, to which she replied, 'I don't think it distracts from my tennis. I am not involved in a lot of stuff. It is ninety-nine per cent less than what everyone says I do. Trust me – if I was not a hundred per cent committed to playing, I wouldn't be here.'

Former Grand Slam doubles winner, Pam Shriver, commented on Kournikova, saying that she had a great coach and that she was desperate to regain her form. Shriver recognised that Kournikova was often unprofessional and that her attitude was not exactly correct for a professional tennis player. Shriver was quoted as saying, 'She is like that a lot of the time off camera. If you talk to people behind the scenes they will tell you that was the real Anna Kournikova. Right now I don't think she can come back. I think she is mentally shattered.'

John Lloyd also commented on Kournikova's attitude. He felt that even though she was having a bad time in the sport, that she should accept this and that in any case she was still making a lot of money. She should also be able to handle difficult questions and media attention because she had always been willing to attract it in the first place.

Kournikova is one of the richest sportswomen in the world, having starred in music videos, Hollywood films, television, magazines and newspaper advertisements. Financially her career has been a huge success. But unfortunately all of these have got in the way of her ability to perform on the tennis court. Her latent talent is still there, having been able to win a singles title on the Women's Tennis Association(WTA) tour. Perhaps it has come to a point with Kournikova that she is so successful elsewhere that she no longer needs tennis to underpin her career.

Opportunities to train and compete

Some have more opportunities than others to play sport, to train and to enter competitions. There are now fewer people participating in sport (see below).

case study 12.10   **Against the odds**

Gail Devers – USA running star
Every athlete has two main obstacles in life – illness and injury.

US running star, Gail Devers, became interested in athletics when she was 15 years old. She was encouraged by her elder brother and soon learned to love the sport, setting herself a series of targets, which she sought to achieve. Like many athletes, Devers has had to cope with both illness and injury. In 1989 she was diagnosed as suffering from Graves disease. It should have been the peak of her career but it left her exhausted. Graves disease is a thyroid disorder and before it was diagnosed she believed that her athletics training was having a negative impact on her body. At her lowest point she even believed that her feet would need to be amputated, but with the backing of her family and her doctor she overcame the illness and won gold medals for the 100 metres at both Barcelona and Atlanta. She firmly believes that whether it's illness or injury, you have either to conquer it, or be conquered.

At an early age Devers got into the habit of setting herself personal goals. Each of these she writes down and is determined to succeed in them no matter how long it takes her. She began her career primarily as a hurdler but has never won an Olympic gold medal. Nonetheless this has not put her off and she still strived to win that elusive gold.

Figure 12.2
'I am willing to conquer every obstacle that stands in my way. No matter how long that may take'
(Gail Devers)

Appropriate Behaviour for an Elite Athlete

The right type of behaviour is important if an athlete is to reach the top and stay there. The following are expected types of behaviour for an elite athlete:

- **Sticking to the rules**. This also includes adhering to the spirit of the rules. Whether you are football player, a gymnast or a skier it is important that you are aware of the rules and abide by them but also that you retain a sense of fair play that should be part of sport.

- **Respect for others**. Any athlete should be respectful to others. Most elite competitors appreciate the skills of their fellow competitors and show respect towards them. Like other situations in life, the more you show respect the more likely it is that you will receive respect from others. It is also appropriate to show respect for the decisions made by officials such as referees and umpires as well as spectators who, in professional sport, are probably paying your wages.

- **Acting as a role model**. Others will look up to you and want to copy you if you are a successful athlete. Others will not only want to copy your skills but will also want to copy your general behaviour. Young people who watch elite athletes will often copy the way they prepare and train but also the way in which they act towards other athletes or to officials. Therefore elite athletes have a responsibility to behave appropriately because they are likely to be copied.

- **Appearance**. Those who follow and watch elite athletes can also copy the way they look. It is important that your clothing is appropriate to the activity and that your conduct and manners are acceptable – again because you may well be copied by young people who are learning how to behave.

- **Awareness of situations**. Elite athletes must be aware that different situations demand different ways of behaving and dressing. A visit to a church for instance may mean that you wear more formal attire but if on holiday casual clothes are more acceptable – remember if you are in the public eye there may well be newspaper reporters following you along with photographers and so it is always necessary to be aware of your behaviour and your appearance.

The Factors that Influence the Effective Planning of a Career

Elite athletes should ensure that they set goals that are going to motivate them but also so that they gain confidence and can plan for the future. Goals can be short, medium or long term.

By setting goals you can:

- achieve more
- improve your performance
- improve your training

- increase your motivation

- increase your pride and satisfaction.

Goal setting is a very powerful technique that can lead to high rewards and increase your motivation levels. By knowing what you want to achieve, you know what you need to concentrate on and improve. You also know what to ignore because these aspect may be distracting.

Goal setting is a useful strategy and one that is widely used in sport for training and performance. Goal setting is a proven way of increasing motivation and confidence and controlling anxiety.

Effective goal setting

For goal setting to be effective there must be short-term goals leading to longer-term goals. For example to win the league cup, the netball team may have to concentrate on winning more games away from home. For this to be achieved, there may be short-term goals of improving the defending strategies of the team.

Motivation can be increased by splitting long-term goals into medium-term and short-term goals, which are more specific and manageable over a short period of time.

SMARTER goal setting

S – **Specific**. If goals are clear and unambiguous they are more likely to be reached.

M – **Measurable**. This is important for monitoring and makes you accountable.

A – **Agreed**. The sharing of goal setting between coach/instructor and performer can give a sense of teamwork.

R – **Realistic**. Motivation will improve if goals can actually be reached.

T – **Timed**. An effective approach is to split goals up into short-term goals that are planned and progressive.

E – **Exciting**. The more stimulating the activities can be the more motivating is their effect.

R – **Recorded**. Recording is crucial for monitoring and, once achieved, can be deleted or checked-off, thus improving motivation.

See Unit 8 Technical Skills and Tactical Awareness for Sport

Goals for the elite athlete must take into consideration the following:

- any changes of coach and/or clubs

- a second career – for example as a coach, teacher, sports centre/gym assistant

- plans in case of injury or illness

- financial goals – financial advice should be sought, preferably from a recognised, independent financial consultant including advice about taxation, pension, savings and insurance.

Being Able to Communicate Effectively with the Media and Significant Others

If you communicate effectively with others, then they are more likely to see your point of view. It is also important that communicating includes listening to others and acting upon appropriate advice. Effective communication skills include:

- **Listening to others** – to gain advice/coaching points and to manage your anxiety.

- **Asking questions** – to obtain all the information you can from experts and to build on your knowledge of the sport/skills and your opponents.

- **Discussion skills** – keeping calm and have a balanced point of view that takes the views of others into account. Communicate your ideas clearly and to back up your points with evidence.

- **Writing** – you may have to write down key points and be able to summarise, for example, coaching points. You need to write clearly and effectively.

To work effectively with other people it is important to establish good working relationships with those around you. You need to get on with coaching staff, managers, advisers and other athletes. It is also advisable to review your relationships with others. For example, if you are not getting on with your coach then think about what you can do to try to improve matters between you. You may decide to 'clear the air' and raise some points that are worrying you, but remember politeness and manners will help you to get your point across.

The media

Any elite athlete must realise that the media play an important part in sport, either to inform or to entertain. The media include TV, radio and the press/print media. The media could be local, national or international and each section of the media has its own interests.

Influences of the media

Television companies spend an enormous amount of money to secure the broadcasting rights to sports events. To view certain events such as boxing the subscriber must often make an extra payment (pay-per-view). Sky, for example, holds the rights to many Premiership football games, which can only be viewed if you subscribe to a Sky package. Digital TV has also influenced sport and not always to everyone's benefit. The collapse of ITV Digital in 2002 meant that many football teams were facing financial disaster, having been promised a considerable amount of money that was then not forthcoming.

The terrestrial channels such as BBC and ITV have lost many of the major sports events and the ludicrous situation arises whereby the BBC's news programme is unable to show a clip of a boxing match because the rights to that match are owned by another company. There has never before been so much coverage of sport on TV but, because of satellite TV dominating this coverage, only those who can afford to subscribe have access to many sports events. Football receives the most coverage but coverage for other sports can be quite limited. Male sport also still dominates, although there is a refreshing interest in women's football, for instance.

The needs of the TV companies have led to revised event programming. Football fans, for instance, are finding that their team may play on a Sunday at 6.00 p.m., which has not traditionally been a time slot for the game. Events at the Olympic Games are often scheduled at unsuitable times because of the demands of TV companies, which are beaming the event around the world across different time zones.

The media have influenced the rules of sport. For instance, in cricket the third umpire in the form of a video replay analysis has come into force, largely due to the influence of TV. There has been a similar development in rugby football. The armchair spectator can now see the event at every angle and the officials' decisions are laid bare for scrutiny, hence the need for new technology to aid the decision makers on the field of play (Honeybourne, 2003).

The extent of media involvement has also influenced the amount of sponsorship and advertising revenue available to participants, clubs and other sports organisations.

Figure 12.3

Advertising revenue is a significant source of income for the elite athlete

This has brought much-welcomed money into sport but some may argue that it has only gone to a small number of participants in a small number of sports and may well have led to the decrease in participation in minority sports.

The media can increase participation in sport. You only have to see the increased activity on municipal tennis courts during the Wimbledon fortnight to appreciate that watching sport can stimulate participation.

Our interest in playing a sport increases when the media highlights the success of UK sports performers. There was a surge of interest in curling, for instance, after success in the Winter Olympics.

Types of media involved in sport include:

- television: BBC, ITV, Channel 4, Channel 5, Satellite, Cable, Digital, factual/fiction /advertising
- press: broadsheets, tabloids, local, weekly, magazines, periodicals

- radio: national, local, commercial
- cinema: documentaries, movies.

Planning and delivery for the media

When appearing or being reported by the media, effective planning will ensure that there are no misunderstandings/embarrassments or misrepresentation of the elite athletes' views.

Before being interviewed or filmed elite athletes must take into account:

- The purpose of the interview (whether it is to promote you/criticise you or just to ask your opinion).
- Likely questions (rehearse some of your answers).
- Sensitive issues – for example you may be interviewed abroad, so it is important to understand what may offend or upset the people of that country.
- The type of speech to use. Is it appropriate to be humorous or serious? Is it appropriate to dress informally or formally?
- Your body language. If you are trying to put an important point across show that you really mean what you are saying by appearing confident. Look the interviewer in the eye and sit or stand upright, again showing confidence.

You might use prompt/crib sheets, or a script that you learn. This would be more likely with an important statement.

progress check

1 How can alcohol and smoking affect physical fitness?

2 Name three prohibited substances in sport.

3 What financial considerations must you take in to account as an elite athlete?

4 What other pressures and demands can affect the elite athlete?

5 Describe three guidelines for appropriate behaviour as an elite athlete.

6 How can goal setting help your career planning as an elite athlete?

7 Explain how, as an elite athlete, you can communicate more effectively with those around you.

8 Name three types of media.

9 What influences does the media have on sport and athletes?

10 Describe how you would plan for an interview with the media after a competition.

UNIT 13

Work-based Project in Sport

This units covers:

- the range and scope of organisations and occupations within the sports industry
- relevant documents and skills relating to sport-based work experience
- planning and carrying out a project during the sport-based work experience
- presenting and reviewing the project

This unit covers material to support Unit 13 of the BTEC First Diploma in Sport. It covers how to identify, plan and complete a practical work-based project and supports your sport related work experience placement. Interview skills will be explored, as well as documents relating to applying for work. It also covers the ability to record activities and evaluate them. During the placement you must complete a project that will be supported by material in this unit.

grading criteria

To achieve a **Pass** grade the evidence must show that the learner is able to:	To achieve a **Merit** grade the evidence must show that the learner is able to:	To achieve a **Distinction** grade the evidence must show that the learner is able to:
P1 Describe three different types of organisations within the sports industry, giving examples	**M1** Explain the skills required for three different occupations within the sports industry	**D1** Evaluate own personal skills and qualities in relation to those required for an occupation in sport, and suggest ways to improve own skills and qualities
P2 Describe three different occupations within the sports industry, and the skills that each require	**M2** Use sources of advertisements for jobs available in sport to identify an appropriate work-based experience in sport	**D2** Present the project, evaluating the benefits and justifying recommendations relating to identified areas for improvements
P3 Identify sources of advertisements for jobs available within the sports industry, and provide three different examples of advertisements	**M3** Relate own personal skills and qualities, to those required for an occupation in sport, identifying areas for improvement	

grading criteria

To achieve a **Pass** grade the evidence must show that the learner is able to:	To achieve a **Merit** grade the evidence must show that the learner is able to:	To achieve a **Distinction** grade the evidence must show that the learner is able to:
P4 Produce an application for a work-based experience in sport, describing personal skills and qualities in documentation prepared	**M4** Present the project, explaining the benefits and making recommendations for improvement	
P5 Prepare for an interview for work-based experience in sport		
P6 Undertake an interview for work-based experience in sport		
P7 Plan a project, listing realistic objectives, proposed outcomes and timescale, to be related to, and carried out in, work-based experience in sport		
P8 Undertake a project in a work-based experience in sport		
P9 Present the project, describing the benefits and identifying areas for improvement		

The Range and Scope of Organisations and Occupations Within the Sports Industry

Sports organisations

Organisations that are associated with sport in the UK can be divided into Public, Private and Voluntary. Most people have to pay taxes to the government, who in turn fund the public organisations. The private sector organisations are usually commercial businesses that try to make a profit. The voluntary organisations are usually run and funded by people on a volunteer basis and do not exist to make a profit.

See Unit 3 The Sports Industry

- Public facilities include the local leisure centre, they are usually run by a local authority and funded via the taxpayer.
- Private facilities include the local private health and fitness club, people often pay a monthly membership fee to use facilities.
- The voluntary sector facilities include the local athletics club. The Youth Hostel Association is another example of a voluntary organisation.

Public, private and voluntary

Local authorities often run the public sector organisations. They can promote sport according to their own particular local needs, such as promoting basketball to improve levels of participation and excellence and to improve basketball court facilities.

The private sector also provides sport according to local needs and often strives to get as many people involved as possible, to raise attendance levels and, very importantly because they are money-making organisations, to improve their profits. An example of a private club would be LA Fitness Health and Fitness Club, who provide the equipment, instructions in fitness activities and personal training.

The voluntary sector too aims to help provide support for local needs. It often involves the promotion of specific sports, such as the local hockey club that strives to get as many people to play hockey as possible and encourages players from all walks of life. Such a club would run teams in local leagues and hold training sessions for their members.

Leisure industry

keyword

Leisure Industry
This involves the products and services that surround leisure activities.

The **Leisure Industry** has grown rapidly over the last 20 years. Many people have more leisure time and are now more willing to spend money on leisure activities. When money is spent continuously in one area the use of facilities and opportunities for its users grow, hence the growth of the leisure industry. Sport is very commercialized, with events and sports competitors themselves being sponsored for large sums of money.

Leisure centres and health clubs

There has been a tremendous growth in the number of health clubs and leisure centres both in the private sector, owned by a commercial company, and in the public sector, run by local councils and subsidized by the tax-payer.

Unit 3 The Sports Industry, page 55

Occupations in the sports industry

The following list includes some of the careers available in sport:

- Sport-centre worker
- Fitness instructor

- Sports coach
- Sports development officer
- Sports scientist
- Professional sports performer
- Sports groundsman
- Sports therapist
- Physiotherapist.

case study 13.1 — Occupations in sport

Using the following websites or contact details, find out the responsibilities involved in, and the skills required for, two or three occupations or careers in sport:

National Training Organisation for Sport, Recreation and Occupations (SPRITO)
E-mail: the.nato@sprito.org.uk
Sports Coach UK
www.sportscoachuk.org
British Olympic Association
www.olympics.org.uk
British Sports Trust
www.thebritishsportstrust.org.uk/
Central Council of Physical Recreation (CCPR)
www.ccpr.org.uk
The Teacher Training Agency (TTA)
www.teach.org.uk
Womens Sports Foundation
www.wsf.org.uk
Youth Sport Trust
www.youthsport.org

Relevant Documents and Skills Relating to Sport-based Work Experience

keyword

Curriculum vitae
This is a brief account of a person's qualitifications, education, previous occupations and experience.

The presentation of personal information

Your curriculum vitae (CV)

Tips for creating the perfect **curriculum vitae** are:

- Keep it simple.
- It must be concise, do not waffle!

- It must be easy to read, avoid jargon and use a spell checker to check there are no mistakes.

- It is a document to display all your best qualities, but be careful not to be too clever or to lie or over exaggerate things.

Your curriculum vitae must be tailored to what the reader is looking for. CV writing is like advertising; your CV must sell you to an employer. You will be competing against other applicants who are also trying to sell themselves, so the challenge in CV writing is to be more appealing and attractive than the rest. This means that your curriculum vitae must be presented professionally, clearly, and in a way that indicates you are an ideal candidate for the job. You will be judged by the way you present your CV because it demonstrates your ability to communicate, a messy and disorganised CV may mean a messy and disorganised person.

You must try to show that you possess the right skills, experience and attitude that the employer is looking for. The employer will have a good idea of what sort of person they are looking for and what sort of skills they need, therefore your curriculum vitae should reflect the job description. The better the match the more likely you are to be called for an interview.

Presentation and order is important. A well presented CV indicates that you are professional, business-like and well organised. You should aim to fit your CV on one side of a standard sheet of A4 paper. A well presented single side of paper will always tend to impress and impact more than lots of detail spread over a number of sheets, you need to keep the readers concentration. Always try to use

Figure 13.1

Suggested curriculum vitae structure

Name . . . .
Personal Details . . . .
Date of birth . . . .
Age . . . .
Gender . . . .
Marital status . . . .
Address . . . .
Telephone number and mobile . . . .
E-mail address . . . .
Education and qualifications: Institution – dates – awards (qualifications e.g. GCSE's and first aid awards/ Duke of Edinburgh Awards) – grades
Work Experience (other than the position you are applying for). Also include part time jobs you have done, especially if related to sport.
Interests: show that you are interested in sport related subjects and do not simply put 'socialising'.

as few words as possible and think carefully about the words you use – make sure they make sense. Never use two words when one will do.

case study 13.2 — Royal Mail

A 2004 UK survey by the Royal Mail postal service of Human Resource (HR) departments in large organisations identified these other CV pointers:

- Incompletely or inaccurately addressed CV's and CV cover letters were rejected immediately by 83% of HR departments.

- CV's and cover letters addressed to a named person were significantly favoured over those addressed to a job title by 55% of HR departments.

- Over 60% of HR departments said that the inclusion of a photograph with the CV adversely affected their opinion of the applicant.

(Source: Royal Mail 2004)

Once you have completed your draft CV, get another person to look at it and invite comments. People such as teachers, parents or friends may point out small errors that could be easily corrected. They may spot problems in the CV that you have missed.

Figure 13.2

Once you have completed your draft CV, get another person to look at it and invite comments

keyword

Cover letters
A letter to accompany your CV which covers the main points and highlights your best experience, skills and abilities in relation to the job you are applying for.

CV cover letters

CV **cover letters** must be very professional and perfectly presented. Use a smart, good quality paper, and ensure that the name, address details and date are correct and personal for the recipient of the CV. Do not use scruffy photocopies – ideally do not use photocopies at all – CV cover letters should look individual and specified for the job concerned.

Look at what the job advert is seeking. Ensure that the key skills, attributes and experience are reflected in the cover letter as well as your CV. Draw the reader's attention to the fact that your profile fits their requirements. Make the cover letter look like a direct response to the job advert and personal profile that is sought.

Keep CV cover letters brief and concise. The reader will make assumptions about you from what you write and how you write it, and from the quality of your cover letter presentation.

Sample CV cover letter

Ensure you lay the letter out neatly on good quality paper, with your own address top right or centre-top. Avoid fancy fonts and upper case (capital letters). Use a single font 10–12 point size (Times New Roman or Arial are best), you could use bold or underlined for the reference or headings if you have any.

CV cover letters for unadvertised positions or opportunities

It is perfectly fine to send a speculative CV to potential employers, i.e. not in response to any advert. In this case you should get the name of the senior person responsible for staffing decisions in the area you wish to apply (call the

Figure 13.3
A CV cover letter

Full name and address

Date

Reference if required

Dear (Mr/Mrs/Ms Surname)

(optional heading, bold or underlined – normally the job title and or reference if they've asked you to quote one)

I enclose my CV in respect of the above reference (or state position advertised and when it appeared). You will see that I have the required skills, capabilities and experience for this position, notably (state two or three attributes briefly).

I look forward to hearing from you.

Yours sincerely (use Yours faithfully if you do not know the name of the person you are writing to)

(Sign)

(And below print your name – not hand-written)

company to find out the correct name and address details, it will often be someone in HR). In these cases you will not know precisely what skills they are seeking, but you should be able to imagine the type of person that they might need. Here are some examples – include two or three in your cover letter that best match your own profile and their likely interest:

- reliable and dependable
- decisive and results driven
- creative problem solver
- team-player
- technically competent/qualified (state discipline or area)
- commercially experienced and aware
- task orientated – you like to complete a job and have pride in completing it properly
- excellent interpersonal and communications skills
- sound planning and organisational capabilities
- loyal and determined.

Speculative sample CV cover letter sample

Again, ensure you lay the letter out neatly on good quality paper, with your own address top right or centre-top. Avoid fancy fonts and upper case (capital letters). Use a single font, maybe bold or underlined for the reference or heading if you use one.

Figure 13.4

A speculative CV cover letter

Full name and address details.

Date

Dear (Mr/Mrs/Ms Surname)

(optional heading, bold or underlined - in this example you would normally refer to a job title, and include with the word 'opportunities' or 'openings', for example: 'leisure assistant opportunities')

I am interested in any openings in the above area and enclose my CV. You will see that I have skills and capabilities that enable me to make a significant contribution to an organisation such as your own, notably (state two or three attributes skills or attitudes you have).

I look forward to hearing from you.

Yours sincerely (use Yours faithfully if you do not know the name of the person you are writing to)

(Sign)

(And below print your name – not hand-written)

As you can see, CV cover letters can be short and very concise. Cover letters need to be, otherwise people won't read them. Writing a short, concise cover letter for you CV also shows confidence and professionalism. The bigger the job, the longer you can make your CV cover letters. Make your key points in a no-nonsense fashion and then finish.

Your CV and your cover letter must sell you and must be tailored to what the reader is looking for. Always keep copies of your CV and cover letters so that you can remember what you have written, in case you are asked about them in an interview. Remember never lie in your CV, not only can this be seen as against the law it will also get you into hot water if you get the job and someone discovers you have lied – you could then lose your job!

Interview skills

You may be called for an **interview** for your work placement and of course you will probably have an interview when you finally apply for a full time job. There are many differing ideas about how to prepare for an interview, but there are some basic tips that all interviewees should bear in mind. Remember interviews are a two-way process – the interviewer has every right to find out more about you and whether you are right for the job. Some interviewers are better at doing this than others. It is well known that some interviewers will make up there mind as soon as you walk through the door, so **first impressions** really are important.

Types of interview vary considerably. There is no standard interview and many interviews develop because of the communication or interaction between the interviewee and interviewer. Interviews are not consistently successful at selecting the right person for a job, but it is still the most favoured way of selection. Getting a mock interview is a good way of getting some advice and practising for the real thing – but remember there is no such thing as a standard interview, so be prepared for anything!

keyword

Interview
An interview is often a formal discussion between a job applicant and employer to fill a vacancy, it is really an oral examination of the job applicant.

keyword

First impressions
A first impression is the initial opinion you form of someone when you meet him or her for the first time. First impressions can be based on a person's body language, clothes, gestures or what they say.

Figure 13.5

It is well known that some interviewers will make up their mind soon after you walk through the door and so first impressions really are important

Figure 13.6

Getting a mock interview is a good way of getting some advice and practising for the real thing

case study 13.3 — Interviews

Things to avoid in an interview:

- Talking too much or too little.
- Yawning – or looking bored or gazing out of the window.
- Swearing or using inappropriate language.
- Sniffing!
- Fiddling with your ear/nose or any other part of your anatomy.

Things to do in an interview:

- Be alert and seem interested (even if you are not).
- Smile and be friendly and polite.
- Listen carefully – if you do not understand a question then say so.
- Answer the questions – try not to waffle!
- Be yourself – try not to pretend that you are someone you are not.

The interview

Interviewers commonly assess interviewees according to their own personal style and approach – people like people who are similar to them. For example, friendly people like friendly people; results-driven people like results-driven people; dependable reliable passive people like dependable reliable passive people; and detailed correct people like detailed correct people.

As an interviewee be aware that even the most objective interviewer – even if aided by psychometric job profiles and applicant test results – will always tend to be more attracted to applicants who are like them, rather than applicants who are unlike them; it is human nature.

- Research as much as you can about the company – products, services, markets, competitors, trends, current activities, and priorities.

- Prepare your answers for the type of questions you will be asked; be able to say why you want the job, what your strengths are, how you would do the job and what your best achievements are.

- Assemble hard evidence (make sure it is clear and concise) of how you have achieved all the things you have done.

- Make sure your CV is up to date and take three copies with you (one for the interviewer, one for you and a spare in case the interviewer brings a colleague to the meeting).

- Get hold of relevant material and read it, such as the company's sales brochures (for example a fitness club leaflet on courses and literature); a trade magazine (for leisure management covering the company's market sector) and a broadsheet newspaper (such as The Times) a few days before the interview, so that you are informed about world and national news.

- Review your personal goals and be able to speak openly and honestly about them, and how you plan to achieve them.

- Get into an enthusiastic, alert and positive mind set.

remember

Proof of experience will put you ahead of those who merely talk about it.

case study 13.4 — Preparation

Make sure you know:

- where the interview actually is
- the time of the interview (punctuality is absolutely essential)
- alternative ways of getting there (just in case the bus doesn't turn up!)
- who you have to ask for
- where you have to meet.

Make sure you:

- do not sit on the edge of the chair or slump in the back of the chair
- do not wave your hands about

- do wear something appropriate for the interview – get advice from friends, a parent or teachers for this

- read what has been sent to you – there may be clues about what to expect in the interview

- get some information about the job / company / leisure centre / sports club

- anticipate questions that might be asked and practice the answers

- work out the questions that you want to ask.

case study 13.5 — Possible interview questions

Question:
'Tell me about your life at college or your time in your previous job'

Answer:
The question is an opportunity for you to demonstrate the qualities that the interviewer is seeking for the job, so steer your answer towards these expectations (without distorting the truth obviously). In your answer, emphasise the positive behaviour, experience and achievements (ideally backed up with examples and evidence), which will impress the interviewer because of its relevance to the requirements of the job. The interviewer is looking for the same capabilities and behaviour in your college life (or previous job) that they want in the job. Your emphasis should be on your achievements, and how you achieved them, that are relevant to the job requirements.

Question:
'What do you want to be doing in 2/5/10 years time? Or: Where do you want to be in 2/5/10 years time?'

Answer:
Say you want to make a significant contribution to whatever organisation you are working for and to develop new skills and abilities. Tell them you hope to become better qualified in whatever way suits the situation and opportunities you have. Say you also want to be better regarded by your peers, and respected by your bosses as someone who can continue to contribute successfully to the organisation.

Question:
'Why do you want this job (or work experience placement)?'

Answer:
Reflect back the qualities required (see job requirements/specifications) as being the things you do best and enjoy. Say why you think the company / leisure centre / club is good, and that you want to work for an organisation like it.

Question:
'What are your strengths? '

Answer:
Prepare three that are relevant to the requirements of the job role. Be able to analyse why and how you are strong in those areas. Mix in some behaviours, knowledge and experience as well as skills, and show that you understand the difference.

Question:
'What are your weaknesses?'

Answer:
Acknowledge certain areas that you believe you can improve in (and then pick some relatively unimportant or irrelevant areas). If you must state a weakness then these are the clever ones that are actually strengths: not suffering fools gladly; sometimes being impatient with other people's sloppy work; being too demanding; refusing to give in when you believe strongly about something; trying to do too much.

Other typical questions:

- What was the last book you read and how did it affect you?

- Tell me about something recently that really annoyed you.

- Give me some examples of how you have adapted your own communicating style to deal with different people and situations.

- Tell me about yourself.

- If you won a million pounds on the lottery what would you do?

- Tell me a joke.

Planning and Carrying out a Project During Sport-Based Work Experience

During your work experience you will need to collect evidence for a work-based portfolio or project. This evidence could include:

- Placement logs or a diary of what has happened and what has been learned.
- Personal accounts of observing others at work.
- Witness style testimonies – from other workers who have seen you complete tasks successfully.
- Points for action, for example related to skills that you would need to develop further.

Your project must list key objectives, proposed outcomes (what you think you will learn or find out), time scales and resources. Part of your assessment will also be on how you present your project to others, listing the benefits to you as the project writer and to the institution. If you wish to get a distinction for this aspect, then make sure that you:

- compare and evaluate the effectiveness of two different methods chosen to present personal information
- evaluate the key objectives, time scales, resources and proposed outcomes for the project
- critically analyse the sports project making recommendations for changes for future activities.

Planning

The key to completing a worthwhile work placement and project is good planning. The documents that you use (recording documents) should be written before the placement.

remember

Keep accurate and clear records of all information that you have gathered during your placement.

Figure 13.7

Keep placement logs or a diary of what has happened and what has been learned

- Keep copies of your CV and job application/letter, as well as notes for your interview preparation.
- Record the aims and objectives and proposed outcomes of your project.
- Organise travel arrangements and accommodation if relevant.
- Organise any specialist clothing needed.

The activities you choose to look at in more depth for your project should be carefully selected. Do not try to be over ambitious. A project that is simple, but well done, is much better than trying to be too clever and not being able to achieve what you set out to do. Discuss your choice of project with your employer. A project that may be useful to the work place, as well as for you, will gain the support of your employer and will also ensure that they help you with the

Figure 13.8

You may need specialist clothing for your placement

information that you need. Your project, if your placement is at a gym club for instance, could be about at what times the gym is used the most and by whom.

Figure 13.9

Your project may be about at what times the gym is used the most and by whom

Key outcomes

Your project key outcomes could be related to specific areas of sport such as:

- coaching or training
- acquiring new skills or techniques
- sports coaching / leadership
- teamwork

■ customer care

■ health and safety procedures.

Skills

The skills that are needed and that you will acquire in your work placement should also be recorded and may include:

■ Practical skills – such as being able to erect a trampoline.

■ Technical skills – such knowing the right quantity of chemicals for a swimming pool.

■ People related – such as being able to work at reception and helping the public.

■ Teamwork, for example – working with others by preparing a sports facility.

Figure 13.10

Skills you acquire on placement may include being able to erect a trampoline

Presenting and Reviewing the Project

Monitor and review

Ensure that you write down what achievements you have made against your aims, objectives and targets. If, for example, your aim is to find out about how the public uses a particular facility, have you found all the relevant information? If you have tried to become more aware of the industry you are investigating, again write down what you have found. You may also monitor:

■ Skills that you have learned at your placement.

■ Activities you have undertaken – this may be related to coaching that you have undertaken.

■ Highlight methods of monitoring, e.g. interviews, witness testimonies, video evidence or tape recordings of interviews.

Review

This may take the form of a diary or a log of what you are doing and what you have achieved as you go along (formative review). You may also summarise at the end of your placement what has been achieved. You may also record what your strengths and weaknesses are and the benefits that have been shown, both to you as a student and for the work placement institution. Your own career development and progression opportunities (what you hope to do next either as a student or as a job).

Personal skills

The work placement may give you opportunities to develop personal skills, for example:

- practical skills of coaching or teaching
- skills related to numeracy, literacy or ICT
- clerical or administrative skills
- qualifications such as coaching awards or first aid
- personal qualities such as improving your communication skills.

Career Development

You will probably be thinking about what to do next after completing the BTEC qualification. You may decide to take the next level and to stay in education full time or you may wish to study part-time and get a part time job. You may decide to enter employment at this stage. Ask yourself:

a. What would I like to do as a job realistically?

b. What do I need in terms of skills and qualifications to do this job?

Presentation of your project

The way in which you present your project will be taken into consideration for grading purposes. The better your project is presented, the more likely you are to achieve a higher grade. The following are guidelines for a good presentation.

- Use the past tense. Record what has been done and what has been found, e.g. it was found that more females than males used the gym from 9.00am until 1.00pm.
- Keep your writing simple and clear. Avoid long-winded sentences.
- Write in sentences and check for spelling errors.
- Make sure you read through your whole project and correct any mistakes – get someone else to look through it to check before submitting the final project.
- Paragraphs should be present and should not be too long or short. Paragraphs should be at least two sentences long but should be no longer than a page in general.
- Use lots of headings to break the project up and to make it easier to follow.
- Number the pages.

remember

Visual Presentations:
- Each slide should include only the main points
- Keep the font size large to enable everyone to easily read the material
- Use colours to highlight the text
- Check for spellings and be grammatically correct
- Do not go on too long and give opportunity for questions from your audience.

You may also be asked to make other types of presentation for your findings, for example a short talk with a PowerPoint presentation. Preparation is crucial if this is going to work well. Stick to the important points of your project and include lots of visual material – photos/video clips/ leaflets etc. Start with an introduction, including the aims and objectives of your project. Use graphs and tables if you have data to present, but again keep them simple and clear. Give your conclusions at the end and relate your findings to your objectives.

Benefits to you and the institution

Figure 13.11

Preparation is crucial if a visual presentation is to work well

Possible benefits for you:

- Improved knowledge of sport.
- Improved knowledge and understanding of sports skills.
- Acquired new techniques in sport.
- Recognised a career path, e.g. you want to be a fitness instructor and you realise what you need to do to become one.
- Identified what progression opportunities (other courses to get qualifications) there are, for example to do a higher level course and to then complete fitness teaching exams.

Possible benefits to the institution:

- You have created new materials for others, for example fitness record cards.
- You have written case studies, for example you have recognised the benefits of exercise to the elderly that will be used in a gym leaflet/prospectus.
- You have done such a good job, that there will be other work placement opportunities.

progress check

1 What is meant by public, private and voluntary organisations?

2 Identify a typical career in sport – what are the responsibilities and skills related to this career?

3 What makes a good curriculum vitae (CV)?

4 Give five guidelines for someone who is going for an interview for a sport related placement.

5 Give four 'not to do' points for an interview.

6 Give a typical interview question and then write the answer that may help to secure the job.

7 How do you record information effectively for your project?

8 Identify how you would monitor and review your project.

9 Choose a career in sport and write down what qualifications and experience you need to get such a job.

10 What makes a good project presentation?

Instructing Exercise and Fitness

This unit covers:

- the principles of an effective exercise session and exercise programme
- planning an exercise programme
- assisting in instructing an exercise session
- undertaking a review of an exercise programme and an exercise session

This unit examines instructing exercise and fitness to complete Unit 14 of the BTEC First Diploma in Sport. It covers the principles behind effective exercise programmes and sessions. The planning of an exercise programme is covered, as well as how to assist in the teaching of exercise and fitness. The unit also looks at material that will enable you to undertake a review of an exercise session and an exercise programme.

grading criteria

To achieve a **Pass** grade the evidence must show that the learner is able to:	To achieve a **Merit** grade the evidence must show that the learner is able to:	To achieve a **Distinction** grade the evidence must show that the learner is able to:
P1 Describe the princples of fitness training	**M1** Explain the principles of fitness training	**D1** Relate the principles of fitness training to a range of clients with different needs
P2 Outline health and safety issues an exercise instructor needs to consider for their clients	**M2** Justify each part of the warm up and cool down	**D2** Plan exercise programmes justifying, the aims and range of activities suggested for three different types of clients
P3 Describe and instruct a warm up and a cool down	**M3** Produce detailed exercise programmes for three different types of clients	**D3** Demonstrate competence in monitoring and adapting exercises to suit different client ability levels
P4 Outline exercise programmes for three different types of clients	**M4** Demonstrate effective communication with selected clients	

grading criteria

To achieve a **Pass** grade the evidence must show that the learner is able to:	To achieve a **Merit** grade the evidence must show that the learner is able to:	To achieve a **Distinction** grade the evidence must show that the learner is able to:
P5 assist in instructing induction, resistance training, cardiovascular training and circuit training sessions for selected clients	**M5** Competently use different forms of feedback in order to review three different exercise programmes and exercise sessions	
P6 Use appropriate feedback to review three different exercise programmes and exercise sessions	**M6** Justify identified personal development needs	
P7 Review performance in the outlining of exercise programmes and in the instruction, and assisting the instruction, of exercise sessions, identify strengths and personal development needs		

The Principles of an Effective Exercise Session and Exercise Programme

Principles of training

A training programme should take into account differences between individuals. An individual's goals must be understood. For example, does the performer want to get generally fit or fit for a particular sport? The individual's current activity level must be assessed and initial fitness testing may be appropriate. The age, time available, equipment available and skill level must all be taken into consideration before the principles of training are applied.

keyword

Anaerobic
A high-intensity exercise where the muscles lack sufficient oxygen to successfully burn fuel.

Specificity

This principle indicates that the training undertaken should be specific and relevant to the appropriate needs of the activity or the type of sport involved. For instance, a sprinter would carry out more **anaerobic** training because the event is mostly anaerobic in nature. It is not just energy systems that have to be specific, muscle groups and actions involved in the training also have to be as specific as possible.

Figure 14.1

Training undertaken should be specific and relevant to the appropriate needs of the activity or the type of sport involved

There is, however, a general consensus that a good general fitness is required before any high degree of specificity can be applied.

Overload

This principle underpins the need to work the body harder than normal so that there is some stress and discomfort. Adaptation and progress will follow overload because the body will respond by adapting to the stress experienced. For instance in weight training the lifter will eventually attempt heavier weights or an increase in repetitions, thus overloading the body. Overload can be achieved by a combination of increasing the frequency, the intensity and the duration of the activity.

Progression

Not only has overload got to occur, but also it should progressively become more difficult. Once adaptations have occurred, then the performer should make even more demands on the body. It is important that progression does not mean overdoing it. Training must be sensibly progressive and realistic if it is to be effective, otherwise injury may occur and there would be regression instead of progression.

Figure 14.2

In weight training the lifter will eventually attempt heavier weights or an increase in repetitions, thus overloading the body

remember

The FITT approach

F = Frequency of training (number of training sessions each week)

I = Intensity of the exercise undertaken

T = Time or duration that the training takes up

T = Type of training to be considered that fulfils specific needs

Figure 14.3

Training must be sensibly progressive and realistic if it is to be effective

Reversibility

This principle states that performance can deteriorate if training stops or decreases in intensity for any length of time. If training is stopped, then the fitness gained will be largely lost. For instance VO_2 max and muscle strength can decrease.

Figure 14.4

If training is stopped, then the fitness gained will be largely lost

Variance

This principle states that there should be variety in training methods. If training is too predictable, then performers can become de-motivated and bored. Overuse injuries are also common when training is too repetitive with one muscle group or part of the body being overused; therefore variance can also help prevent injury.

Methods of fitness training

Warm-ups and Cool-downs

Warm-ups and cool-downs are very important aspects of any training programme:

- The warm-up enables the body to prepare for the onset of exercise. It decreases the likelihood of injury and muscle soreness. There is also a release of adrenaline that will start the process of speeding up the delivery of oxygen to the working muscles. An increase in muscle temperature will help to ensure that there is a ready supply of energy and that the muscle becomes more flexible to prevent injury.

- The cool-down is also important for effective training. If light exercise follows training, then the oxygen can more effectively be flushed through the muscle tissue and oxidising lactic acid. Cool-downs also prevent blood pooling in the veins which can cause dizziness.

Figure 14.5

Exercise client warming up

Aerobic and anaerobic fitness training

Aerobic capacity can be improved through continuous, steady state (sub maximal) training. The rhythmic exercise of aerobics, continuous swimming or jogging all are good for aerobic fitness.

Anaerobic training involves high intensity work that may be less frequent, although elite athletes will frequently train both aerobically and anaerobically.

keyword

Aerobic
A physical exercise which improves the efficiency of the cardiovascular system in absorbing and transporting oxygen.

Figure 14.6

This low-intensity exercise must take place over a long period of time from 20 minutes to 2 hours. The intensity of this exercise should be 60%–80% of your maximum heart rate

Aerobic and anaerobic fitness training methods

Interval Training

This is one of the most popular types of training. It is adaptable depending on individual needs and sports. Interval training can improve both aerobic and anaerobic fitness. It is called interval training because there are intervals of work and intervals of rest. For training the aerobic system, there should be slower intervals, which is suitable for sports like athletics and swimming and for team games like hockey or football. For training the anaerobic system, there should be shorter more intense intervals of training. The following factors have to be taken into account before the design of a training session:

- Duration of the work interval should be between 3 – 10 seconds at high intensity for anaerobic and 7 – 8 minutes for aerobic.

- Speed (intensity) of the work interval should be between 90-100% intensity for anaerobic and moderate if aerobic.

- Number of repetitions. This depends on the length of the work period, but if repetitions are short, then up to 50 repetitions is appropriate for anaerobic. For aerobic, 3 – 4 is more appropriate.

- Number of sets of repetitions. Repetitions can be divided into sets, if 50 reps then these could be divided into sets of five.

- Duration of the rest interval. The length of time that the heart rate falls to about 150 bpm. Aerobic training will require a shorter rest interval for effective training.

- Type of activity during the rest interval. If the energy system is anaerobic, then only light stretching is needed. If it is aerobic then some light jogging may help to disperse lactic acid.

Fartlek Training

This is also known as speedplay training. This training is good for aerobic fitness because it is an endurance activity. It is good for anaerobic fitness because of the speed activities over a short period of time. Throughout the exercise, the speed and intensity of the training is varied. In an hour session, for instance, there may be a walking activity which is low in intensity to very fast sprinting which is high intensity.

Muscular strength, muscular endurance and power training

For strength and power training, the performer needs to work against resistance. The training is effective only if it is specific enough. In other words the training needs to be targeted depending on the type of strength that needs to be developed, for instance explosive strength or strength endurance.

Circuit training

This involves a series of exercises that are arranged in a particular way called a circuit because the training involves repetition of each activity. The resistance that is used in circuits relates mainly to body weight, and each exercise in the circuit is designed to work on a particular muscle group. For effective training

Figure 14.7

For strength and power training, the client needs to work against resistance

different muscle groups should be worked on, with no two muscle-groups being worked on one after the other. For instance an activity that uses the main muscle groups in the arms should then be followed, for example, by an exercise involving the muscle groups in the legs. The types of exercises that are involved in circuit training are press-ups, star jumps, dips and squat thrusts.

Figure 14.8

Score at the end of the circuit may be related to time or repetitions and are a good way of motivating in training

Circuit training can also incorporate skills in other activities. In football for instance, there may be dribbling activities, throw ins, shuttle runs and shooting activities. The duration and intensity depends on the type of activities that have been incorporated. An example would be a circuit with one minute's worth of activity, followed by one minute's worth of rest. The whole circuit could then be repeated three times. The score at the end of the circuit may be related to time or repetitions and can be a good way of motivating in training. It is also easy to see progression in fitness as the weeks go by, when more repetitions can be attempted or times are improved.

Weight and resistance training methods

In circuit training we have seen that it is the body weight that is used as resistance to enable the body to work hard and to physiologically adapt to the training stresses. For strength to be developed more resistance can be used in the form of weight training or against other types of resistance, such as the use of pulleys. Weight training involves a number of repetitions and sets, depending on the type of strength that needs to be developed.

Plyometrics

This type of training is designed to improve dynamic strength. Plyometrics improves the speed in which muscles shorten. If muscles have previously been stretched, then they tend to generate more force when contracted. Any sport that involves sprinting, throwing and jumping will benefit from this type of training, as will players of many team sports like netball or rugby.

Plyometrics involve bounding, hopping and jumping, when muscles have to work concentrically (jumping up) and eccentrically (landing). One type of jumping used in this training method is called in-depth jumping, which is when the athlete jumps on to and off boxes. This type of training is very strenuous on the muscles and joints and a reasonable amount of fitness must be present before this training is attempted. As usual, it is important that there is sufficient stretching of the muscle before attempting this type of training.

Flexibility Training

This is sometimes called mobility training. It involves stretching exercises of the muscles and this can help with performance and to avoid injury. There are two types of flexibility exercises:

■ **Active stretching**. This is when there are voluntary muscular contractions that are held by the performer for 30 seconds to one minute. When the muscle is relaxed at the limit of the stretching range, muscle elongation may occur if this practice is repeated regularly. So the more you stretch the more flexible you will be! As long as the stretching is under control and muscles are suitably warmed-up before stretching begins. One method of active stretching is called the ballistic method.

case study 14.1 — Ballistic stretching

The subject actively uses the momentum of the limb to move the body through a wider range of movement. This is achieved through a bouncing type movement and should only be attempted by those who are extremely flexible such as gymnasts or certain athletes because muscle tissue damage is easily experienced with such active stretching.

- **Passive stretching**. This technique incorporates an external 'helper', who pushes or pulls the limb to stretch the appropriate muscles. This is obviously potentially dangerous, so the subject must be thoroughly warmed up and should go through some active stretching to begin with. Gymnasts often favour this particular type of stretching. One type of passive stretching is called proprioceptive neuromuscular facilitation (PNF).

case study 14.2 — PNF

This method tries to decrease the reflex shortening of the muscle being stretched, when the muscle is at its limit of stretch:

- The limb is moved to limit by subject.

- The limb is then taken to passive limit by partner.

- Just before the point of real discomfort, the muscle is contracted isometrically for a few seconds, then relaxed.

- The muscle will then be able to be stretched a little more during the next stretch.

Planning an Exercise Programme

keyword

FITT
F = frequency of training (number of training sessions each week)
I = intensity of the exercise undertaken
T = time or duration that the training takes up
T = type of training to be considered that fulfils specific needs.

Although each individual's needs may differ greatly, there is an overall structure that all training programmes should follow. The principles of training outlined earlier in this unit should be taken into consideration as well as the **FITT** principles. Planning is crucial if any programme of training is to be effective. The essential components of any exercise programme are:

- identify the individual's training goal
- identify the fitness components to be improved
- establish the energy systems to be used
- identify the muscle groups that will be used
- evaluate the fitness components involved

- use an exercise / training diary
- vary the programme to maintain motivation
- include rest in the programme for recovery.

The main factors to consider include an assessment of the client's activity levels and lifestyle. There should be suitable screening that involves a doctor's referral if appropriate. The exercise programme must also take into consideration whether the clients are exercising as a group or as individuals. What is their current fitness level? What experience have they had before? It is very important that each individual's need is taken into consideration so that the effects of exercise can be maximised.

Assisting in Instructing an Exercise Session

At the start of the session it is important to:

- set up the equipment correctly and check for safety
- establish good relationships with your clients – use effective communication
- carry out screening activities – check whether there are any current health issues/injuries
- ensure that clients are aware of emergency procedures / recognition of fire exits etc
- set out the objectives of the session so that goals can be identified and recognised
- use appropriate warm-up procedures
- ensure that correct and safe techniques are demonstrated/reinforced
- motivate clients with encouragement and through personal and shared goal setting.

Unit 11 Fitness for Sports Performance

During the session you should:

- continue to motivate and project your voice appropriately (for example if speaking to a group in a hall the voice must be projected so that all can hear the instructions)
- regularly check on the clients' understanding / progress and adjust if necessary
- feedback continuously on technique and skills
- adapt activity to the varying levels of ability – ensure that all levels of ability are challenged

- give opportunities for re-hydration (plenty of water must be available throughout the session).

At the end of a session make sure you:

- ensure that there is a suitable cool-down (see earlier in this unit)
- give feedback about objectives
- give opportunities for questions and comments regarding the session
- give ideas/extension tasks that clients could be carrying out on their own
- summarise the session briefly then organise the departure of clients
- check equipment and then put away safely.

Undertaking a Review of an Exercise Programme and an Exercise Session

Evaluation is the process of analysing the sessions you have planned and delivered. This can help exercise teachers and coaches to identify what went well and what could have been improved upon. Effective evaluation is essential if progress in exercise instruction is to be made. Good exercise trainers are always trying to improve what they do. This involves them in thinking about and evaluating the exercise sessions they have planned and delivered, identifying strengths and weaknesses and learning lessons for the future.

Figure 14.9

Observing and working with other exercise instructors will improve your own practice

The instructor must also take into account developments in exercise training practice and take part in regular exercise/coach education to develop their practice further and to add to their training skills. This could include attending courses, conferences, reading journals or other relevant publications, as well as observing and working with other exercise instructors.

When evaluating an exercise session and programme it is important to review not just the way in which a session is delivered, but also the way it was planned. The key to really effective instructing is to plan well. It is important to take into account how the participants felt about the coaching session. Their views are important and probably more objective than the coach's own views. Their views could be sought via verbal feedback or a written evaluation.

Figure 14.10

It is important to take into account how the participants felt about the coaching session

It is important to record the evaluations both in terms of self-evaluation by the instructor, evaluation by other trainers and the clients themselves. Remember the whole process is meaningless if these evaluations are not acted upon.

■ The elements of the coaching that has received favorable evaluations should reinforce good practice, and this practice should continue and develop.

■ The issues that arise from poor evaluations should be addressed and become part of an action plan to improve.

■ Progress should be reviewed and there should be a development in coaching practice, as well as an updating of the personal action plans and goal settings accordingly.

Unit 12 Lifestyle and Sports Performance, page 229

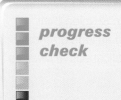

*progress
check*

1 Name the main principles of training.

2 What is meant by the FITT principle?

3 What is circuit training?

4 Describe why plyometrics affects muscle power.

5 Why is flexibility training so important?

6 Why are warm-ups and cool-downs so important?

7 What factors must you consider when planning an exercise programme?

8 Identify what should happen at the start of an exercise session.

9 What sort of feedback should you give during an exercise session?

10 What makes an effective review of an exercise session or an exercise programme?

Glossary

Aerobic – A physical exercise which improves the efficiency of the cardiovascular system in absorbing and transporting oxygen.

Amino acids – These are present in protein. There are eight amino acids that the body is unable to make for itself and these are called essential amino acids for example leucine and threonine. The essential amino acids should be part of our dietary intake. The other 12 amino acids are called non-essential, for example glycine and glutamine.

Anaerobic – A high-intensity exercise where the muscles lack sufficient oxygen to successfully burn fuel.

Attitudes – These are thoughts that we have towards something or somebody. These thoughts include beliefs, feelings and how we behave towards something or somebody.

Arousal – This is a term used for the intensity of the drive that is experienced when an athlete is trying to achieve a goal. High arousal can lead to high levels of stress, both physiologically and psychologically.

Complex skills – These include a slip catch in cricket, or a pass by a midfield player in hockey who has to make lots of decisions before she passes.

Court games – These games include tennis, squash and volleyball. There is usually no contact between the players because they are kept apart by a net, although in squash both players occupy the same space.

Cover letter – A letter to accompany your CV which covers the main points and highlights your best experience, skills and abilities in relation to the job you are applying for.

Curriculum vitae – This is a brief account of a person's qualifications, education, previous occupations and experience.

Ecological footprint – This is the impact or effects that man has on our natural environment, some of which may last for a very long time.

Evaluation – This follows monitoring and usually occurs at the end of a process. An evaluation takes into account the overall strengths and weaknesses of the programme and factors that have affected the results.

Extrinsic motivation – This is the drive that is caused by motives that are external or environmental. These motives are rewards that can be tangible or intangible.

Extroversion – Seeks social situations and likes excitement. Lacks concentration.

Glossary

Field sports – These are often associated with rural areas but not always. Sports such as shooting and fishing are field sports and are linked with killing animals for food, although the point of most field sports is the competition between the human being and the animal he or she wishes to kill. Many people who participate in field sports describe the 'thrill of the chase' as the most enjoyable aspect of this type of sport. Others oppose this activity and view it as cruel and unsporting because the animal has no choice in its participation and it is not a fair competition.

First impressions – A first impression is the initial opinion you form of someone when you meet him or her for the first time. First impressions can be based on a person's body language, clothes, gestures or what they say.

FITT
F = frequency of training (number of training sessions each week)
I = intensity of the exercise undertaken
T = time or duration that the training takes up
T = type of training to be considered that fulfils specific needs.

Haemoglobin – This is iron-rich protein and transports oxygen in the blood. The more concentrated the haemoglobin, the more oxygen can be carried. This concentration can be increased through endurance training.

Hazard – Something that has the potential to cause harm.

Hypothermia – Hypothermia results from a reduction in the body's core temperature. If the core temperature drops to 35°C or below then you are deemed to be suffering from hypothermia. If the core temperature continues to drop then there is a real risk of death.

Insertion – This is the end of the muscle attached to the bone that actively moves, for example the biceps insertion is on the radius.

Interview – An interview is often a formal discussion between a job applicant and employer to fill a vacancy, it is really an oral examination of the job applicant.

Intrinsic motivation – This is an inner drive or need to want to do well and succeed and to feel good and enjoy the activity.

Introversion – Does not seek social situations and likes peace and quiet. Good at concentrating.

Invasion games – The object of these types of games is to invade the opponent's territory, as if you are at war with the opposition – which of course you are not! Rugby, netball and football are examples of invasion games.

Kinaesthetic sense – This is the feeling or sense that we experience through movement.

Leisure

'An activity, apart from the obligations of work, family and society, to which the individual turns at will, for either relaxation, diversion, or broadening experiences.'

Leisure industry – This involves the products and services that surround leisure activities.

Manipulation – The term 'manipulation' comes from the Latin. 'Manipulate' means 'to handle'. It covers a range of techniques, using the hands to realign the structural system of the body, relax the muscles and improve circulation.

Monitor – This involves taking notes of developments as they happen. It is an ongoing record of progress or lack of progress.

Motivation

A need or drive to do something with determination, for example to keep turning up to hockey practice and hopefully to be picked for the next game.

Neurotic – Highly anxious and has unpredictable emotions.

Notational analysis – This involves taking notes about a person's or group of people's performance during the activity. The notes serve as important information to use to assess what went well and to identify areas for improvement.

Origin – This is the end of the muscle attached to a bone that is stable, such as the scapula. The point of origin remains still when contraction occurs. Some muscles have two or more origins, for example the biceps muscle has two heads that pull on one insertion to lift the lower arm.

Participation rates – This refers to the number of people within a group who are involved in sport compared with those who are not.

Personality – An individual's behavioural chracteristics that make him or her different from others.

Recreation – The active aspect of leisure. Recreation involves a state of mind and involves us viewing the activity as not work but active enjoyment that helps us to relax and escape stress.

Reinforcement – There are various types of reinforcement:
- **Positive** – this is the giving of a stimulus to ensure repetition of behaviour, for example a badge for swimming.
- **Negative** – this is the taking away of a stimulus to ensure that the right behaviour is repeated, for example not giving any verbal praise if the performer shows the wrong movement.
- **Punishment** – this is the giving of a stimulus to prevent a behaviour occurring, for instance dropping a performer from the squad for not trying hard in training.

Risk – The chance that someone will be harmed by a hazard.

Risk assessment – Risk assessment is the technique by which you measure the chances of an accident happening, anticipate what the consequences would be and plan actions to prevent it.

Saturated fat – A saturated fat is in the form of a solid, such as lard, and is primarily from animal sources.

Simple skills – These include a sprint start in swimming, for example where there are very few decisions – other than to dive – that have to be made.

SMARTER goal setting

S – **Specific**. If goals are clear and unambiguous they are more likely to be reached.

M – **Measurable**. This is important for monitoring and makes you accountable.

A – **Agreed**. The sharing of goal-setting between coach/instructor and performer can give a sense of teamwork.

R – **Realistic**. Motivation will improve if goals can actually be reached.

T – **Timed**. An effective approach is to split goals up into short-term goals that are planned and progressive.

E – **Exciting**. The more stimulating the activities can be the more motivating is their effect.

R – **Recorded**. Recording is crucial for monitoring and, once achieved, can be deleted or checked off, thus improving motivation.

Sport – This involves competition between individuals or teams that is organised and includes physical activity.

Sports equity – This is concerned with fairness in sport, equality of access, recognising inequalities and taking steps to address them. It is about changing the culture and structure of sport to ensure that it becomes equally accessible to all members of society.

Stable – Does not swing from one emotion to another.

Target games – As the name suggests, the aim of the game is to hit certain targets. They involve accuracy of judgement often called 'marksmanship'. Target games include golf and archery.

Target group – This represents the type of people on whom one wishes to concentrate for an activity session.

Unsaturated fat – An unsaturated fat is in the form of a liquid, such as vegetable oil, and is from plant sources.

Vasoconstriction – This occurs when the artery walls reduce their diameter. The vessels can therefore help to change the pressure of the blood, which is especially important during exercise.

Vasodilation – This occurs when the artery walls increase their diameter.

Veins and venules – These carry blood at low pressure and return the blood to the heart. Their walls are less muscular but gradually increase in thickness as they approach the heart. The vena cava is the largest vein, which enters the heart through the right atrium. The smallest veins are called venules. They transport the blood from the capillaries. Veins contain pocket valves that prevent the backflow of blood.

Index

Index

Index

Index